SILENT
RAIN

SILENT RAIN

Amaro Bhikkhu
Talks & Travels

ISBN: 974-89658-2-1
Printed by: Craftsman Press, Bangkok, Thailand.
Tel. 253-3009, Fax: 253-3298

This book is lovingly dedicated to the
memory of my father – Tom Julian Horner
('The Pope of Bull Terriers') – who passed away,
aged 80, during the time that this book was
being composed.

Contents

… it is not a miseffectual whyacinthinous riot
of blots and blurs and bars and balls
and hoops and wriggles and juxtaposed jottings
linked by spurts of speed:
it only looks as like it as damn it …

James Joyce
Finnegans Wake

Foreword

I hope you will enjoy this book. You probably won't like it unless you feel like listening to it the way you would listen to the rain, now pattering, now beating, on your window on a dark and blustery night. That kind of listening can be marvellous. It's the way that contemplatives attend to consciousness.

Here Ajahn Amaro is not so much telling us how to attend in that way – how to meditate – but presenting the patterns that a contemplative mind moves in. It's like saying: "You know how to do this! Remember? It goes like this...." There are methods and techniques of course, and many excellent books on the subject; the drawback with that being that it can create an artificiality, because we try to do it, with all the anxiety and need to achieve that we are conditioned into ... and all we really witness in ourselves is the sense of trying ... and because of that joylessness, the sense of failing or not getting the point. In between these covers you learn in the same way that a child learns to speak – by listening to the voices around her or him.

Not that you have to agree with what the voices are saying either. Here and there I found myself thinking, "That's a bit of an exaggeration"; or "The Buddha didn't put it like that." But that's life, isn't it? Even contemplative life is like that: and that's where Ajahn Amaro is doing his learning – through listening to the rich variety of teachers and teachings that we are privileged to have access to in this age. Attending out of interest; just to understand the patterns that consciousness weaves – without believing in any of them.

This may come as a surprising approach, because Ajahn Amaro has been trained, and lives, as a forest monk according to the conventions of Theravada monasticism. And most people would assume that Theravada monasticism is about affirming the same approach to the Buddha's teachings as established by Venerable Buddhaghosa Mahathera fifteen hundred years ago. The Theravada scholastic tradition has been concerned to present the teachings in a consistent way and to preserve them against false interpretation. By its own lights it has been successful. However, the more you meditate, the more you realise the relativity of words – that they only set up resonances rather than convey absolute meanings. And unless you study and practise a lot, under a wise teacher, it's easy to practise according to misleading interpretations of such key terms as 'cessation', 'attachment', and 'not-self'. These terms, fingers pointing at the moon of bliss, peace and wholeness, can set up resonances that drive us deeper into the negative and fragmented state that the Buddha was trying to pull us out of. Without refuting a more scholastic approach, the line of practice of the forest monks has set about keeping the moon in mind and getting your own finger working.

You've probably guessed that Ajahn Amaro is a friend of mine. He began his training in the forest monasteries of North-east Thailand under Venerable Ajahn Chah in 1978 and came over to England in 1979. We were at Chithurst Monastery then, with Ajahn Sumedho in the teacher's seat. I thought that

Amaro talked too much, but he certainly put a lot of effort into meditation, helping out with all the manual work in the monastery and exemplifying the refined ethical standards of a good bhikkhu. My grudging admiration of him went up a notch when he spent a month retreat in the back of a derelict police van in our woods with just a sleeping bag and a bottle of water. I'd softened up a bit by the time we were living together again at Amaravati Monastery (for seven years). He still was a bit long-winded, but you could always rely on him to help out and back you up in the many duties that establishing a monastery in the West entails. He kept cool and played it straight, and had the patience with confused people that I lacked. In 1994 when he got round to putting this book of his talks, essays and poems together, I was back at Chithurst (in the teacher's seat) and he was spending more time in America. He asked me to help edit the book. He still talks too much – but by this time, I'm nearly as bad.

I hope you enjoy the book.

Ajahn Sucitto
Chithurst Monastery
October 1994

Preface

In the way of spiritual life, creation tends to happen through response to circumstances rather than from any self-propelled initiative.

In the summer of 1993, whilst I was doing some teaching in Detroit for a few days, I was asked if I had ever written a book. I replied, "Yes, but it's long out of print." "Could it be reprinted?" came the inquiry. "Theoretically yes, of course...."

Before I knew it donations for such a reprint started to be offered in quantity. The book in question, by the way, was *Tudong – The Long Road North,* which I had written in 1984 following a long walk that I had made through England. We had only printed a thousand copies at the time and they were long gone by now.

When I mentioned to some other supporters in San Francisco a few days later that reprinting *Tudong* was in the air, they suggested: "Why not put together a collection of more recent stuff instead?" "Good idea," I thought. "That makes sense...." On returning to England I talked the possibility over with Ajahn Sucitto – the monk who looks after all our publications – who responded by saying, "Great. You could include some of those travelogues, and maybe some poems of yours...." It thus gathered momentum and its own life began to unfold.

As the text selected itself and grew I began to think of illustrations that might be used to round out the book. There were a number that had already been produced for various Sangha publications, and ones that I had drawn over the years for members of my family. I gathered these together and found a few that seemed to match the different moods and themes of the book.

What you are now holding in your hands therefore is the confluence of all these elements. More than anything else it is a scrapbook – a simple cross-section through the world of someone who, in this late 20th Century time, has chosen to live as a Buddhist monk. In putting this book together, every effort has been made to render it as accessible as possible. If, however, at some point its meaning or reason escapes you, hopefully the music will tide you over.

Amaro Bhikkhu
Troy
November 1994

Acknowledgements

Every book is the result of the collective effort of many people; in books of spiritual content that are for free distribution those efforts are made solely out of love and generosity, and they therefore lend a certain glow to any volume thus produced. A large variety of kind and generous offerings have contributed to the production of this book and, rejoicing in the good that has been done, I would like to express my gratitude to the following for their assistance:

To Buddha-Dharma Meditation Center, Drs. Wanchai and Jaruwan Sangchantr, Dr. Chate Wansom, Dr. and Mrs. Vinai Pira, Drs. Aungchoye and Sunthorn Thrupkaew, Adirek and Dao Dulyapaibul, Dr. S. Boonjarern, Drs. P. and P. Jantra, Dr. and Mrs. Yongsuk Lertratanakul, Dr. Uraiwan Chuntharusmi, Dr. and Mrs. K. Kitiphongspattana, Dr. and Mrs. Pakorn Sirijintakarn, Drs. C. and B. Supapodok, Dr. and Mrs. C. Luangsuwan and Viruch B. Yongsmith for their financial support of this book; to David Babski and Richard Smith who masterminded the typesetting, layout and printing; to Jennifer May and Thelma Knott, Anagarikas Irene and Laura, Bhikkhu Nyanavutto and the City of Ten Thousand Buddhas who patiently transcribed all the Dhamma talks; to Catherine Spencer who deciphered and transcribed the Indian diary, and to Jeannie Bendik who typed in the entire edited manuscript at amazing speed and then asked for more; to Bhikkhu Khantipalo who prepared the various drafts; and finally to Ajahn Sucitto for his help in editing and for his (characteristically unique) Foreword.

I would also particularly like to thank Nancy Sloane Stanley for the use of her 'Tudong' illustrations again; and Stephen Mitchell, Red Pine, Brother David Steindl-Rast, Bhikshu Heng Chau, Andy Price, the Buddhist Publication Society, Cannongate Press and numerous others for the use of quotations and renderings from their work. This book is a collage and therefore derivative of the wisdom of many people; it has not been possible to follow up on the author or translator of every single quotation contained here so, for those whose work has been made use of between these covers, I hope it is found that the words have been used respectfully. Everything quoted here has been employed both to express truths that I have not had the ability to articulate myself, and out of a deep sense of their usefulness to the world.

If anything contained in this book is of benefit, all my teachers and the other contributors should be considered as the source. If anything herein is harmful, has been quoted out of turn or has been expressed in a misleading way, the responsibility is mine alone and accordingly I ask for your forgiveness.

AB

Trust, Mystery and Ritual

From a talk given on the Easter retreat, Amaravati, 1992

AS THE DAY BEGINS, we ready our minds; we come together, compose ourselves and open our minds to the coming day. How today will be is unknown to us, isn't it? We might be eager and interested, hopeful, curious, inquisitive, enthusiastic; we might be feeling depressed, weary and downtrodden, fearful and threatened by what we might have to face during today; or maybe we have mixed feelings – hope and fear mingled together and stirred up with the general run of habitual patterns of thought. How did you go to bed last night? Did you go to sleep all bright and joyful, warm and cosy at the end of the day, full of the delights of the Dhamma or were you weeping into your pillow? However it was, we simply reflect, we look very closely at what happens to be here.

We experience constant changes of mood: feelings of inspiration and desperation, hope, disappointment, positivity, negativity, coherence and distraction, disintegration. We look at these and tend to think everything is going well or everything is going badly. But the position that we take with all of this in practising Dhamma is to reflect upon it; to observe the changes in nature within our own minds just as we observe the changes in nature in the world around us. Night: the qualities of the dark, dimness, the silence, stars, privacy and rest. This fades out and then there's light, colour, personal contact, moving and functioning with other human beings, the need to engage and to be involved. The formal meditation of the early morning changes into walking, eating, working, then shifts back into formal meditation again. In the midst of all of this we come to the place of silence, the place of inner quietude.

We try to use all of the aspects of our experience to bring us to a realisation of that stillness, where the habitual buzzing of thoughts, moods and emotions is understood and not given solidity, is seen as transparent. This is why we learn to reflect and to bring such obvious things to mind as the body and the breath. We keep bringing the mind to settle upon how the moment feels, what the nature of our experience is right now. To witness the patterns of consciousness that are there and the silence within which it all occurs, the stillness within which it all moves.

Moment after moment through the day, look – reflect that there is just this: the colour of the grass, the feeling of the breeze, the eating of a piece of toast, taste, it is just like this. A drink of water is just like this. The body feels like this. Nameless dread, anxiety feels like this. Buoyancy, ebullience and energy feel like this.

It's not that one is trying to homogenise all our experience and pretend that it's all the same. What we discover instead is that we're able to experience everything clearly, in a perfect context. We're not trying to see it all as void of flavour but to have a heart-rooted realisation of the integrated nature of it all, the orderedness of the whole mental and physical world.

This is part of the usefulness of morning and evening chanting: coming in to the shrine room, bowing, waiting, ceremonial respect for religious figures, religious persons – these are all patterns that we use that have a certain power. To participate in a ritual takes us into a timeless space, it connects us with a timeless reality. We're performing actions that have been performed thousands, millions of times before by millions of people all over the world. These same words have been recited, these same gestures have been made countless times so, at that moment even if only to a small degree, we are at one with all of those who have ever made those same gestures, performed those same actions and aroused those same aspirations. We're attuning the heart to that archetype and we're acknowledging the order that is there. We are, in a very formalised way, linking up our own consciousness with that universal orderedness. This is why we chant and bow together. The shrine is arranged in a symmetrical way, a way that is beautiful to the eye, it's not just a disorganised heap of objects, but it has symmetry, proportion, the colours are chosen, the flowers are fresh.

If we take the ritual as an end in itself we miss the point. It's become superstition. In the same way, if we dismiss ritual altogether we miss the point. If we think that the flowers are all-important – beautiful, fresh flowers are all-important – then, when the flowers fade or they're not arranged as perfectly as we would choose them to be, then we suffer. But if we say, "Flowers are impermanent; they're just plants' sexual organs, of no interest to the serious, committed meditator; they are impermanent, unsatisfactory and not-self, chuck them out!" – this is not the point either. Flowers have beauty, they're naturally uplifting. Their delicacy and symmetry – they are a natural expression of the purity, balance and wonderful nature of the universe. So we use flowers and suchlike forms to help evoke that same quality in our own hearts. The Buddha sits always upon a lotus flower. We use these in endless places, carved on shrines, woven into carpets, painted on our clothes, woven into designs, because of the uplifting, inspiring archetype that they embody. Participation in a ritual, using such forms, ideas and traditions helps to keep reminding us in the same way. They help to keep arousing that faith or trust, even though this can occur in a very unconscious way.

The thinking mind can be quite critical: perhaps we don't like the words, or feel that we can't chant, or the melody could be a little more exciting, or could be in a different key. But the whole process is pitched at a much more fundamental aspect of our life than that. A group of human beings joining together in one voice evokes the quality of Sangha, 'the perfectly unified assembly'. It awakens in us the recognition that we are capable of acting with one mind, one body, one spirit. We have our own personalities, our own gender, age and dispositions, yet without negating those we are still able to find channels of harmonisation. It is crucial for us to recognise that such devotional practices and rituals help us to contact that. A mind which is given to faith, to devotion, is also a mind which is open, a mind which is ready to receive – this too is a crucial aspect.

When we look forward to the coming day, if we've already written in what we expect to achieve or what we expect to experience, then we'll make that happen. We create the world out of our expectations, fears and hopes. We limit our experience by the patterns of what we anticipate. Instead of following this habit, we try to open the mind and ready ourselves for everything. We don't know how today will be – the future is always mysterious to us. The heart which is open and ready will be capable of learning from everything. It will be able to make use of whatever it is that arises, however things turn out to be. We recognise those particular things we hope for, those things that we fear, but hope and fear happen right now. Leave the day open, leave the future open as an infinity of possibilities.

This can be frightening to us; we like to predict the future and have it all written in, because it makes us feel secure. Even though we know it's un-likely to turn out that way, even if our prognosis is that things are going to be terrible, having *something* to expect makes us feel more comfortable than not knowing at all. But to consciously not know is actually the much more realistic approach; it's much more honest – we don't know!

If we face the unknown when our life is very much ego-based and self-centred, then the unknown is frightening, terrifying, we feel threatened. The sense of self and the quality of fear are very closely related with each other. In one of the Upanishads, the Hindu scriptures, it describes the beginning of the universe: in the beginning there was simply the Absolute, the mind of the Absolute present in the infinite dark. Then within the mind of the Absolute there arose the thought "I am", and immediately following that thought there came fear. Immediately following that fear there came desire.

When out of the purity of the unattached mind some self-based thought arises, as soon as that thought is grasped the 'person' is then separated off from the rest of the universe. And with 'me' separated off there is the feeling of vulnerability, "Anything might happen to me." We need protection. We need comfort, affirmation, and reassurance; so then desire arises to placate that sense of lack and vulnerability. So the whole Samsaric cycle begins.

The less that we live from the basis of ego – from I, me and mine – when we're faced with the unknown, the experience is not one of fear but one of wonder, mystery. The universe is still incomprehensible – we can't categorise it, conceptualise it or name it, we can't explain how and why everything is, or even describe what one thing really is – but rather than that lack of ability to define being something threatening we find it wonderful, dazzling, beautiful. The mind and the universe have an awesome, terrible beauty – there is wonderment.

It's a challenge to live without expectation, to let go of our prospects for the day and for the future, but this is a liberating act. It is an attitude which frees us, opens us up, and enables us to change and to learn. Without this, Samsara continues – we constantly recreate past habits – with this openness, faith and readiness to be with the unknown we can change, the heart can be transformed, purified – Awakened.

In Spite of All

In spite of all the heated breath,
The angry skies and stormy seas;
In spite of passions ripe and hot
That flicker through the mind
And trot around each other
Blind and fraught, (furied, signifying naught),
In spite of this and all of these;
In spite of all the agitations,
The greed and lust,
The confrontations;
In spite of all the heat that's spent,
I know in truth I am content.

A falling leaf spins through the air
And through my open window where
It lands upon my lap –
"O joy! A wish! A wish……. a wish?"

Nothing to wish for,
Not a thing.
My head's a blank, an empty ring;
Nothing stirring there, no waves,
Like the clear and empty blue that paves
A still and peaceful ocean sky,
The silence between you and I.

Silence in the midst of change,
A silence beautiful and strange,
Silence in the forest deep
Where chickens scratch and lizards creep,
Where crickets ring and night-birds call,
Silence deep – in spite of all.

(Roi-Et, North-east Thailand, 1979)

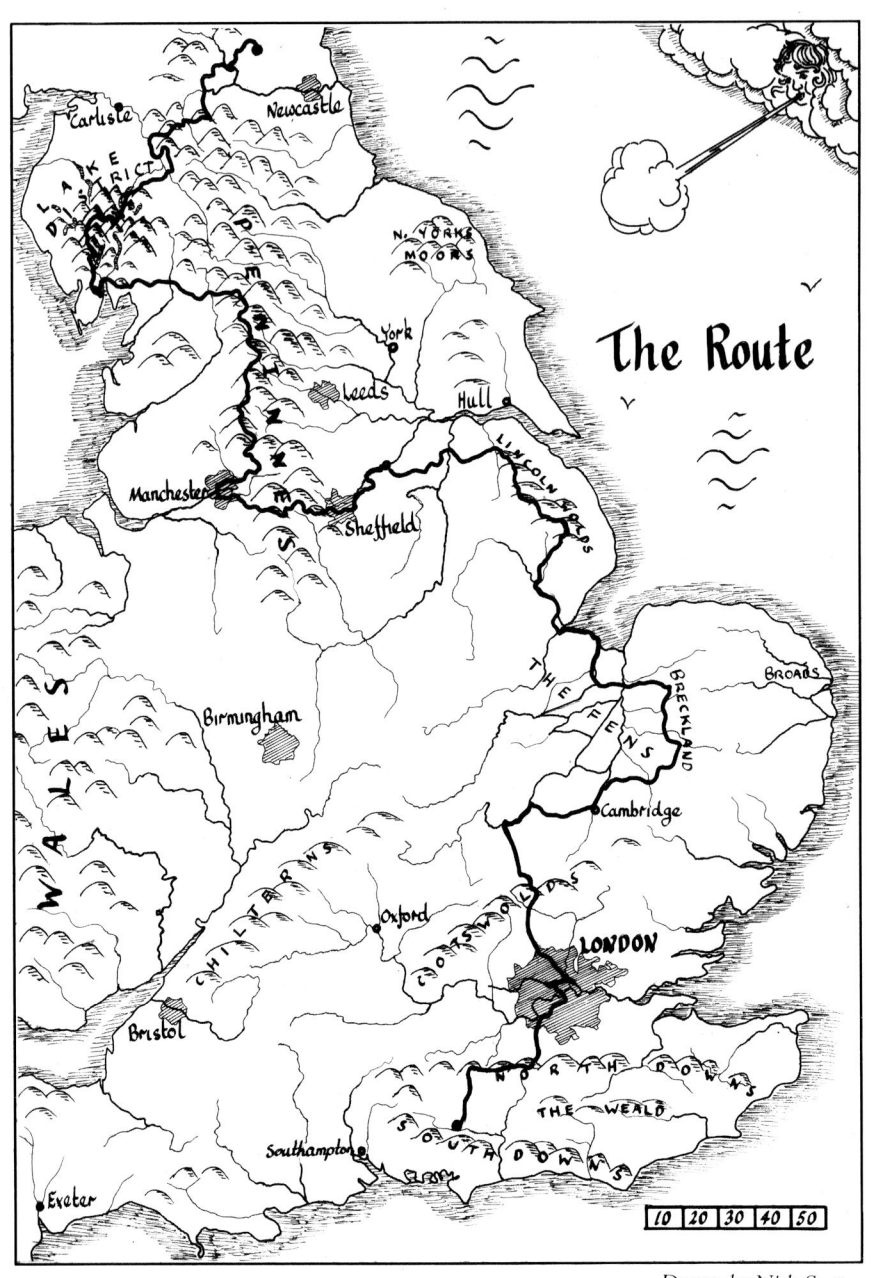

The Route

Drawn by Nick Scott

The Long Road North

PART ONE – FROM SUSSEX TO THE WASH

Having spent some of my early monastic years at Chithurst, in 1982 I asked Ajahn Sumedho if I could go on a long 'tudong' walk to our new branch monastery at Harnham in Northumberland. The plans for the walk took shape over the next few months and, in the spring of 1983, I set off with Nick Scott, a friend and supporter of the monastery. The following passages are taken from a longer account of the walk which was published in 1984.

"In actual fact, there is nobody going anywhere, there are just conditions changing."

Ajahn Sumedho

IT IS NOW THE MORNING of the third day, Nick is trying to get a fire started, it rained heavily last night so the damp twigs are difficult to burn.

We are in a little wood south of Guildford, not far from where the A3 goes over the Hog's Back. The road is a constant roar in the distance. These first few days have been truly beautiful: leaving Chithurst in the rain, it poured most of the day. The land we passed through was almost all woodland; oak and young beeches began to glow when finally the sun appeared. Nick gave me a fine waterproof before we left so I find walking in the rain as lovely as in the sun; just as having the refuge of Dhamma in the rain of conditions, great joy arises in the heart.

I try to use the Ajahn's phrase, about no-one going anywhere, as a constant reflection.

> Who is walking?
> Where is there to get to?
> Who does this walk belong to?
> Who does this mind belong to?

Talking yesterday with Sri about how to live with paradox: to be attached as a good mother to her child, to be detached as a good Buddhist; the appearance of a journey but going nowhere.

It is such a comforting reflection that we have: as long as you are going some-

where you are living in the desire to get there and the fear of not making it; you feel a twinge in your knee, your arm goes dead, your shoe begins to rub – EEEK! goes the mind. Dying into every step, seeking no future, life is painless.

We camped our first night under a great beech in the Land of Nod. The young

23

We camped our first night under a great beech in the Land of Nod. The young green of the new leaves quivered in an amazing flickering dance, the evening sun and spring wind, the earth and the old tree. It must seem funny to see, in the space of one night (which is just one exhalation to a tree), these little pink critters come bustling up, clump down against the trunk, leap up, run around, tent, fire, tea, sleep, up, fire, tea, tent down and zip off again, all in the time it takes for a breath to leave your lungs. A lady who dropped in at Noy Thomson's house later on told us that the Land of Nod was a dangerous place; nasty people with sawn-off shotguns roaming in the woods. It felt like Tusita Heaven – or like, when I took my pack off, the bliss of release that the Buddha found when he put his burden down under the Bodhi tree.

★ ★ ★

Tudong is certainly a good teacher: as soon as you are drawn into the journey as a material thing you become struck with the pain of always having to get on to the next place, got to crack on, get up and go. The true journey, from distraction to awakening, steals all the tension and dukkha from whatever is happening in the senses. Being so much, so obviously, on a physical journey makes the distinction crystal clear: the urge to move, nowhere to go.

Sunshine
the open road
going nowhere.

★ ★ ★

We walked from our lakeside camp feeling somewhat drained from all the bustle of London. We did not have far to go that morning, just to a rendezvous with Paul Dolby and Peter Da Costa in Shenley, a few miles down the road. We arrived, sat down in the porchway of the church and had a breather; Nick took his clock out – nine-thirty exactly – we looked up and there was Paul, rounding the corner, his hand held up in greeting. Shortly afterwards Peter appeared and we all went off in Paul's car to find a picnic spot.

It was overcast but quite bright as we organised the seating arrangements and the food. Paul, a chef in a St. Albans hotel, had prepared a great feast; napkins, table-cloths – *avec du tout*. In the monastic life, food – the one meal of the day – can take on a peculiar importance. It is the primary medium of support given by the laity to the Sangha: people like to make sure that the Sangha is well looked after, and offering food is the most immediate means of ensuring this. Also, because we are celibate, penniless renunciants, the meal is often the most striking thing which happens in the realm of the senses throughout the day. Whether one likes food, dislikes it or is indifferent, the meal-time always seems to be a major event.

As Paul began to offer the dishes it started to rain but, as can be the way with hungry people and food, we were not deterred. With no immediate shelter obvious and convincing ourselves it would soon pass over, we gave the blessing and began to eat. It poured. The heaviest rain we had seen so far sluiced down upon us, merciless. We sheltered beneath umbrellas and

About three-quarters of the way through the meal, Nick suddenly remembered a barn which we had passed on our way to the picnic spot. He began to look uneasy but said nothing. He had covered most of the gear but was soon up, exploring the possibilities of a dry place.

"So it's raining," I thought, "we'll dry off sooner or later." I carried on eating, determined not to be moved by the whole affair. The rain poured on, beating onto our brollies and pattering into our pasties. Eventually the rain faded out and we upped sticks and removed ourselves to the barn which Nick had found. Amazingly it was abandoned, with a good roof and a thick layer of dry hay on the floor; we laid out our wet things and made ourselves comfy for the afternoon. We sat and watched the rain, which had gained strength again, drank warming coffee and talked.

All this rain is bringing us a mass of greenery, everywhere we go the country is thick, wet, lush and beautiful – tall banks of shining green and deep, deep mud. Peter joined us for the day's walk and we set off towards Ayot St. Lawrence; the footpaths are so muddy I am finding it hard to keep up with Nick, sliding about in my sandals and scouting for the driest patches. It is easier once your feet are completely wet and muddy as you do not care so much, but until then there always seems to be a compulsion to find the driest way.

As we passed some houses near St. Albans we were invited into the home of a lady called Josephine. She had spotted me walking down the street and had thought that I might be her long-lost cousin Jeffrey who is with the Hare Krishna movement. Although good-hearted she was **very** eccentric and I felt a bit wary and uneasy. My English reserve and fear of the unknown rose well to the fore; after a while, however, the fear died away and we had a lovely time together. She offered us tea and we had a good talk; I did not say much, listening mostly to her and Nick. At one point she set about guessing our ages, looking at the wrinkles around our eyes. She got both Nick and Peter's right to within a year or two and then came over and stood in front of me. Lowering her head to my level and staring into my face.

"Seventeen! But you can't be – how old are you?!?"

"Twenty-six…. Er … I meditate a lot." I replied a little nervously.

After tea we said goodbye and got back on the road again. It was a fine afternoon. We left Peter in Wheathampstead and camped for the night a mile or so south of Ayot St. Lawrence. Nick found a quiet meadow surrounded by woods – a soft green solitary square – in front of us a lovely evening sky, sheltering nearly half a moon, sat shining over a wall of larches that linked arms at the field's edge.

Happiness at the end of the day: Peter had helped to carry our packs, we had met the remarkable Josephine, picnicked in the rain and now we sat, caped against the midges, well-sheltered underneath the moon.

Evam.

As we left Paul Hendrick's house in Suffolk and walked on down the road, I realised that I had fallen into something of a rut in recent days: getting caught up in places and schedules and worrying about the pain in my feet. As I began to put more effort into using the walk for awakening, turning to emptiness, I felt a smile appearing for the doubts and anxieties, feelings of inadequacy. Once a few miles of long straight lanes had passed beneath my feet the clouds had cleared. If you let your eyes close, drifting off the path is inevitable.

We have now moved from the great flatness of the Fens into the country of the Brecklands; low undulating sandy heaths where Nick has been finding a mass of interesting plants. In the ancient past these parts were heavily wooded, but early man's excessive deforestation leached the soil. A few thousand years of these poor conditions now make it a unique environment and many rare species abide here. As Nick pointed out, however, it does not take long before even the Breckland is ordinary: like oxlips, tudong or anything else, the exciting becomes the mundane and only the unconditioned mind can recognise the perfect joy in that.

When we are walking through the country, all through England, if you turn your ear there always seems to be a lark singing nearby – as endless and omni-present as the shining of your true nature. Always it is there – listen – remind-ing you of the total joy and emptiness of it all. Even the death and sadness one sees: the squashed animals on the road; the spent beer cans and tubs of Colonel Sanders'; the frightened lady in Stoke D'Abernon and lonely old 'Mum' who asked, out of the blue –

"Do you know of the poem that goes:

> 'She walked through the fields wearing her gloves,
> Fat white woman that nobody loves.'?"

It almost made me cry, the beauty and sadness of it. How difficult our lives seem and how perfect, in true reality, we are.

Even though we walked all day on country lanes and on a good straight path beside the River Nene, I was finding it very hard to concentrate. That familiar gnawing angst of 'something's wrong' hung ever in the background and, on reflection, I put it down to be the karmic result of having had a long lie-in that morning. Despite the sun, the waving river-banks of soft grass, I felt persis-tently wretched; patience and a lot of sitting I decided would be the best cure. We reached the sea-wall at the mouth of the river that evening; sitting in the last of the day's sun we sheltered from the wind, warm but blasting inland from the sea. It was after ten o'clock and still twilight when we turned in, the first stars had appeared and there were no clouds; I got up from my sitting mat, stuffed my hands into the pockets of my foam-filled waistcoat, stretched my back and looked around.

"Yup," I thought, straightening my knees, blinking at the stars and evening sky, "despite a nameless discontent, blabbering aimless streams of thought, a clutch of painful gnawing doubts, everything is just as it should be."

By the next dawn the wind had dropped so we sat on top of the sea-wall and watched the early sun; up on top a long time the sky was clear and soon the air felt quite warm again. I find it continually amazing now to realise that this world is just a shadow or a gesture of the Unborn; I look around, look at my-self – it is so convincing, seems so real, so important, yet always in the back-ground there is the silent balm, the endless song of life's true nature: the real real, calling from afar, reminding you – "not so, not so".

— To a lady seen from the train —

O why do you walk through the fields
                                in gloves
   Missing so much and so much ?
O fat white woman whom nobody loves
Why do you walk through the fields in gloves,
When the grass is as soft as the breast of
                                doves
   And shivering-sweet to the touch ?
O why do you walk through the fields in
                                gloves
   Missing so much and so much ?

                        Frances Cornford

Living in the Dhamma

From a talk given on a retreat at Amaravati, November 1992

'LIVING IN THE WORLD OF DHAMMA' means seeing things in a very clear, direct, straightforward way; immediate, direct looking at our own experience of the pure reality of each moment, at what constitutes the experience of our life.

There is an oft quoted phrase of the Buddha, "Mindfulness is the path to the Deathless, heedlessness is the path to death; the mindful never die, the heedless are as if dead already." This is almost the motto of Amaravati; it is also a favourite phrase of Ajahn Sumedho, he has used it over and over again as a reflection, hence it has ended up being the title of a book of his talks.

What do we mean by 'being alive' and what do we mean by 'death' here? Obviously what we are talking about in this instance is not whether our bodies happen to be alive, we are talking about it on a more spiritual or symbolic level. Mindfulness being the path to the Deathless means that when we are mindful we see our perceptions thoughts and feelings very clearly, and we see the context for them. We begin to perceive, or at least intuit, the quality of silence out of which all thought and feeling comes and into which it dissolves – the stillness within which all movement occurs – the silence behind all sound, within all sound.

The word 'Deathless' refers to this fundamental reality, this timeless, primordial quality, and when this is realised – when we are mindful and we are aware of that – then the response to thoughts, feelings and all the objects which are born into the mind is that of non-attachment. We experience the phenomenon of birth and death because of identification with thought, the body, with feelings and emotions. This is why every morning in the chanting, we recollect "The body is not self, feeling is not self … etc." – the source of dukkha is identification with the body, with feelings, with perceptions, conceptions and consciousness. We pound this into our minds, put the suggestion in there over and over and over again because we are so habituated to identification.

The only reason why we think of ourselves as being mortal, of having been born and being destined to death, is because of the identification with the body and so on. Bodies are born, bodies die, thoughts are born, thoughts die, perceptions are born, perceptions die, but that which knows thought, perceptions, moods and memories, that which knows all the attributes and feelings of the body, that quality is timeless, it is always there, it does not move, it is not born, it does not die. You do not have to believe this, but this is the way that the Buddha spoke about it.

★ ★ ★

The more that we use the meditation, the more we investigate the more we will keep coming to a direct realisation of this Truth. So when we say "Mindfulness is the path to the Deathless, the mindful never die," it does not mean that if you are a mindful person your body is not going to die – it means our body will die but it was not really ours anyway! This is the tricky and delicate manoeuvre whereby we are able to escape from the illusion of birth and death.

There is a beautiful saying by the Sixth Patriarch of the Zen tradition, called Hui Neng:

"In this moment there is nothing which comes to be,
in this moment there is nothing which ceases to be"

– in one single moment there is nothing which actually arises, the arising of things has to take place over time; in each moment there is just THIS, this particular pattern of images. In this moment there is nothing which ceases to be because cessation also has to take place over time....

…"thus in this moment
there is no birth and death to be brought to an end,
therefore this moment is the absolute peace
and though it is just this moment
there is no limit to this moment
and herein is eternal delight."

This means that if we look at life from the perspective of here and now, if we step out of the time-bound perceptions of beginning, continuing and ending, in that very **now** there is no coming, no going, there is no birth, there is no death.

We sometimes think of the here and now as a minute, insignificant little line between a vast past and a vast future; however, the more we observe the mind the more we realise that the here and now is that which is vast and the past and future are like vague mirages. The now is vast and immeasurable, in-finite, that is why Hui Neng says, "there is no limit to this moment", it goes on for ever, and in that timeless presence there is the quality of delight, the natural joy of the free mind.

"Heedlessness is the path to death, the heedless are as if dead already": this means that when we are not mindful, we keep identifying with things that we are not, we keep claiming things to be ours or who and what we are, but which we are not. In that identification with the world of things and mental objects, as they pursue their cycles of coming and going we feel that **we** go through those cycles as well. So as the body ages and gets sick then we think, "**I'm** aging, **I'm** sick"; if we are facing painful or negative experiences in life then they are taken to be who and what we are: **my** problems, **my** world is falling apart, **my** difficulties, **my** diseases, **me** being criticised, **me** being mistreated, **me** being oppressed, and this all seems to be very real. We like to be identified with a healthy body, a young attractive body, with affirmations of success and goodness; but if we heedlessly take that to be ours, then it is as if we were holding on to a wheel, if a wheel is turning and we hold on to the rim as the wheel goes up with success and health and youth and good fortune, then we are still holding it when it goes down the other side – when it goes down into criticism, failure and fragmentation – you know the system!

The great Western dream is to get to the top and then let go – we just get the up bit and we don't get the down – we assume that we will always remember to let go when we get to the top so then the wheel goes round but we are not holding it. That means I can identify with the good bits but when I get to the bad bits they are 'not mine'. Sometimes this system works but, having tried it myself quite often, I realise that we are not so sharp that we can remember to do that every time. That is why heedlessness takes us to death. When we meet with the dying side of the cycle we think it is real: if the body is ageing and is sick and dying then we think, "I'm dying, my life is ending, it is over, what is going to become of me? Will I disappear? Where will I go???"

The process whereby we recognise the pain of attachment and, if we want to be free, the complete necessity to let go is therefore encapsulated in that simple verse.

★ ★ ★

If we are mindful we do not suffer and if we are not mindful we do. If we do not want to suffer we just have to learn how to be mindful and the more supportive conditions we can find in our lives to help us learn how to be mindful, the better. That is the key issue, whether we happen to be in Thailand or England or America or Africa, or whether we happen to be a man or woman or young or old or healthy or sick or a monk or nun or a yogi or a school teacher – all that is immaterial. What is crucial is how mindful we can be – that is the hub that everything else in life revolves around. If we can get that right then everything else good follows.

Mindfulness is not something that is developed in a single particular way, although there are of course exercises and attitudes which help to cultivate it. It can be there in formal meditation and also in the work that we do around the place – we can always employ attention and care, easefulness about what we are doing.

I was talking with someone today who was saying how he found that, when he was what he called 'being mindful', he started to get really clumsy and that he could not do things as well or as fluidly as when he was thinking about something else. Oftentimes we find this is so because we take the idea of mindfulness to mean that we have to do everything in a very deliberate way. "Now.

I. am. walking; Now. I. am. eating; Now. I. am …" but that very way of labelling every experience can make the whole process extremely cumbersome and
difficult. We become self-conscious about what we're doing and any naturalness in our actions seems to be smothered or obstructed. What we mean by
mindfulness is the quality of presence of mind – there does not have to be a
categorisation of what we are doing, it does not have to be phrased in verbal
thought. The man speaking with me said that some of his most fluid and free,
totally harmonious moments are when he is playing sports. You are in some
very tense or testing situation, you find that you do some marvellous move that
you did not even think of beforehand, the body responds to the situation,
works out a course on its own and fulfils it in a completely harmonious way –
without thought. He was saying, "It is strange that things go best when I seem
to be most un-mindful." I replied, "I think you've got the wrong end of the
stick – it is actually a perfect kind of mindfulness when, with wisdom and
awareness, you let go of self-concern and are just letting life live itself."

Mindfulness is very much a matter of getting out of the way of things.
Sometimes we can take the idea of doing things mindfully and turn it into a
tremendous burden for ourselves and everyone around us. I have known many
people drive their family and friends to distraction over this – our efforts to be
mindful can be incredibly annoying to the people around us – if you are determined to eat your supper 'mindfully' while everyone else is just being normal,
you feel as if you are doing it the 'right' way and you don't notice the fact that
your family are becoming homicidal around you – it is definitely something to
take into account! To be mindful means to live in a fluid and easy way and simply to have our mind on what is happening, it does not mean we have to behave
in any particular fashion. With the meditation practice – *samatha* meditation, using some sort of object like the breath to aid in concentrating the mind,
or with *vipassana*, opening the mind and letting oneself be with whatever
thoughts or feelings come up – in both of these aspects one is employing that
quality of easeful attention.

★ ★ ★

One of the things that we often come across in meditation is that, even
though we might develop some ability to let go and free the mind, there is something in us that does not want to be free, that quite likes to have something to
wrestle with, something to push against or some kind of familiar feelings around
to identify ourselves with. It can be quite a challenge to let go; even though we
know that it is the right thing to do or we know that to hang on to something or
to continue to push against something is just protracting our imprisonment. In
a way we are afraid of freedom, we are scared of the responsibility of freedom.
We prefer the devil that we know – even when the door is open and the way out
is clearly in front of us, something in us prefers to keep looking in the opposite
direction so that we will not take up the option of freedom.

To let go is hard to do because we are very frightened by the unknown.
Many years ago, when I had just arrived in the monastery in Thailand, I had a
dream (set in the Wild West) where there had been some kind of battle. There

were some friends of mine who had been imprisoned in a stockade. After the battle had been won by us, the Indians, I went running into the fortress looking for my friends. I came upon the cell where they were and flung the door open, came bounding in and said, "You're free, you're free, you can go! We won the battle."

Rather than being delighted, however, they looked up at me nervously and carried on with the things they were busying themselves with. I thought, "Funny..."; I walked over and said, "You are free, you can go. Look – the door is open." One friend whom I had known for many years was sitting over in the corner with his back to me doing something with his hands. I went over to him and said, "You can go, you don't have to stay here any more." He looked up and said, "Well, er ... I am kind of busy at the moment." I looked down and saw that he was knitting – I had never known him to knit before but at that moment it was desperately important to him to be knitting. So he said, "I'm sorry, I can't leave right now," so I thought, "Oh well, never mind, leave them to it. I'll just prop the door open and be on my way."

When we let go and turn the mind towards relinquishment, emptiness, non-attachment, we can experience a quality of bereavement – the feeling of estrangement, not having familiar things around and no longer being able to think of life in the same old way. Such a quality of emptiness can feel like desiccation or blandness; we can feel a sense of dying or that the fire of our life is going out.

The spirit of living is something that we can put a lot of emphasis on and give a great deal of energy to over the years, so then we wonder, "Am I doing this right? Is this really the right thing? Everything seems to be so vacant, insubstantial." It takes a lot of courage to see that actually all that is dying is self-centred thinking. And in that dying, what is being actualised is an awakening to the true reality of our own nature; the eye is being caught by the peel that's been cast away rather than noticing the essence which is being revealed.

This principle is displayed in the symbolism of fire within Buddhist and Vedic scriptures. There, when a fire is described as going out, as in the word 'Nibbana', it is not seen as something dying and going into extinction, rather the fire element is regarded as returning to its primordial, immortal, omnipresent state. The fire element, the innate energy of the object, is withdrawn back into the thing which had been on fire, it returns to its original nature. We can think of the mind in the same way: when the mind flows out into acquisition, fear, and worry, into aversion and attraction, into ambition, views and opinions about things, into chasing pleasure and escaping pain, these are the flames! The mind on fire – the flames aleaping. When we restrain those out-flowing tendencies of the mind, this is not death but real life at last. The en - ergy of the mind is contained and is allowed to rest, aware and bright in its primordial and unconditioned state. We are no longer wasting mental energy, no longer sending energy wildly out into the sensory world; instead we are containing it, retaining it. We are no longer trying to, or needing to, define our being solely in terms of external qualities and activities; we are defining it far more in terms of spiritual qualities, that which is timeless, knowing and not mortal, that which is infinite and universal within us.

★ ★ ★

In Buddhist meditation there is a lot of emphasis on understanding the body because it is such a focus for our attention and a key place of identification: its health and its energy, its age, its gender, its appearance and so on. It is therefore important to be aware of how much mental energy flows out in identification with the body. We have a vast variety of different ways of contemplating it: the different elements of the body – earth, water, fire and air – or to think of it in terms of organs and bones and skin and muscles and blood and so on. This is all to do with learning to see that which is the physical basis of our being in terms of a whole natural order, rather than seeing it in a very personalised way. We are restraining the habitual way of thinking of it and seeing it as a part of a whole web of being; it is part of a vast process of integration and disintegration.

When we see the body in this much more objective way, it brings us to a quality of coolness, steadiness of mind. Then, whether the body is healthy or unhealthy, whether it is young or old, whether it is attractive or unattractive, those processes or those different attributes that it can have occur according to time and place and we do what we can in response to them. If we get hungry, then we eat; if we get sick, then we find some treatment – but it is not something that we seek for absolute satisfaction in. It is a great relief to no longer expect the body to be comfortable or to be perfectly healthy or to be arranged according to some kind of ideal. We can just let it be what it is – it goes through its cycles, it has its own nature – we can take care of it and look after it and be with it until it dies but we are not making anything out of it. It is just a simple aspect of nature like any other living thing. It has its good qualities, its bad qualities, its beautiful and its ugly qualities, and we cease to make any great drama out of it.

Sometimes in the Theravada tradition the meditations on the body can seem like a very narrow-minded way of viewing the person; it is often remarked that in the Theravada approach towards meditating on the body it is seen as something which is inherently dangerous and attractive and that we have to dismember it with our thoughts because of the power that it has to delude. That is only one aspect of it, however, and one can view it in many different ways.

If we see a person who is physically attractive to us then the initial approach is to contemplate the perception of the body just as a physical body and to take it apart into its different elements and to look at it in that way – that is the 'Hinayana' or personal approach: "This is attractive, it's dangerous, the mind should not get attached to it; quick, take it to bits, get it out of the way so we will avoid the trouble."

The 'Mahayana' or grand approach, the next step along, is to say, "Well, here is a living being who experiences pleasure and pain and hope and fear and happiness and unhappiness. What can be done in order to help this living being to transcend suffering and to be liberated?" The person is then seen not just in terms of attractiveness or unattractiveness of the body but seen as a living being needing help.

The last level of appreciation when we meet another being is recognising that here is something inherently divine, pure, which is Dhamma, totally spiritual.

When we meet another person we can contemplate the experience in these different ways. One is opening the mind to the whole spectrum of being, from the mundane and physical to the altruistic, to the ultimate. This is the way that we can also relate to our own body, our own being: this is just a bag of bones, blood and flesh and all sorts of other unspeakable things; and yes, here is also a living being who has feelings of pleasure and pain and who aspires to transcend suffering and ignorance; and yes, here is also a completely perfect and pure aspect of Nature. All these realities are true and one has to keep an eye on all of them. If we just focus on one aspect and say, "I am this," we miss the rest.

We need to include them all – from the most humble to the most elevated and pure – then the way that we appreciate ourselves and the way we appreciate others around us has a wholeness to it, has an integrated quality. We are not just acting on a part of the picture, we are living with the whole and because of that our actions and the way we live are always going to be harmonious with the things and people around us.

★ ★ ★

The 'outflowing' of the mind is what one is witnessing in meditation when the mind surges off into sights and sounds, opinions, thoughts or feelings. It is most important to get acquainted with what that is like for the mind: the attention pouring out into different things. One can see how, first of all, there is just a vague thought or a memory, or a shape that you notice, and it is quite ephemeral; there is nothing very much there, you just remember some event. Then it catches our attention and, as the mind goes into it; suddenly what was just a vague and insubstantial thing comes to life – and our attention has brought it to life. We have breathed life into that thought with the act of attention. As we give attention to it and it comes to life, then the whole flow of feeling along with that increases and develops – whether the feeling is pleasant or painful or whatever. It comes into being and the whole thing starts to gain momentum. If there is no mindfulness, then that feeling conditions self-centred desire; if it is a pleasant feeling, a desire for more of it; if it is a painful feeling, a desire to get away from it. Then that desire turns into attachment and the attachment turns into what is called 'becoming' – like a wave gathering strength – then, as the attachment and the becoming increase, we find ourselves thoroughly caught up with some melodrama and carried away on the whole cycle of birth and death. We are born into a memory, a hope or a worry, born into a piece of music or a feeling; and if we are born into it then we die with it when it comes to an end. Suddenly we find ourselves stranded and lost in another world.

If, when we have given something our attention and the thing has come alive, and the different feelings of pleasure or pain are there, then, if there is constant mindfulness and concentration, the concentrated mind will contain the feelings. If there is mindfulness it will surround and hold that feeling. There is a knowing that "this is a feeling of pleasure" or "this is a feeling of pain", and there is wisdom. We understand it, we know that this is not going to last. "This is just a feeling, it is not me or mine, it is not who and what I am." So that feeling becomes a basis for liberation: rather than carrying us into a whole cycle of hope and disappointment, the cycle of birth and death, if mindfulness, concentration and wisdom are there, that same feeling will take us to deliverance. If there is wisdom then we realise – "This is a feeling" – and we follow it as it goes through its cycle of life. Then, as the feeling fades, there is nothing there creating more momentum around it. The feeling fades like a sound and then there is silence. That condition dissolves into the Unconditioned and there is peacefulness, clarity, the joy of the free mind; this is what we mean by Nibbana. All conditions of mind, all patterns of consciousness end in Nibbana. They will lead us to Nibbana if we let them – if we don't let them they won't!

The way we let them lead is through mindfulness and concentration – this is the process we give ourselves to – learning to recognise the power of attention. Then, even if we cannot restrain our attention from going into things initially, we can still bring our mind to the feelings that have arisen and then let any feeling or experience take the mind to the realisation of Nibbana, the energetic silence, to the quality of living stillness that is the very fabric of this life.

The Long Road North

PART TWO – FROM THE LINCOLN WOLDS
TO THE PENNINES

W E HAVE LEFT THE FEATURELESS LEVELS and vast skies of the Fens far behind us and are now sitting on top of Hoe Hill, an old mound near the Bluestone Ridge. Around us the Lincoln Wolds lie folded in gentle green rumples, the barley is billowing in the wind and the sun is shining brightly. It is hard to imagine that the world could be any more beautiful than this. It was only a few hours ago, however, that we were chased from our campsite by hordes of hungry midges, the skies were lowering, the wind cold and rain was threatening to lash us. It was only a short while before that that the same valley seemed like paradise … it only goes to show.

★ ★ ★

The last three days have been quite a mixture for us: sunny ambling, picnics, campfires, an irate farmer; rolling through gentle valleys, windy hills, meadow churches; fears and worries, warmth and light, peace and agitation; one and all in the sky together like the sun and clouds.

The afternoon that we left Hoe Hill we joined a path called 'The Viking Way', which wanders north-south through the Lincoln Wolds. We have stayed with or nearby it ever since then. Like the North Downs Way, it is an official long-distance path but, predictably, the marker for it is a little viking's head with a two-horned helmet thus: ♈. This fellow we have named 'Sven' and we have enjoyed his company for this part of the trip. As we have been aiming to reach Brigg on Thursday we have been able to go at a very gentle pace, often stopping to sit and meditate and take in the glory of our surroundings.

That first evening we found an abandoned farm near a small nature reserve called Red Hill; it was very broken down but the barn had a good roof so we decided to spend the night there. I am always a bit nervous of "appearance of irate farmer with shotgun" whenever we spend the night camping in the corner of some farm or in such places as this. Neither that night, however, nor the following morning did anyone appear, and after we had eaten we ambled on.

It was another hot day and the countryside was beautiful. As we approached Ludford Woods, where we had planned to stop, we could almost hear the Siren's song of the midges, calling out for us to join them amongst the trees; it was wet and humid with dense undergrowth and dark. We declined the invitation and carried on, finding a large barn off the road shortly before the village; it seemed a good place so we decided to stop there. We lit a fire under the huge lean-to as it had begun to rain and, despite ever more present fears of 'the farmer' and the sound of a shotgun nearby, no-one appeared. The next morning we were clearing up to go and, as I rounded the corner of the barn bearing two dead but smouldering logs from the fire, my eyes fell upon a small flock of sheep and a farm-lad, clad in a blue boiler-suit, hands in pockets, ambling along beside them. He did not see me and I quickly turned around; I scurried through the barn to see Nick (who was in the middle of his yoga routine), and told him what was up, my heart pounding furiously. I started to pack and suddenly realised that I was completely terrified. "This is ridiculous," I thought, so I paused for a few moments and stopped, slightly amazed at the intensity of my fear of 'being caught'. The lad looked like the most amiable fellow in the world and, as it turned out, a few minutes later he drove off and we never saw him again.

Later that morning, whilst Nick and I were sitting at a crossroads, a policeman pulled up in his car and said hello; he made conversation with us, asking our names and where we were from. Thinking that he was just curious about us, I was quite surprised when he asked for our dates of birth as well; as we were talking I felt quite at ease and we chatted happily away. Afterwards Nick told me that they would be checking up on us (having had some experience of his name being taken in the teenage days of his south coast jaunts with his young pals Tombstone and Weasel). They would look to see if we had a record or if anything suspicious had happened in the district – "like a barn burning down". "Oh dear," I thought, trying hard to convince myself that we had been really thorough in putting the fire out; imagining the Lincolnshire Constabulary appearing at Chithurst with a warrant, or arresting us in an ambush further up the Viking Way.

Later on we sat on a windy hilltop, with the trees and all the land around blown wildly and buffeted; we found a sheltered corner and I reflected on the doubt: you do not know exactly what is going on, as from whence the wind comes and where it will go you cannot say – all that is certain is that the wind is blowing, whatever will happen, will happen. What can you do but find a sheltered spot where there is some peace amidst the storms?

Bright and breezy the afternoon; we pressed on through Tealby and Walesby and stopped for a while in the old wayfarers church up on the hilltop. Silence hovered – greeting us as we walked in, blessing us as we sat, unmoved in parting as we left; it was still windy outside and heavier clouds were coming from the south-west. As we crossed over Lincoln's highest ridge we were rained upon but our path took us down into a sheltered valley and soon the weather cleared. We camped and, after making tea, sat until quite late. A crescent moon had appeared by then, together with a star. I watched as they sank behind the hill leaving the night alone to be lit by a few pale constellations. It was midnight and, feeling very clear and peaceful with the fading of the day's traumas, I went happily to sleep.

Curiously, it was the following morning, after all the doubts, fears and worries seemed to have vanished, that 'irate farmer' (but without shotgun), eventually appeared. For once we were camped right on a public footpath and were, I (incorrectly) thought, completely 'legal'. He came at about eight o'clock, pulling up in his Land-Rover in the field across the stream. Immediately he started shouting at us, bawling loud abuse and furiously brandishing his crook;

"Aha," I thought, "Buddha as wrathful deity." As I felt we were there quite rightfully it was not difficult to be calm with him. He came over to us very angry, but after talking for a while he saw that we had meant no harm and were very sorry to have caused offense. Nick spoke very kindly to him and I was amazed to see his mood dissolve as rapidly as it did; he even became quite calm and quiet as they talked about the land and the running of his farm.

"They're always like that," said Nick afterwards, "come on all irate but are really friendly underneath. Their farm is the dearest thing to them, it's their life, so it's understandable that they feel put out when someone just moves in – sets up like they own the place." The thing he was most upset about was the fire, which was embarrassingly and unnecessarily big; we explained that it was all dead wood we had picked up and that we had tried to do no damage to his farm. When we parted company he was quite friendly, but I still felt a bit guilty about the fire, having followed the Viking rather than the Buddha way in my wood-gathering exploits. I had not been very mindful of either what we really needed or the respect due to the land as someone's private property. I realised that we should be more sensitive and careful, especially about fires, and not to go about things in such a heedless way as we have done on occasion up to now.

It is good to see that when you wander off the track it only takes a while before the karma ripens and you get to taste the fruit. Guilt and remorse for being selfish, intrusive and clumsy; all the angst which comes from having lost your path. All this feeling is exactly what makes us resolve to do better in the future: to keep to the path, since to struggle in the rough is both painful and exhausting. *Hiriottappa*, moral sensitivity, guardian and protector of the world.

★ ★ ★

From Brigg there were only two bridges over the River Trent within twenty miles of us and the closer of them was a motorway. Nick felt inclined to take this but, since a motorway is illegal for pedestrians, eventually I decided it would be wrong. This meant we had to walk a further four miles north and through the edges of Scunthorpe rather than through the open country. Nick bowed to this choice without a murmur and I was glad – the noble way may not always be the most direct but every step of it is in the peace of innocence.

★ ★ ★

Now that we are well into the journey I have found that I think very little in terms of getting anywhere: we have walked north, south, east and west; fast and slow; have had to rush, had to wait and have taken a host of small detours, often for very little reason. All of this combines together in the walk and helps dissolve any idea of progress or a goal. At any one time we are somewhere aiming to be somewhere else, but the very physical nature of our day's activities, the variety of places, moods and weathers we have been through, always return one to – "Well, here we are." The memory of our departure from Chithurst and the fantasy of our arrival at Harnham occasionally flicker by – remote mirages, unconvincing, with their irrelevance so clear they fade almost as soon as they arise.

★ ★ ★

As we walked along the pathway in the park at the edge of Sheffield, through the neat lawns and flowerbeds, we passed a young man with a burly dog straining on its lead. Nick stared down at the panting beast and his curiosity was aroused.

"What an incredibly ugly dog!" he proclaimed. "What is it?"

"It's a bull terrier," the young man replied. "They are supposed to look like this."

Conversation having begun, the two of them chatted on as we walked along. At some earlier point on the walk Nick and I had been talking about the different worlds we live in: how one can be skilled or expert or even famous in one field, yet unknowing or unknown outside of that. I mentioned how surprised we had all been in our family when we began to realise that my father had become an internationally famous journalist and judge of dog shows, and yet, within the home, he was just the same as when he had been a farmer. I suppose it must have sounded to Nick like a boast when I told him you could mention my father's name to any dog-breeder and they would know him. We sat down to rest on a park bench and he decided to put me to the test....

"Tan Amaro's father is a dog man. He says you are bound to have heard of him."

"Oh? What's his name?"

"Tom Horner."

"**Tom Horner**! *The* bull terrier man! Well, fancy that – of course I've heard of him. Fancy meeting Tom Horner's son in the local park."

I suspect Nick was considerably humbled by this response. It is true that most dog-breeders have heard of my father but to pick a bull terrier owner was unlucky. This is the breed in which my father is most expert; he has bred them, shown them and has written a well-respected book about them.

We sat and chatted together for a while and at last parted company, the young man still shaking his head with incredulity at our meeting.

"You were right, bhante," said Nick, "I am **very** impressed."

Smiling quietly, we carried on down the path out of the city.

★ ★ ★

It was quite late when we pitched the tents and we watched the sky as it cleared; by twilight there were no clouds and we looked forward to a fine day to cross the last of the big hills.

By the next morning things had changed and all my hopes of basking in sunshine on top of Kinder Scout (whose continually foul weather is legendary) were dashed. The day broke with heavy cloud, which descended to meet us as we climbed the hill. Following the track called Jacob's Ladder we walked into the whiteness and soon were soaking wet. We decided to go straight over the pass and thus avoid the summit. We resolved that it was much wiser to be buddhas than world conquerors – it was very wet and windy, visibility was less than twenty yards and the top of the hill was a trackless plateau of peat-bog – the obvious thing was to go through it as directly as possible and take a path straight down the other side. As we crossed over the pass I suddenly realised that in a way I had got my wish after all, but the sunlight of wisdom does not need a cloudless day to shine.

★ ★ ★

Our walk through the city of Manchester was something I had slightly dreaded; I had prepared myself to be kicked to pieces and never leave the place alive, but after all the spreading of Dhamma, together with the mountain of good wishes and blessings we were carrying, in the end it all went very smoothly. Contained and keeping an even pace, I determined to hold wisdom as my refuge rather than the absence of any immediate threat. Our route took us through the inner city, a mass of broken and dismal streets, through Old Trafford and the docklands stuck between Salford and central Manchester. We crossed the black and bubbling ship canal, passed through the lanes of towerblock estates and finally entered the genteel Jewish confines of the borough where Carol Batton lived. As we walked through the town you could see that people simply react to the sight of you out of their conditioning: little children go, "Wow"; slightly larger ones say, "What are you?" "Are you nuns?" "Are you Spanish?" "Are you a Egypt man?"

"That skin'ead's wearing strange clothes."

"It's Jesus."

"Jesus."

Groups of teenage girls tend to laugh, giggling as you go by.

"Will you look at the state of that!"

Older boys bellow insults, incomprehensible, unfamiliar, from passing cars, across the street.

A pair of punks said, "Hi", and a couple of old men smiled warmly.

The pattern of all attention simply comes out of our conditioning; by being resolute in non-contention with the effects you have on people, you can walk through it quite untouched. It was all very peaceful, I could feel the habitual reaction of fear to threat and derision fading, evaporating as we walked; illuminated from the inside by offering peace.

Hot and sticky in the valley, although it was evening by now, we headed up into the hills again; tromping along through farm-tracks, out into the open. It was getting dark and we were beginning to notice more and more abandoned farm buildings around. As there was a lot more climbing to do before we would be able to find a good place to pitch the tent, we opted to spend the night in a derelict house. It was long since unoccupied and in use as a hay-barn. We clambered through the hay-bales to the first storey and sank, completely worn out, to the floor. How good to be stationary and cool. We remained immobile, slumped on our packs, until some energy arrived; we sat and meditated for a while and it was nearly midnight when finally we turned in.

A clear bright morning ran in through the empty window and shook me from my sleep. It was looking to be hot again so we decided, as before, to walk early and late, taking a long break at midday. We followed the Pennine Way up into the hills and found a good spot in the shade of a thorn tree by a reservoir. All through the afternoon a stream of walkers passed us by, maybe even a dozen every hour. I do not know what people think when they see us: we are obviously somewhat different from the crowd, travelling the same road but on another wavelength – treading to the beat of the Deathless Drum.

After six hours under the tree we decided it was time to move on. As we walked I found myself with a bad attack of the 'getting somewheres', which I had not seen since before we got to London. It was quite funny to see the mind figuring out what fraction of the journey we had done (eight-thirteenths), how much we had to go and all along knowing there is no-one going anywhere at all. Sunshine, cool breeze, good path, good boots, doing what you most want to in the world, but the untamed mind is always keen to be concerned with something, someone or somewhere else.

Through the lands of Wuthering Heights and down into the valley, we carried on up the next hill to camp in the breeze. Finding a midge-ridden marsh and no breeze on top, however, we kept going until we reached another abandoned farmhouse. We cleared ourselves a space amidst the rubble and broken glass and settled in, thankful to the farmer and the house-builders for the use of a shelter for the night.

★ ★ ★

Walking in the dales, on the Pennine Way and around has been good for meeting other travellers. Most of the time, conversation only begins when we ask for water or arrive at our destination; here, amongst so many other walkers, I am often taken to be simply strangely dressed and people talk to us quite freely. There is always a camaraderie between members of the same group and interest in how you are doing. Being so obviously hikers we are part of the family and people are very open with us.

As we followed a broad track between some reservoirs above Rochdale, we saw a man with a tripod photographing the valley; now brilliant and hazy in the afternoon heat. It was plain that he was keen to meet us and, as we went by, he introduced himself. We stood together for a long while, listening to his gentle Orkney accent and telling him all about our walk. Before we parted he took some photographs and promised to send us copies. He was a truly gentle man and it had obviously meant a lot to him to meet us.

Another touching gesture made that day was the gift of some ice-cubes from a lady in Hebden Bridge: having just climbed a steep, long, cobbled lane, the two of us rested on a low stone wall, sitting there very hot and sweaty. After a while Nick went to ask for water at a house; the lady took the bottles in but was gone for a long time. When she returned, she explained that she had been trying to break up ice-cubes to put in the water.

"The big-necked one were quite easy but t'other one gave me a load of trouble."

Eventually she had given up, filled a margarine tub with ice and offered that to us instead. Very grateful, we drank many mugs of the delicious liquid – cool Yorkshire water like nectar in a hot and dusty throat.

It had been roasting all day and that evening, after long, hot and humid hours, the sun mellowed to a glimmering orange fire. It rested for a moment as a red balloon bulging on the hill-crest; lingering long before it disappeared, gently and as if for ever, beneath the blue slumber of the hills.

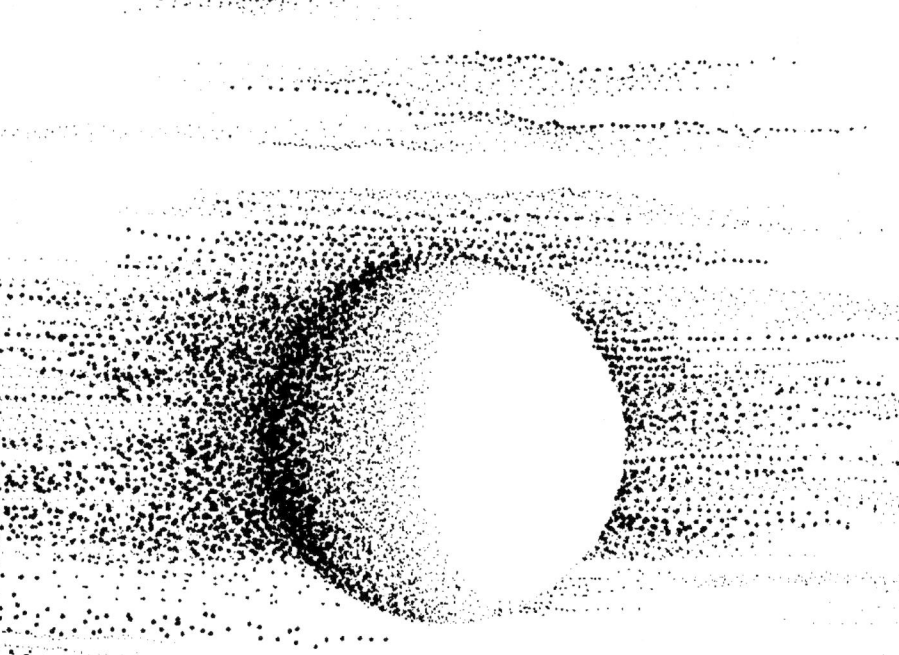

I

"The bower of sleep is a double-edged sword,"
a golden cord. Quiet,
we pick our way along parks and watersides,
canals and rivers, under trees, finally through floral boroughs,
polite streets, to bring us here.
And, insofaras separated I exist,
I feel the point of all projection worn away –
a smooth stone smooth
at the bottom of a stream.
Sh-sh-sh-shadows
shawdo, shadow of the Unborn –
a smooth stone dissolving in the bottom of a stream.
Cultivating; rotating, but in the heart of silence.
A dog-like mind tends to bark louder when it's chained,
behind windows, when it's reined;
smart old silence, emptiness, a sea –
less the friend of absence than of light –
transparency.

(Chorlton-cum-Hardy, June 1983)

In the Refuge of Sangha

From a talk given at Chithurst during the winter retreat, February 1991

THE BUDDHA'S FIRST DISCOURSE after the enlightenment, which we recited this evening, the Dhammacakka Sutta, is something which always touches my heart. There is something moving and significant about the recreation of that moment when the Buddha's dispensation began. In the chant itself it describes how, after the Buddha had given this talk, the earth quaked and the "ten thousand-fold universal system shook and quaked and rocked and a great measureless light surpassing the beauty of the gods spread throughout the world". We can feel a small echo of this in our own heart when we go back to that moment of the first transmission, the first conveying of the Buddha's insight to other people. Because at that moment the Buddha realised that one of the bhikkhus with him, Kondañña, had understood the Teaching; the eye of Dhamma had opened, he saw the Truth, the Path. The Buddha then exclaimed, "Kondañña knows!" So from that time forth, the monk's name was changed from Kondañña to Añña-Kondañña – 'Kondañña who knows'.

That night in the deer park in Benares, these half dozen wandering monks sitting gathered together, what an earth-shattering little scene that was, unbeknownst to the people just half a mile away. But at that moment, something happened that has since transformed the lives of millions of people. We in this little group of people gathered here, we inherit the result of that moment. That was the moment the Sangha began, because Kondañña's response to the eye of Dhamma opening was immediate: "I would like to become your disciple." He asked to be accepted as a disciple, one of the Buddha's children. He was born of the Dhamma.

So, all these centuries further on, we are part of that family and we inherit the blessings, the benefits, the treasures of it. We are children of the Buddha and we inherit the Buddha's legacy.

The Sangha is something we describe in the daily chanting as "giving occasion for incomparable goodness to arise in the world". This is something that is good to contemplate: why is existing together as a group so important? Why such a big deal about it? How come a group of people who live a simple life together, who observe kindness and restraint and so forth, how come this is such a blessing? Why is this an incomparable field of merit, a fertile ground for goodness to develop in? Why is it such an important thing for the world?

For myself, I can see that if I didn't have like-minded companions to help me in the spiritual life, I never would have gained remotely the understanding or the peace of mind that there is in my life; it would have been impossible to develop any kind of spiritual qualities without the presence of such companionship.

When I was growing up I was always very interested in mystical things, the inner aspects of religion and understanding. It was tremendously important to me to understand what lay behind everything, to understand the *meaning*. I thought about these things often and felt that I had figured out a lot. I would get into intense discussions on esoteric, profound, obtuse philosophical points for hours on end, ablaze with interest and an emergent understanding. Alongside that, however, there was also tremendous emotional turbulence; uncontrolled anxieties, fears and passions were all swishing around in my mind along with everything else.

Even though there was a strong spiritual impulse from a young age, still the confusion coming from instinctual desires, fears and insecurities meant that all the attraction towards Truth, wisdom and understanding that was there, the valid insight that was there became confused, corrupted and sidetracked and taken up with secondary things, or got drawn into being lazy or choosing oblivion rather than true knowledge of the spiritual Way.

I had been studying at London University. When my degree was finished I took the opportunity to leave England and head off into the East, on my spiritual quest. Up until that point I had always felt that making my own piecemeal spiritual path was quite sufficient; I wasn't consciously looking for any kind of institution or group to belong to. In fact I had quite strong anti-establishment feelings, I always felt that just to be a free spirit was the ideal: "When love beckons to you, follow him … when he speaks to you believe in him," as Khalil Ghibran put it. Well, 'love' was leading me to some disastrous places.

Even though I made efforts to live a free and spiritual existence, trying to maximise on the qualities that I respected – being a harmless, friendly, kind, generous etc. person – this didn't seem to help me a great deal with the confusion that was in my mind. Also spending time amongst people whose values were very worldly and were based upon distraction had a very negative effect. It became clear that just having a nice philosophy and nice principles but without having something that helped that to be actualised, led to a place where I found all of my ideas and aspirations were wasted, burned up. I began to feel a lot of despair. I seemed to be doing all of the right things according to my own formula, yet the result was extremely painful and disappointing.

One of the things that I had always cherished was the quality of harmony and friendship. I found that being a force of concord between people was an important ethic in my life. I always felt very hurt by people who were determined to conflict. When coming into contact with the Sangha in Thailand, I found that the quality of harmony or friendship was the very basis of that community. The word 'Sangha' means "those that are together". Its whole essence is in being separate individual people joined together in harmony: "As friendly and undisputing as milk with water, looking upon each other with kindly eyes."

The initial attraction towards the Sangha was the realisation that, "Here is a group of people who are putting into action the spirit of what I respect and find most important and precious in life. Here are people who are learning to live harmoniously with each other." The other aspects of Sangha life, the qualities of renunciation and devotional practices, adherence to rules and so forth, those things were all very secondary to me. I didn't really take them in at first, because what was most important was the communal spirit, the training of the heart to live harmoniously with others. This is what caught my interest and drew me into the community. This was slightly unusual because most of the other people in the Sangha were people interested in meditation, who had wanted to find a teacher, who had studied Buddhism and wanted to try and experience life as a monastic.... For me all of that was stuff that came later – the spirit of community was what I really longed for.

I suppose I knew in my heart that what I needed more than anything else was an environment in which to make use of the potential that was there within myself. I could see that a lot of the good things that were within me and other people were just being wasted. And I could see that this was a tragedy, and would only lead to sorrow in the end.

So the beauty of the Sangha is that we have people around us who are like-minded who can support us in our spiritual life and encourage us with their presence. I remember being at Wat Pah Nanachat, the international monastery, in Thailand and my mind being incessantly filled with unspeakable thoughts – steamy passions and worries – my imagination would go wild thinking about this and that. I used to feel guilty about receiving people's offerings. As a Western monk, even as a novice, people were very devoted, kind and generous, so I would think, "If they knew what was going on in my mind, they would be horrorstruck." I would express these reservations and feelings to the monks there and say, "You know I feel this is a bit of a sham, these people think we are all so pure and holy. What is going on in my mind is pretty profane!"

Then, when the monks explained, I realised that a monastery is not for 'saints', it is for 'sinners'. If we were all pure, enlightened beings there wouldn't be any need for monasteries. Monasteries are here for those that have potential and a lot of defilements and confusion. Monasteries exist so that the potential that is there has a chance to ripen, to develop. If we feel that as soon as we shave our head or come and stay in a monastery we are supposed to be absolutely bereft of unwholesome or anxious neurotic feelings, or anything less than totally pure radiant love, wisdom etc., then we create a lot of problems and confusion for ourselves.

A monastery is a place where we allow our confusion and our defilements to be understood. We allow into consciousness all the habits of our mind that we have lived with through our lifetime. A monastery is where we study these, where we look at them; we learn to see what these are. Where do they come from? What is that which is good? How do we develop it? How do we bring that to fruition? What is there that is bad or unproductive? How do we let it end? How do we allow it to go to cessation? A monastery is where we learn to do these things, that is what it is for.

So the point is not to feel guilty if we are not thinking beautiful thoughts but to be able to reflect upon the whole – the faults and the problems along with that which is beautiful, loving and wise.

★ ★ ★

As I began to understand this, I began to see that the people supporting us didn't expect us to have totally pure minds or to be without faults or problems. They were glad that there were human beings who were ready to lay aside choice, worldly joys and comforts, and who were ready to search within their own hearts to develop the good. This is what people support us for: not for the things that pass through our minds, but for the aspirations that we have to develop and cherish the good. Whatever we need to go through in order to do that is all right – everything that goes through our minds is all right. We can experience months, years of despair, turbulence, doubts, anxieties, passions – hundreds of years of Siberian low – it is all right. Whatever the accumulations of our karma are, that is the material we have to work with.

So the Sangha is a gathering together of people who are encouraging each other to have the strength and fortitude to keep going, to fulfil the resolution that we have. I know that even if I had been taught how to meditate and do all the right things, if I hadn't had the companionship and the support of the monks and the nuns I would have slung the towel in long ago – of that I have no doubt whatsoever. I would have given up the whole thing, hit the bottle or ended up in some dope-den in Bombay, or just found a little corner to crawl away into to forget the whole thing. One has high ideals and nice illusions about life, but so many times there has been that feeling of, "I can't stand it any more, I give up." So many times that feeling has come up, but one of the most important things about being part of a whole collection of people, is the sense of honour or affiliation with other members of the group. That sense is what stops us, and says, "Well, if you give up then you are robbing other people of the encouragement to keep going; your resolution will contribute to the resolution of others."

All-night meditation vigils are a great teaching of this: you think, "What is the point of all this?" Or you are living in a monastery with someone you can't get along with, there is constant conflict and you are tired of thrashing away and dealing with your feelings of irritation or aversion; or you are madly in love with someone and you can't stop thinking about them, and yet you don't want to make a big thing out of it…. That quality of being part of the group and expressing devotion towards the communal aspiration is what provides us with the check that says, "No, don't give up, don't throw it in."

To give up the aspiration in order to surrender to a passing feeling would be tragic, something deeply regretted later on. At the moment of wanting to give up, it is quite obvious that, "I can't stand this any more, this is too much, I'm going to explode, I've got to do something, get me out of here! Something which makes a difference – eat something, steal something, go run round the forest half a dozen times – **something**, anything to make a difference." Then, because we have paused to take into account the community's values, we realise that that thought, that feeling is not as absolute as it pretends to be.

The quality of Sangha empowers that sense of honour in our heart which says, "You can let go of this, you don't have to believe this, you don't have to follow this." Now, one can look upon this as being intimidated by the group, as a weakness or inhibition – "You know, if you were really strong you wouldn't be intimidated, you wouldn't be afraid of upsetting the others saying, 'Tut, tut, tut, naughty girl, you should behave, be good, don't do anything bad that upsets the rest.'" One can look at it in that way, as inhibition, but one can also see it as being that which truly protects and guards our heart; the quality of virtuous restraint and gentleness, it is the quality of desirelessness and fearlessness.

When we act out of our passions, there's a certain gratification at the moment of getting what we want, and it is **really** pleasant. Like when Babou the cat was calling out two doors away, wailing helplessly in the cold with all the rest of group in here. Then came the incredible satisfaction of getting through both doors – Venerable Buddhadaso getting up to open both doors – and the sheer delight of not only finding the Venerable Brahmano's lap but also that he had his sanghati wrapped around him, so he got Brahmano's lap and a woollen blanket. The purring was shaking the whole shrine room – one happy cat – "Ooo, not only out of the cold, but YES! This is as good as it gets."

We can feel just like that when we get what we want – there is a moment of satisfaction and thrill. But then shortly after, as we are all acquainted with, there is the feeling of, "Is that it? You mean that's it? All this time I've been wailing for **this**? Oh no, oh what an idiot, what a disappointment, it's just so ordinary." You've said what you wanted to say, you've got what you wanted to get. You've broken out, you're free, and then … "This is it?"

So this is why I feel in my heart that the Sangha is something that we need to deeply treasure, respecting it as an institution and as an entity in itself. Without the Sangha and its communal aspiration so many of us would just fall away, caught into our desires, our worries, fears and distractions. Those qualities which are pure and noble within us would be lost, or not given the opportunity to fulfil themselves as they do in this situation here.

Once we generate that reverence in our hearts, things can become difficult, because that reverence is something that we sometimes prefer not to have around. Often one would really not like to be a member of the Sangha, thinking, "If only these other people were not around, I could get on with my own thing. If I didn't have a meeting to go to; if I didn't have these rules to keep; if I didn't have these other people hovering in the background, then I could do my thing." It is hard to sustain that respect because it frustrates the self-centred lower mind. That frustration is hard to bear. But what such respect does do, if we do bear with it, is bring us to experience the true wealth, true richness, true joy in life. We find a heart which is light, free, which is beautiful. Which is unobtainable just through the gratification of desire.

Gratification can mimic that same fullness but it cannot really match it. So the presence of the Sangha is a source of support, it is like having a sea that buoys us up; it is like being able to float – when our resolve weakens then we have the community which is there to keep us breathing, which will hold us up when our strength and interest in the spiritual flags and wanes.

In an ideal world we shouldn't need this, if we were all enlightened beings we wouldn't need this but, because there is work to be done, we need friends. We need to connect with people who respect what is good, spiritual and pure. Those connections will help keep us alive and maintain that capacity within us for the good qualities of our hearts to flourish.

The Long Road North

AFTER A WHILE we dropped down off the hills and, passing through the richer lowland farms, walked along a disused railway line in the valley bottom, side-by-side with the river and the Leeds and Liverpool Canal. Down in the valley it was hot and there was not a breath of wind; we decided to camp high for the night and aimed for the distant point of Flasby Fell, looming hazy and dark to the north of us. "Maybe, with a bit of luck, there is an inch of air astir up there." We crossed the canal, the knot of roads and railway, and began the long climb. Once again what we had estimated to be an easy day turned into one long and sweaty; our boots finally coming off at twilight. It felt very good to have endured through it though, carrying on until the very end was reached. As it turned out, even on such a high and open hill, there was only the slightest of breezes. These parts must be another story in winter but right now the air just seems to hover, still and heavy, too hot by far to move. Some rain came in the night but, by daybreak, what wind there had been had gone. The valley below us was filled with mist and only the tops of the far ridges were visible. I would have felt like the half-sketched figure of a Chinese landscape in such a scene, had the image not been marred by the fact that I was scurrying busily about, gathering all our bits to be on the move, hurrying away from the midges.

We crossed over the hilltop and decided to take a level-ish path to Winterburn Reservoir. Down along the valley edge the morning was cooler, the sun not having penetrated the mist, and we found it this way for most of the day. It was actually just a pleasantly warm July day, but if you wanted to walk through it heavy-laden you were going to sweat. We stopped on the edge of the reservoir and laid our wet things out on an old stone wall. My robes were clammy from several days' perspiration and our socks were soaked from the grass. A few hours in the sun and wind and things were much fresher. It was such a lovely day; it kept reminding me that there is nothing inherently wrong with the world, it is just a matter of what you do in it: if you choose to walk you get hot – can you really blame the weather for your discomfort?

Later in the afternoon we followed the lane up from the reservoir and saw an old farmer coming up the track towards us, hobbling along gently on two walking-sticks. Being English, we soon got around to talking of the weather.

"A bit hot," we said.

"Aye – expect it is, if y' walkin'."

So gentle and old, he could hardly hear or see; he had spent his life farming this valley and was obviously enjoying the slow fading of his years. We talked a long time together and, when he smiled, he reminded me of my old Jewish grandfather: so ancient, had worked so hard; when something tickled him you could see an impish spring-like grin run through him and you felt yourself melt away inside.

That afternoon continued hot and humid; we sweated, cleg- and fly-chased through the valley. The river bottom was dry, and the thought of the windy tops of Pen-y-ghent was very inviting. We stopped by Litton village, where the path up the valley-side began and Nick went off to fill our water-bottles. I sat on my pack in a farm gateway and waited. Much time passed; he seemed to have been gone for an age and I assumed that he had got into conversation with the farmer in the nearby house. About twenty minutes later he rounded the corner and, looking up, I thought, "What, no water-bottles? No water-bottles, no pack??"

"We have been invited for tea, bhante," he said, smiling a cheesy smile. Having gone in search of orange juice as well as water, he had sought out the local post office. For once he was disinclined to get into a chat with anyone, hoping to get the stuff and get over Pen-y-ghent as soon as possible. Nature has a way of putting the brakes on for us whenever we get too caught up in the impetus of our plans: the postmistress was very interested in where Nick was going, what he was doing and soon they were deep in conversation. Once he had started to tell her about the walk she called her husband to come and meet him too. After enough time just talking about it all the husband suggested that Nick go and fetch me and we have some tea together. That seemed like a good idea, so in a little while there we were, in the garden of Litton Post Office, sipping tea, talking of monastic life and enjoying the summer afternoon. All three of them there, Janet Taylor, her husband Geoffrey and a young guest of theirs, were very interested in religion.

Hours disappeared; we carried on and on and it was late when our conversation drew to a final close. They invited us to stay the night, and for a meal on the following day. Janet and Geoffrey were quite inspired by the whole thing and said it was likely that they would visit the monasteries before too long.

After they were all gone Nick and I sat in the dark of the living room, not sleepy – the air was still electric from the inspiration of our talk. Phrases and thoughts from our conversation flickered through, the night was quiet and eventually we found ourselves asleep. With the morning I awoke from a long and lovely dream about Ajahn Chah: he was laughing uproariously in the midst of frantic people, mussing Nick's hair and talking kindly to us. As he now is in Thailand – his body paralysed, speechless, spoon-fed and chairbound – just seeing his face, so loving and good, made a golden day's beginning. Andrew, one of Janet's sons, arose early and made some tea. Janet, although she had said she would not be getting up, talked with us a little and joined us for a cup before we left.

Andrew came with us as far as the path up to Pen-y-ghent and, being an agricultural botany student, had a great time with Nick, talking and being instructed about the local plants. In amongst the limestone pavements, on the borders of the lane, many rare and interesting things were growing. When we had been at the house, Geoffrey had shown us a book about this valley, written by a vicar of Litton in the last century. Amongst other things, in it was told the story of the Lady's Slipper orchid: this delicate flower of rare beauty once graced the area in large numbers but, even by the time the old book was written, the poor thing had been collected almost to extinction. The villain of the piece, apparently, was the then professor of botany at Edinburgh University; he had offered "a guinea a root" to those who undertook to collect specimens for him. This was indeed a princely sum for those days and very hard for the locals to resist. This flower is now the rarest plant in Britain and the last remaining site where it grows in the wild is a secret known only to the few. Each year a dozen flowers arise from the fragile root-system and are fenced and guarded twenty-four hours a day. It is said, though, that a Litton farmer knows of another place where the orchid grows; tucked away in some nook of the dale, unbeknownst to the world.

Nick and I donned our packs and headed down the steep western side of the hill. After a short time we cut away from the main track and found a good place to stop, in amongst the boulders of yet another limestone pavement. As there is a big layer of it in this area you tend to find matching outcrops of it on opposite sides of the hills. The one on this side of Ingleborough seemed much wider and there were great expanses of smooth white rock. They are called pavements because the erosion by water in the cracks of the limestone splits the rocks into great rectangular chunks. Flat, and separated by deep fissures known as grikes, it is in these grikes that the plants peculiar to the terrain grow.

It was still quite early when we arrived, there was a warm breeze carrying the thick mauve scent of wild thyme up through the valley, the evening light and the soft turf to sit upon made it a perfect resting place. We sat for a long time before Nick went off to explore the pavement. I took the opportunity to write a batch of postcards to the family and the faithful, easily gathering inspiration from an occasional glance over the valley of Twistleton. Pretty views and summer evenings make a poor refuge, however; as soon as the wind dropped, a mass of midges appeared and were, in no time, swarming all around me – oh well. Happiness is a fickle friend, no more than freedom from midges; freedom from suffering is another story.

I opted to sleep out that night; the windy afternoon had cleared the air and I woke, soon after dawn, to an empty sky and grass-heads wagging over me. Again, though, it was a very midgy morning; I sat on the rocks and wrapped my robes all around me. Even though one feels compassion for the little creatures' hunger, it is at times like this I am very grateful that the form of the Buddha's enlightenment is in the realisation of our limitations: he did not sit out in the open but beneath the Bodhi tree; he used just a reasonable amount of shelter from the harshness of the world. Such a precedent reminds us that it is not in conquering the world, but in recognising the real that genuine liberation lies.

★ ★ ★

We have come down from the moors and are suddenly back amongst small farms and country lanes – packed now with dog-roses, fox-gloves, honeysuckle and swarming flies – high summer is definitely with us. Last night the two of us slept out by an old canal after the sweatiest spell so far; soggy robe for a pillow at the end of a long day.

We had both rested well in our little camp under the rowan trees, up above the craggy valley in the northern tip of Lancashire. The sky was already clear by early morning so we set off promptly to reach Barbon before it got too hot. That little valley was the border with Cumbria, so once across it, with a last stretch of moorland, we descended for a couple of hours and were soon in amongst the gentle hills and woodlands of the coastal area. Following a small river valley down into the village, I waited in the shade while Nick went to do some shopping. An old farmer came by and said good morning. He was a sweet old fellow; I asked him a question about the village, he tried to remember the answer but it just would not appear.

"Can't do anythin' about, can you? Old age. You just can't remember things so well. Got arthritis too," he said smiling.

"Well, if you were sixteen you would have good reason to complain!"

"I'm not doin' so bad though – if I live 'til next April I'll be eighty. If y' take it easy, go a bit steady, y'll live to a good age. If y're satisfied y'll 'av a good life. Only thems as wants to be rich is never satisfied."

The lanes took us further down into the valley and we stopped for our meal at the water's edge after fording the River Lune. Under the dense greenery of an old sycamore we spent the day, watching some stoats at play on a fallen tree and the splashes of salmon as they leapt up to catch the passing insects. We did our washing in the river and laid our things out to dry over the hot, smooth rocks beside the water. Nick went for a bathe down at the deeper stretch.

The walk from the Lune to this canal bank was hot and sticky; wet and smelly, we were like magnets for the flies – for long stretches there were clouds of them, buzzing frantically about our heads. Whenever we stopped and cooled off they would diminish, and whenever the sweat began to flow again they would increase: what a sweet and simple equation for our existence. At one point we were climbing a long hill past a dairy farm. From behind us we heard the farmer's voice.

"'Ow far 'av y' come?"

We talked a little as we went along, he climbing the hill behind us with his dogs. He told us there was a small reservoir over the other side which we could visit if we liked.

"People not supposed to go there wi'out permission, but I give y' permission. It ain't ma place but I'm supposed to look after it," he smiled, nut-brown and bright-eyed. We said goodbye as he turned into a field about half-way up the hill. So hot and sweaty by the time we reached the top, Nick and I found ourselves almost irresistibly drawn to the lake. Before we knew it we were swimming there, with long happy strokes in the cool of the water; watching later the darts and dodges of electric, needle-blue dragonflies as we sat drying off in the sun.

★ ★ ★

The evening that we arrived at the old canal we had passed through a village called Endmoor, which mostly consisted of new houses clustered around an A-road. I sat on my pack whilst Nick went to ask for water. I was waiting on the pavement of the main street and a small group of teen-aged girls went by, talking loudly amongst themselves. I looked at the ground and heard only bursts of their conversation; I could not figure out if I was being derided or ignored. When a small stone skidded past me, having been thrown from their direction, I guessed that it must have been abuse. I had been prepared for this kind of thing in the big cities, but meeting it here, in the Cumbrian hills, had taken me by surprise. I was slightly amazed and ruffled by the situation but let it pass; they carried on walking up the street. Nick returned with the water-bottles and we sat a while on the pavement talking. Still somewhat on edge, I found myself buying into the whole feeling – hurrying up the hill as some village lads came by, calling out to us loudly from their moped. We tromped up the hill and heard them shouting, "There's bulls in that field," and suchlike, up from the street below. By the time we reached the top, I was astounded at how frightened I had become. We saw two of the boys circle around the hill to the farmyard we were aiming for; I thought, "Oh no, oh no."

We sat for a rest on the hillside and I looked down there below; I realised that it was only fear creating the situation. You realise that it is just the habitual grasping of conditions which makes things seem a problem; whatever you need to meet you will meet, and liberation is just a matter of acceptance. This is how things are, how could they be otherwise? On reflection, even on a gross physical level, it was obvious that two teenagers on a moped were not going to be much of a threat. As it was, we walked down the hill and past the farm without a sign of them; as the evening and the next day wore on, I saw the fear demon, which I had carelessly fed, fade once more into oblivion.

★ ★ ★

Another of the good teachers of this time has been the bugs: high summer in England is a huge festival for the many-legged. Everywhere nowadays, wherever you move, there are always insects and little creatures to be taken into account: if they like to bite, there is the dissuading of them; if they like to land on you, wander in your ears, crawl on your mat, fly into your mouth, land in your drink, or walk precariously on the parapet of your alms-bowl – you have to watch out for and take care of them. Having to be careful and patient with that which is most irritating; having to respect the hunger of a midge; having to give up your convenience to make way for another being – these are all great teachers of humility. Everyone gets hungry, no-one wants to be disturbed; why am I more important than you?

It is a good reminder that the earth is a shared concern and that our training is to disrupt the lives of others as little as possible. One recognises that with the birth of a physical body, without a doubt it will be an agent for the death of others. When we walk through the long grass, on the paths and moorlands, countless moths and little bugs fly up; you find their crumpled bodies in your socks, between your toes. How else could it be? Walking in the world we are bound to do some damage, however hard we try to be gentle. Our reflection though is that we walk for peace; at least we are not starting any wars. For every handful of little beings we disturb, countless millions are untouched by our passing.

II

Space,
vast and beautiful,
thunders in the silence;
peace.
Out beyond the stars and black,
what lies?
The limits of my human eyes:
mirages, the tricks of light,
shimmer, flicker, undulate.
Wind blows
below the stars,
silver leaves do not resist:
wind blows – they move,
and when it rests – they still

(On the slopes of Ingleborough, July 1983)

The Source of Creation

From a talk given during the Easter retreat, Amaravati, 1991

AS MONASTICS, we are often asked where creativity fits into our way of life. The tone of a monastic environment is very simple. We aim at as simple a life as possible, so people wonder where the creative instinct fits into all this. It is often difficult to understand why, for instance, music does not feature in our lives in the monastery when it seems to be so intrinsic to most other spiritual traditions of the world.

Since it is so often asked of us, naturally it is something that we contemplate and of course, as individuals, it is something that we are involved and concerned with, and consider in our own way. Often the assumption is that, since the monastic life represents the epitome of spiritual life, we have to strangle the creative impulse or the capacities that we have, our talents, inclinations and creative abilities. All of that has to be hidden away or discarded, and looked on as distractions, unnecessary for enlightenment.

This is not really a healthy approach. Many of the people in the Sangha have creative backgrounds and are very artistic. The other day I was talking to an anagarika who had been helping in the Italian Vihara for the last few months. Though there were only 4 or 5 people in the vihara, amongst the group there was a former anagarika living locally who was a jazz pianist and singer; the anagarika who visited us used to play the saxophone; Ajahn Thanavaro used to be a drummer and Ven. Anigho was a lead guitarist in a well-known band in New Zealand. These facts came to the attention of the members of the Sangha here in England, who politely asked if the artistes had ever got together. The reply was, "No, no! And if we did, I never told you so!!" So it is not as though the people who are attracted to living a monastic life are bereft of the inclination in these directions. This place is stuffed full of poets, artists and musicians of one sort or another and you might have noticed that, generally, we are not a repressed bunch of people. So how does it all fit together?

The Buddha was often criticised in his own time as a life negator. There is something within us that is very strongly affirmative towards life and our existence as human beings. That 'life affirmation' is highly praised and given a lot of energy and support in our society. In our own time, as in the time of the Buddha, to be enthusiastic about life, to take one's life in both hands and really make something of it is to be highly praised, and we celebrate someone who has "done something with their life". And so the Buddha's whole approach towards spirituality – promoting renunciation, celibacy, simplicity, non-accumulation and so forth, has attracted much criticism. People used to call him an annihilationist, someone who was denying the spirit of life and the spirit of all that was good and beautiful in the world; someone that had a big downer on life, a nihilist philosophy – "It's all pain," "It's all a dreadful mistake," "It shouldn't have happened in the first place." "You have to minimise your life, grit your teeth and wait until it's all over, and the sooner the better!"

It was felt that the Buddha really held that kind of a view. He was questioned on it and he once replied that his Teaching did tend more in the direction of the nihilist than the affirmative: "My Teaching is much more in the direction of desirelessness, of coolness rather than in the direction of desire, of getting, of possessing, of accumulating."[1] Yet it would be incorrect to call the Buddha-Dhamma a nihilist philosophy; it is not life-negating.

The Buddha said that because of the way that we are conditioned as human beings, we tend to drift into the two extremes of, on the one hand affirmation – affirming and investing in conditioned existence and seeing the beauties, delights and good things that life possesses in terms of what can be achieved or derived by conditioned existence – or, on the other hand, criticising the conditioned world as a dreadful mess, a mistake which one wants to get away from. The Buddha pointed out that these are two extreme positions that we fall into and are points of view on life that do not actually respect the true nature of things, because they are bound up with the view of self, the view of the absolute reality of the material world, and of time.

This is not seeing things in a clear, true way. What the Buddha was always pointing to was transcendence of the conditioned sensory world, of selfhood, and the illusion of separateness. When we sit in meditation and look into the nature of our own minds, we can see how much the mind will grasp at anything. Depending on our character, sometimes it will grasp at positivity – affirming things to get interested in and excited about – or it will grasp at negative aspects that we don't want to bother about or that we want to get rid of. But any kind of holding on or pushing away, however subtle, affirms the sense of self. Even if the impulse is destructive or nihilist, we still operate from the view there is something here which is 'me' or 'mine', which 'I' want to get rid of and not experience, it's an intrusion upon 'me', a corruption in 'me', and I don't want to bother with it. I want to get rid of it.

Sometimes, when the mind has a really perverse streak, we can even bring pain upon ourselves; we can actually know that something is wrong, is going to bring pain to us or to those around us, but we go ahead and do it anyway. "I know it is wrong, I know I am going to get into trouble; I know it is going to hurt; I know I am going to get criticised for it, but I am going to do it anyway!" – the 'spitting at God' impulse – "And I don't care if you are the Creator of the Universe!"

Sometimes we will do anything to bolster the sense of 'I' and keep it alive, pushing against or holding onto something just to feel there is someone here who is pushing or holding, because this very powerful sense of ego, of 'I', is terrified of non-existence, of dying, of non-being.

The Buddha was not pointing to life affirmation, or negation, but to the understanding of existence, and of life – to seeing clearly the true nature of things. When we see clearly, then we don't define fulfilment by material achievements or creations or things. It doesn't have to be demonstrated by the material world, or by experience and possessions, feelings or associations. The Buddha's insight is very much into the ability we have to hold the material world: to experience life and the people around us that create the fabric of our life; to be able to harmonise with that completely without being deluded by it. It's rather like being awake in a dream. We know that we are dreaming, that everything around us is simply dream-stuff, but we can be in accord with the dream without being deluded by it.

People often say, "If the Buddha was beyond suffering, why did he bother to live in such a miserable way?" "Here is a being who was liberated, incapable of suffering – so why did he choose a life of celibacy and renunciation, living as a mendicant, walking around the Ganges Valley barefoot for 45 years, giving his time up to teaching people who, for most of the time, understood very little of what he taught?" He himself said that it was going to be incredibly difficult to communicate his understanding to people. Many people assume that someone who is completely liberated can really 'enjoy' life – go out and have some fun. They think, "Once I get enlightened, I am really going to have a good time." One of our Australian bhikkhus, who had been a guitarist, expected to get enlightened after a couple of months of meditation so that he would be able to play **really** well. "It will really do wonders for my technique!" – this is what he thought. "Get this enlightenment cracked, back on the road, go to the top of the charts, make a lot of money and be happy!" If we are completely beyond suffering and nothing in the world could make us miserable, then surely we could have a little bit of a good time?

But the Buddha had realised what it takes to have a good time. He lived in the way of completely fulfilling everything in life that he saw was conducive to happiness. **This is really worth contemplating**. Why did he choose to renounce, why did he choose celibacy, why did he choose simplicity and homelessness, just living on alms food? What one sees is that the Buddha's vision of life was very different from that of the rest of us. When he was enlightened he had insight into the nature of the world. Our worldly mind-states do not allow us to see it that way, but the Buddha realised the limitations of the satisfaction that comes from the sensory world, although it is gratifying and pleasant enough; he saw that the true happiness, the true bliss in life, is in being free from the illusion of self-hood and separateness. "The greatest happiness of all is to be free from the sense of 'I am'."

This does not mean self-destructiveness, wiping oneself out, but to realise that 'I am' is just a thought in the mind; anything we define ourselves as, any characteristic we claim to be, or think we are, is but a half-truth. When the mind realises and is aware of this, then we are blissfully content, blissfully happy. And so the Buddha simply lived his life in a way that respected this realisation, this sense of purity and simplicity. When someone asked him about this, saying: "You monks really live a rough life. I could not live like that. You seem to be so hard on yourselves," the Buddha answered: "Who do you think enjoys life more, the Tathagata or King Bimbisara?" (the local king). "Well, the king of course: a lovely palace, surrounded by beautiful people, lovely music, delicious food to eat, and he can amuse himself whenever he wants to." The Buddha said, "I can sit experiencing uninterrupted bliss for seven days continuously without a moment's break; do you think King Bimbisara is capable of that?" "No!"

Despite the pleasures that we can experience through sound and sight, feeling etc., the bliss of the free mind, the mind which is unattached, far exceeds any other. The Buddha taught this realisation of emptiness.

When we talk of 'emptiness' or the empty mind, it is not a mind devoid of feeling or objects or of any experience. It is not everything vanishing and the mind being an empty space where nothing else is happening. But it is a mind empty of the sense of 'I', of ignorance, of grasping and rejecting. When the mind is empty there can still be sight, sound, feeling, smell, taste, touch. It can all be there, but there is no grasping. Everything that we see, hear, taste, touch, think, remember, every mood, every aspect of ourselves and our world, every particle of it, is experienced as a pattern of consciousness in the mind. And so to understand and realise emptiness, is to be able to see that reality, that actuality.

It is almost, in a sense, seeing a transparency of experience, the dreamlike, mirage-like nature of our world of experience. The Buddha's description of emptiness, and what that takes us to, is a mind which is fresh and alert and can respond freely to life.

This is where, in a sense, creativity comes in to our life as monastics. By giving up the need to have fulfilment expressed in terms of artistic creations or a beautiful home or bringing up children or anything of that nature, by living with a mind which is unattached, empty, and free, everything which is creative, or which needs to be created or said or done, arises from that pure clear space. It arises with a freshness and naturalness that gives it tremendous beauty, simplicity and loveliness. Thomas Merton talked about this when he used the expression 'Divine Silence' or 'Silence of God'. Thomas Merton was a Trappist monk who wrote a great deal in the 1950s and 1960s and was very influential amongst modern Christians. He said that "The monastic life is a life wholly centred upon this tremendous existential silence of God, which nobody has ever been able to explain, and which is, nevertheless, the heart of all that is real.

"The value of the monks' Public Prayer is therefore not drawn so much from its sound as from the deep silence of God which enters into that sound and gives it actuality, value, meaning. The beauty of Gregorian chant and that which distinguishes it from every other kind of music, lies in the fact that its measured sound, in itself beautiful, tends to lead the soul, by its beauty, into the infinitely more beautiful silence of God. Chant that does not have this effect, no matter how great its technical perfection, is practically without value. It is empty of the silence of wisdom, which is its substance and its life."[2]

This relates to the same principle that the Buddha pointed to: when the mind is awake, still, and pure, then every action is invested with that divinity, that sacredness. This has also been the basis of a lot of Buddhist art, particularly in Japan. People have also extended this into spontaneous art in more recent times in the West, trying to find the point where art and life meet (or collide!) with each other, and investigating which is life and which is art. Which is the real thing? One modern composer, John Cage, writes outrageous, weird pieces: his 'Living Room Music' is the sound of people in a living room moving all the furniture and cushions around; or his most famous piece – 4'33" – is a pianist sitting with their hands over the keys for four minutes and thirty-three seconds without touching them. What you hear is the distress and indignation of the audience, whispering and trying to find out what is going on; that is the music! So our concept of what is music, what is art, is challenged.

I have something of a creative streak myself, I suppose. When I was younger I used to have fantasies about being a great writer; find myself a garret and go and starve in it and create unique masterpieces – be some marvellous, compelling figure like Kafka or Rimbaud and produce pithy, obscure wonders. I used to sit down and get deeply into some piece of writing, but then I would realise, to my dismay, that I didn't have anything to say. I kept realising that, although I could put words onto paper and express things, I didn't know anything, and I really didn't have anything worth saying. So I realised that this effort was foolish. Why not wait until I had something to say and then maybe the writing would happen! I was suffering from what I call the 'Roy Jenkins effect': he was once asked if he had had any regrets about his political career. He replied that he used to say that he would have been fulfilled if he had become Prime Minister – but then he realised that he had never really wanted the job itself, he had merely wanted to *have been* P.M. I wanted to be known as a great writer simply for the prestige and the identity alone, like Roy Jenkins.

As the years went by, I found that in monastic life there are long periods of time when one is not expressing anything in any formal way. In our formal sitting and walking meditation there is no material expression but, more importantly, the way that we talk with other people and move around, this is its own expression, and in a more tangible sense. During the run of life in a monastery there is a time for us to do things like giving Dhamma talks, or writing for the Newsletter; these are art forms. I was asked to write a book a few years ago after I completed a long walk from our monastery in Sussex to our monastery in Northumberland. People said, "Please keep a diary," so I started writing. It was about 250 pages long by the time I finished. I then designed it, arranged the photos and illustrations, and organised the lettering. I had a great time. Since then various opportunities have arisen when something needs to be done, and I find that it creates itself. On the birthdays of my mother, father, and two sisters, I draw birthday cards for them. If I sit down to draw a picture for myself, just because there is a spare moment, it is terrible. But if there is a reason, a cause for it, then amazing little pictures seem to appear – exotic and colourful. What arises is elicited by the occasion, by the person it is for, by the moment and the mood. It does itself! When the ego gets out of the way, that which needs to appear seems to manifest. It is in accordance with the time, the place, the situation and so it does itself.

For instance, at the end of last year, the nun who was supposed to be editing the children's magazine 'Rainbows' threw up her arms in despair crying, 'I can't do this, it's too much!' I found myself volunteering to help. Not only did I help put the thing together, but I created illustrations for a whole week. Yet, when there is nothing to be drawn, written or created, then I don't feel that I should be creating something to show people that I am an artist or am this, that or the other. Perfection or talent or fulfilment of ourselves as human beings does not have to be manifest. The free mind is the truest, purest affirmation of Truth, of the very heart of life. Whether that manifests as material things or as actions that we perform, or whether it doesn't, we realise that that is not the important thing.

If something needs to be done then it happens; we find that we are not holding back or being unkind. If people don't need a hand, then we know how to restrain, how to hold back. But if we see something that needs to be done, then we come forth and we find that that which is necessary, which accords, is what appears. As soon as a sense of self appears in anything we do, then the whole thing takes on a much more clumsy and discordant tone. One can see very strongly when there is self-consciousness or self-assertion; it stands out. When it is absent, there is a real fluidity in the person, a freeness, an easiness; every gesture is magical, beautiful.

[1]"Now the view of those whose theory and view is 'I have a liking for all things' is close to lust, to bondage, to relishing, to acceptance, to clinging. But the view of those whose theory and view is 'I have no liking for anything' is close to freedom from lust, to non-bondage, to non-relishing, to non-acceptance, to non-clinging." (M. 74) Ñanamoli translation, Buddhist Publication Society.

[2]From *Thomas Merton, Monk and Poet*, by George Woodcock, Cannongate Press.

The Arahant

The lone remaining wall
Of a long-since fallen house,
No more inside, no more outside,
No more trespass for the mouse;

Where a doorway and five windows
Allow the winds to pass
Unobstructed as they billow
Through the woods, across the grass;

Where sun and moon and starshine
Illuminate the scene
For all the folk that pass it by
When wandering in the green.

"I wonder who the person was
Who built this mighty house,
That's now a bramble garden
And a home for grub and louse?"

A broken ridge and rafters smashed
Lie strewn across the floor
And all that stands, quite ownerless,
Five windows and a door.

(Chithurst, 1983)

The Long Road North

PART FOUR – FROM MORECAMBE BAY
TO HARNHAM

THE OLD MEN AROUND THESE PARTS really love to talk – being
friendly, gaffing about past times and the way things are seems to be their
province. A little later in the afternoon we met another old fellow and stood
for ages chatting together on the pavement by the coast road. Hearing of his
life, the local tales (how his brother had seen the one German prisoner who
managed to escape in the war, skulking along the railway tracks, making his
way to the coast), telling us of the paths we could take and a whole lot more
besides. It became quite an uncomfortable exchange though – I found that I
wanted to get on and could feel this reflected in his wanting to get through:
the more my ear closed and I wanted to get away, the stronger his efforts to
penetrate. All this wanting led to little peace of mind and we ended up having
to prise ourselves apart. Oh well.

Down by the sea there was a good breeze, so at first the afternoon was cooler
than we had known for a long time. We followed the old railway line down
the headland and, after a long sweaty tramp, arrived on the beach below
Conishead Priory, home of the Mañjushri Institute. After sitting there for a
little while we made our way through the small woodland up to the main
house. As we emerged from the trees the towering, pinnacled building
loomed above us. Block upon block, wings, turrets and curling towers stood
stacked up high before us. We swung the great front door open as the gong for
puja filled the air. Evening light streamed through the kaleidoscope of stained
glass windows and, down the long broad corridor before us, Western Tibetan
monks and nuns scurried about, getting ready for chanting.

★ ★ ★

During the day, when we were sitting by the river, Nick mentioned that there
had been a message from Mañjushri that we were to call Harnham when we
arrived. Both of us found the idea coming into our minds that we were going
to be asked to hurry up and get to Northumberland as soon as possible. Nothing was said between us but, as I sat after the meal, I heard the familiar whispers of Mara, patterns of speculation and projection, running around in the
mind. "When he says this, I shall say that" – practising lines for the scenario.
As wisdom was telling me not to buy into this, I promptly brought up the
worst possibilities for the situation. I had not realised how attached I had become to the idea of how the walk would end and how upsetting any other al-
ternative would be. I sat there, reflecting on the journey, the Journey and the

priorities of monastic life. Of course, you just do what your teachers ask and you let go of what you want – if I was told to get on a bus and arrive at Harnham the next day, that would be absolutely fine. After a while of cutting off ideas about the walk in this way, I found the panic beginning to abate and, by the time I was due to make the call, I felt almost at ease about it all. As it was, predictably, we had only been asked to ring in order to allay the rumours of us needing to arrive at Harnham early.

"Just whenever, venerable. However long it takes is O.K."

Thus Ajahn Anando's voice assured us. There had been some comment misunderstood earlier on, really he had not been at all concerned about the time. I must confess, even though I was prepared to do anything, I felt quite relieved that things were going to carry on as we had planned. It was a good lesson in seeing how attachment to ideas of the future secretly crystallise and solidify; you forget that anything can happen at any time – that plans are only 'flowers in air' and that death comes without warning.

★ ★ ★

We walked a little way out of town and up into the hills which look out over Morecambe Bay. With numerous rests and refreshments, and a raucous bellow from a passing motorbike ("another garbled message from the Buddha", quoth Nick), we finally made it to a heathery hillside and decided to stop for the night. Inadvertently, Nick had planned our route on Noy Thomson's map and then had returned it to her; consequently we had to guess the position of our destination for the next day. It felt pleasantly adventurous, sleeping just off the edge of our map. We turned in while it was still light, our attempt at sitting meditation having rapidly dissolved into a fog of sleepiness. We slept out but were roused by rain in the early hours. It was only a small shower but enough to tell us that the weather was on the change. In the morning light we were amazed at the clarity of the air: after two weeks of haze and mist, now we could see for miles. Hills, long left behind and forgotten, suddenly reappeared on the horizon, and we could see the industrial towers lining the coast, way away to the south. The horizon of the Irish Sea magically appeared and the

Old Man of Coniston stood out clear in the north – a silent greeting for the new day – from nowhere the Cumbrian mountains were all about us, their straggly crags spread in all directions.

★ ★ ★

Earlier today Noy remarked how delighted she had been when I told her that essentially there is nothing wrong with pleasure: that the feeling of pleasure arising from good action was one of the benefits of the religious life. As we were walking along, Lydia spoke:

"I was just thinking how pleasurable it is to be alive in this time, in this place – do you think that's wrong?"

Out of nowhere I heard myself reply. "Finding true happiness in the world is an art, not a sin."

Cultivating the art of finding silence in the midst of sound. Sitting by this tarn at the end of the day, watching this pen move across the pages: motion but stasis, silence but sound, darkness but light.

As we had walked, the air to the west cleared, so we stopped at the cairn on the last peak before we dropped down. The shadowy figure of the Isle of Man, which we had speculated on before, was now quite clear; we could see the south-western-most tip of Scotland as it jutted out into the sea, and, in be-tween the two, the distant shape of the hills of Northern Ireland. We sat a long time taking it all in – the vastness of the scene and the fathomless age of these rough old mountains. Millions upon millions of years, rain and snow, sun and wind, have beaten them into a huge and awesome mass. Steep valleys and rocky peaks; long ridges where, until the sheep and the climbers came, only the swifts and ravens were to be found – swooping in fearless parabolae, gath-ering their evening feed, or floating on black wings amongst the crags.

It was a blisteringly hot day, no clouds at all, but with a cool and steady breeze. Completely happy, feeling blessed to have made it, the four of us arrived at the tarn. Filled with a warm peace as I sat there, thinking what a fine and strange crew we must seem – two middle-aged ladies: one in white, perched neatly on a rock; the other, small and oriental, struck with the majesty of the great tarn, its glowing hills, the azure sky, slowly weaving a T'ai Chi sequence down at the edge of the water; a tall red-bearded man, stretched on the turf after a swim; and the orangey-brown pyramidal form of a Buddhist monk, contemplating the Wonderful.

After the ladies had left us I too went in for a swim; quite a few days had passed since my last wash and it felt good to be wet and refreshed again. After a nod to any aquatics who had been disturbed by our passing, I followed Nick up the hill to the Helvellyn ridge. It was quite late and no people were to be seen. On the climb to the top I felt like Christ on his way, carrying his cross up to Calvary – weight, heat and a dust-dry stony path. Nick miraculously managed to collect water from a small springlet on the way up and, before too long, we were enjoying the broad span of the path which runs almost level to Helvellyn peak. It felt as if we walked in the sky, there were steep drops on either side and the path ran like a ribbon; hazy blue, heaving ranks of mountains lay spread out to our left and right.

The haze of the day had settled just below us. All around the mountains were muffled in thick mauve with only the peak of Skiddaw poking out. The line seemed to solidify as we walked along, the darkness of the haze and the crimson and gold of the sunset drew together into a dense interface. From the hilltop above where we planned to stop we watched the descent of the sun – squashed oval and then drawn pearlike as it crossed the line, finally disappearing behind the coastline of Stranraer. The bands of colour remained unmoving – as the ends drew in, short flushes of violet and green appeared, rays launched from the departed sun like a great wheel pivoting beneath the horizon. All of this flickering in the silvery sshh-h-h h h of the mind, silent and unmoving.

When I telephoned Ajahn Anando about our plans to see him at the Allendale retreat house, he gave me the shocking news of the explosion at Chithurst. Apparently towards the end of the ordination of the three new nuns and four anagarikas, Sam Ford's car had blown up. Hannah Renshaw, Colin and Jane's two year old, had been inside and, although her father had managed to pull her out, she had been very badly burned. There was a doctor at the monastery at the time and he had been able to help. It was stunning news, and all through the morning on our walk to Armathwaite, thoughts about Chithurst and speculations on what was happening went through my mind. We were getting so used to the continual mounting of auspicious and wonderful events, flowering and growth, as though our life was charmed, then suddenly King Yama carries someone off right in the midst of the big day. It had been Ajahn Sumedho's 49th birthday, two of the new nuns had been waiting for several years for their ordination and many people had come to be there. You forget that death is always close at hand.

After an intense but lively visit to the Holden's house in Ruckroft, their two boys, Stephen and Darren, walked to Armathwaite and waited on the bridge with us until Mo Robbley arrived. When she appeared, the boys said goodbye and left us to find a picnic spot by the river. Her son Ravi and her new baby Aidan were with her; they had come down from their little place north of Brampton as it had been too far off our route to visit. I do not know if it was the news from Chithurst, Mo's quiet nature, or just my tiredness – but we hardly seemed to speak at all. We sat by the water, under the trees, grey sky, cool; I had to search for conversation, things to say and talk of … nothing wanted to appear. An hour or so later Mo and her boys left, needing to run some errands for the farm. Nick went into the village to shop and make a few telephone calls; when he got back he told me that Hannah had died early that morning. Sudden and unexpected death makes much of our lives seem so petty, a cold trump which outplays any card we hold. I contemplated death through the day, as we walked up out of the valley to the edge of the fells over Croglin; contemplating death, the suffering of separation and the only thing to do – recognise the fact and abide beyond it. As we sat on the hillside, wrapped up for a grey windy evening, I chanted '*Anicca vata sankhara*' and '*Aciram vatayam kayo*', not quite sure if I got it right; little, and maybe not quite right, but good enough – truly warmed by the heart which listens.

★ ★ ★

Nick and I were welcomed in and given tea as soon as we arrived at Throssel Hole Zen Priory. Reverend Chu Shin, the guest-master, showed us around and found a place for us to keep our things. We met the Prior, Reverend Master Daishin, and a few of the others, talking for a while before the evening meeting began at seven twenty-five. They run a pretty tight ship here and there is a lot of form, ritual and etiquette to fit in with. It was a very good feeling, being with them all; sitting, listening to the chanting in the zendo and talking with the monks afterwards. We are sleeping in the zendo along with the novices and lay-people, so we had to be in, with lights out, by ten o'clock. I think it must have been the first 'bedtime' I have had since my early teens. I lay awake a long time, sleeping lightly for short stretches and, not being allowed to rise before the bell at six, lay obediently in my place until it was time to move. Their morning session is much longer than the evening one, with several devotional chants, including one for Kanzeon (Avalokiteshvara), the Prajña Paramita Sutra, the succession of the Patriarchs and several others. I am enjoying the clarity of their forms and the crispness of their lifestyle here; it is a good exercise to step along with a different dance for a while.

★ ★ ★

Bright sun with a cool breeze. We followed the lanes until we met an old railway line: now a track of grass and flowers; we tromped speedily along, rosebay willow-herb, thistles, bell-flowers, and a thousand waist-high coloured heads, fences, stiles, steep banks, deep grass; feet fairly flying through the dewy mass. It hardly seemed a moment since we joined the old track before we were cutting off it, dropping down through a raspberry bush and onto the back lawn of some old friends of Nick, Richard and Rachel Glover.

★

We crossed over and found a flat patch beside the water, screened from the upper part of the field by a small hillock. In front of us lay a last filament of the wood and up above a dark blue August sky. It was a quiet spot to mark the ending of the day; we sat until twilight, feeling free in the cool air.

Erecting the tent in the dimness – barefoot between the thistles – me clambering into my bag, protected from the night; soon peacefully asleep, yet waking moments later to my alarm and a sliver of moon in the early morning sky. Nick did not stir as I bustled out from the tent, and there was no sound from him as I sat nearby, listening in turn to the sound of the stream, flurries of thought and the quicksilver hush of the mind.

★

Half a mile from the road on the southern shore, we found a good flat space and an abandoned house beside the path. We downed our packs and sat on top of the small cliffs. We looked out over the water: waves driven in the evening wind, sitting under the pines, watching the sporadic splashing of those annoying fishes who have always vanished by the time you look for them. I closed my eyes and, after a while, a huge splash was heard; Nick hit the water down beneath the cliffs – kerrspish-pash-sshwoosh – and came up bristling and refreshed.

A fisherman rowed across from the other shore and the evening sun settled over the lake, it disappeared behind a cloudbank just above a spinney in the north-west. After a sitting and a sleep I awoke to see it rising again; a furnace into scarlet gold, barely watchable, spraying colour across the water: fat patches of shimmering pink, outrageous orange and crimson burning clouds – dawn of the last day. I half-expected a heavenly choir to start up and complete the scene; but for the wind, though, there was only silence.

The moment passed and the sky, its dramatic flurry over, soon calmed to a sedate yellow-grey and became cloud-filled and simple once again.

★

We had about six miles to go that morning and, although our route was straightforward and easy, I felt grumpy and unsettled. Having seen this tetchiness before, I did my best not to act on any irritation I felt. But being with only one other, of course Nick became the villain. "Hopeless, selfish, bum, bumbling…" – a familiar tune – but it takes a lot of care not to become entangled in it. I had realised before that as long as you fail to see people as perfect they will irritate you; however, it takes a lot of careful footwork to remain free when such a mood comes to visit.

As it was, the road rolled away under our feet. I sat by Throckrington Church griping at Nick, waiting for him to reappear after visiting the graveyard plants – "Come on Nick, this is RIDICULOUS" – a car came by, packed with five young men who looked as though they were on their way to shoot something. The driver hesitated as he saw me at the roadside: as they drove by I smiled weakly and was given a V-sign by the boy in the back seat. Right on cue, like a flag saying, "How ugly is aversion?" A mirror, and not a pretty sight. It did not take long for the negativity to evaporate after that.

★

"Shall we?"

"Let's."

We took the path down the hill and detoured past an old cave, famed for having had Bonnie Prince Charlie spend the night in it during his flight from England. As we clambered over the rocks we saw a young woman seated in the cave mouth with a young man about to take her photograph. Nick said hello to them and we began to chat. The young woman's face had a slightly amazed look on it; she explained that five minutes before, she had, for no apparent reason, been thinking of a visit she once paid to Green Gulch Farm, a Zen Buddhist centre in America. Obviously struck deeply by this coincidence, they said they would like to visit the monastery some time.

"Always welcome," we said, and, waving goodbye, set off on the very last leg.

Through bracken along the hillside, down the slope; one step at a time; up onto Farmer Wake's land: image of arrival. Nick dropped behind as we topped the hill; down we go to the gate. Hook and chain – through the gate – onto the drive, here we are: arrival. Climbing up the final hill – David's head above the grass, bobs up to our left; seeing us a moment later he leaps, hand-clapping around the corner. Our little crowd is there: Dave and Jenny from Doncaster, a crew from the retreat, Marianne and Kristian, Virginia, Nancy, Jeanne, the children; all the others across the grass; hooped garlands arch above us, petals strewn beneath our feet: arrival – image of arrival – arrival.

"Welcome, Venerable," a glittering smile shining from Ajahn Anando. Stoop –
unbuckle my sandals – my pack is taken; into the shrine room – radiant, white
– before the Buddha-rupa. Bell-ringer, ringing done, Tan Thanavaro holds my
mala beads; fix my robe; bow – the Buddha, bow – the bhikkhus; set the
rosary round the shrine; smiling faces –

"We made it"

Evaṁ

III

Humid swirling, distant hills,
the day that Hannah Renshaw died.
Locked in talk, intense and tight –
disquiet, shadows quivering.

Half discerned, a gentle sound
carillons in the turbid air;
from nowhere dances wee Janelle,

skipping, "*Merrily*, joyously and unconcerned,
through the joists, *merrily*, amid the bricks and building blocks.
life is Glimpsed from the corner of an eye and ear;
carefully, delicately, *but* on scaffolding she treads.
a dream".

Skip, clapping, skip, clap, skip, clap, ski^{pp}ing.

"*Merrily, merrily, life is but a dream*".

(The Holden's garden, August 1983)

Beyond Being and Non-Being

From a talk given on the winter retreat, Chithurst, January 1991

WHEN WE TALK ABOUT THE GOAL of Buddhist practice, about enlightenment or Nibbana, we use the term 'realisation' as being the most accurate way to approach it. Often one sees the term 'getting' enlightened, or 'becoming' enlightened; this is good and meaningful enough in ordinary speech but it also has connotations which are obstructive or misleading. Whenever we think of 'getting' something or 'becoming' something, it always implies that what there is right now is somehow lacking, there is 'me' that is missing something and I have got to get some kind of experience or some kind of quality that is going to make me complete in the future and then, once I have got it, it is going to be mine and I can keep it. There are many characters who have 'got' enlightened and then their enlightenment has wandered off and left them rather bereft and despairing for months or sometimes years.

So when we think and talk about enlightenment it is much better to use the word 'realisation', because it is pointing to the fact that we are discovering what is here already; we are realising, real-ising that which is already true, that which is the fabric and nature of our own being. Any thought of getting or becoming is what ties us to the incessant cycles of birth and death; this is what is called the *bhavacakka*, the cycle of becoming, because anything we get we can lose or we become anxious about being separated from – ownership is suffering. Thinking in terms of realisation, discovering the Truth, lends itself much less to the idea of ownership. The Dhamma, the ultimate reality of things, has no owner and this realisation of Truth is the fulfilment of our life. You do not have to take this as a proclamation, but I would say that this is the goal, the fulfilment of our life. Everything else that happens in life that we achieve or create, bring forth into the world, these are all secondary to the realisation of Truth, to this quality of seeing and being Dhamma.

Knowing the reality of things does not seem like very much. Our worldly tendencies and our habits of seeing always tend to focus on the objects, beings and places, the achievements, triumphs and disasters of our lives as

80

being the real, substantial, important aspects and something as ephemeral or intangible as realising Truth, on a conceptual level at least, seems a bit flimsy and simple-minded.

Buddhism gets criticised a lot by people who take the position of life-affirmation. This has been the case right from the very beginning when the Buddha first started teaching – particularly because of being a religious tradition with a monastic order of celibate monks and nuns. This renunciant lifestyle gets quite a pounding from people, who are not necessarily worldly or indulgent, but just those who see value in the fulfilment of life on the worldly plane: the qualities of a loving relationship, of having children, of creating music or beautiful things, planting gardens, trees, building houses, forming friendships, creating networks of wholesome activity, learning, teaching, nursing, healing the sick, helping the dying – these are all tremendously appealing, important and positive things in life. There is something very deep, very instinctual in our hearts which does appreciate and celebrate this – that loves life, that wants to live, to laugh, to love – and this seems to be the very fabric and essence, the spice and purpose of life, to live life to the hilt, to the full.

In the last 'Inquiring Mind', a Buddhist newspaper put out in America, they had an article about Ajahn Sucitto and Ven. Vipassi teaching a retreat in Massachusetts. This article went to great lengths to make sure that people knew that both these monks had lived very 'full' lives before they became monks; which is a polite way of saying you have done everything you could think of and then some before you became a monk. People are very scared of the idea that you would become a monk before you had really done **everything**, tried everything out. The idea is that life is to be lived, everything is to be tasted, to be experienced – Rajneesh was very keen on this kind of practice: doing absolutely everything to the limit and learning from that. The true learning experience in life is described as to take it all on, to swallow it whole and watch the results – so this does make what we do here at this monastery look a bit strange! Maybe I am sounding like an advert for Dionysiac hedonism (brandy will be served in the kitchen after the evening meeting), but it is a very powerful streak in our minds, it strikes a powerful chord.

The other day I ran across something that D.T. Suzuki wrote in one of his books on Zen Buddhism, it went something like, "The spirit of freedom, which is the power behind Buddhism breaking through its monastic shell to ever more vigorously bring enlightenment to the masses, is the life impulse of the universe," then he says something like, "The spirit of Buddhism has always been intellectual, moral and spiritual freedom, thus the moral aristocracy and the disciplinary formalism of primitive Buddhism could not bind our freedom, our spirit for very long,"[1] so **we** are right out of the picture! I am not criticising D.T. Suzuki but just saying that there is a strong tendency in people's minds to think, "Well, if you are living a very restrained, renunciant life you really must be missing out on a lot; you are not respecting all that life offers, these bodies are fertile, they are designed to produce offspring and you have creative talents – we can do, we can speak, we can create – why not!" Because I draw pictures for birthday cards for my family and occasionally write poems, I find that this is one of the few things about my life that my family can relate to. My mother is always encouraging me to create more masterpieces; I have got pads and pads of drawing paper and crayons and pens and ink, an incredible stash of stationery to do my creations on. I regularly get a burdened feeling when I look at this pile of stuff in my desk-drawer, "Oh dear, I suppose I should create something." I like doing that kind of thing but one sees that for people with a more perceptually based perspective on life, what you create becomes the most important thing – "After all, you can draw such nice pictures, you can say such nice things, why not? You are robbing the world by not producing offspring, poems, pictures, etc. etc. etc."

This question had long puzzled me and struck me deeply when I first arrived at the monastery in Thailand. I was reminded of it this morning, since we have been having readings from 'The Life of the Buddha' and we have just got to the time of the Enlightenment. Oftentimes as a Westerner we think about enlightenment as meaning having a mind which is happy all the time, regardless of whatever is going on and whatever we choose to do – this is a very very attractive proposition! After the Buddha's enlightenment he sat for a week rapt in meditation, experiencing the bliss of deliverance and, after that absorption into bliss, he emerged and then what did he do? He spent the whole night contemplating Dependent Origination, the law of dependent arising: ignorance conditioning the arising of desire, attachment, birth, death, suffering and so forth; contemplating its arising, contemplating its cessation, backwards, forwards, up, down, all night long.

Now, if you were enlightened and had just become completely, irreversibly free from suffering, it's possible to imagine you might think, "What a relief! At last that's all over – no more suffering, marvellous, amazing." And you might think, "Let's go eat pancakes!" or "I wonder what that nice young lady who brought me the milk rice is doing tonight, maybe I'll pop round and see her." Or, if you were of a less sensual character, with a bit more nobility: "Now I'll go back to my kingdom, encourage my old father, give him a bit of support and then help take over the kingdom and run a really good little country for the rest of my life."

But we can see that, far from having this reaction, with his enlightenment the Buddha experienced life from a completely new dimension. He was seeing things in a way that he had not seen before, he was seeing what the rest of the world could not see. It's rather like when we come into a new situation – an institution, a school or a family, a monastery – we are a stranger and we suddenly find ourselves in the midst of all kinds of webs of relationship, power-trips, struggles, gripes, loves and hates and personality conflicts going on; we are an outsider for whom all this has no value and yet to all the people involved in that place it's all terribly real and important. We are not a part of it, however; we are not caught up in the value system.

One can also see enlightenment as simply growing up; as an adult one stops being able to play with dolls and toys in the same way that one did when one was a child, it becomes impossible. It's also like having solved a puzzle that everyone else is still deeply involved in trying to unravel; you can see the answer, whereas everyone else is anguishing and fretting and rushing about and discussing how to find it. Or that lovely feeling of understanding a clue in a crossword – when you have got it and the letters all fit in the right places, "Ah! I see!"

At the enlightenment, the Buddha stepped out of the worldly perspective and could see from above the world – *lokuttara*. There is a wonderful passage in the scriptures that describes this insight of the Buddha and the way he saw things after his enlightenment: He saw that the worldly mind cherishes conditioned existence, it cherishes becoming; it opens itself to and welcomes conditioned existence, it welcomes becoming. The urge of the world, of worldly thinking, is always to become other: to get to the next thing, to progress, to develop, to have, to keep. It cherishes, relishes conditioned existence; but the problem is that what it relishes brings fear and what it fears is pain, because that which is the very basis of conditioned existence is also the basis of suffering.[2]

This was the insight that he had with Dependent Origination – he saw how ignorance was the originator of all problems in life; how the reality that we give to our thoughts, feelings and emotions, to our memories and perceptions, is the true creator of all our difficulties. He also saw that if we believe in conditioned existence, if we believe in everything that happens in our senses, then we will believe in our suffering and we will possess it, we will own it, it will be ours. But with the ending of clinging, the ending of attachment then suffering ceases.

This is perhaps a difficult insight to comprehend and really digest. In the same passage he says something like, "Liberation does not come through loving conditioned existence but neither does it come through loving non-existence. One who is liberated abandons craving for being without relishing non-being...." Now where is that? You do not find that one in the 'A-to-Z'! "Liberation comes from abandoning craving for being, without relishing non-being."

The worldly mind can only see that either we are or we are not, something is or is not, but the Buddha is talking from a position which is neither this nor that, neither being nor non-being, neither existence nor non-existence. On hearing this sort of thing, maybe our mind starts to go into a flap, just goes blank or thinks, "What on earth is this about? I mean, come on, let's be serious, let's hear something useful, shall we!?" But from my perspective this is the most useful and powerful tool for insight that we have with which to understand and live our lives.

It is, however, something that is very intangible; conceptually it is not graspable, it evades our intellectual faculties. It is also the very reason why in his life the Buddha was constantly criticised for being a nihilist – because of not saying, "This is the Truth," and stressing some kind of metaphysical pattern or grand cosmology. Instead he kept talking in terms of Nibbana, which just means 'cooled' or 'blown out', like the blowing out of a flame. Nibbana can also be translated as 'extinction' and to many people the concept seemed nihilistic. "Life has got to have a bit more to it than just extinction to look forward to!" But he refused to go along with the eternalists, people who were philosophi-cally life-affirming, yet he also refused to go along with the annihilationists, those who were philosophically life-denying; he kept pointing at the fact that the Truth is other than either of those two fixed positions.

There is a lovely story from the Theravada tradition concerning a seeker called Kamanita.[3] He, having heard of the Buddha's reputation, was passing through Rajagaha on his way to meet him at Jeta's Grove in Savatthi. At nightfall he put up in a potter's house; little did he know at the time that the monk that he was sharing his lodging with that night was the Buddha himself.

Kamanita, after a while, started enthusiastically telling his fellow lodger how he was on his way to meet the Buddha. The Buddha sat there listening and didn't let on who he was – "Tell me about this great master and his teaching," he said. So Kamanita goes on for some time, telling the story of his own life and extolling all the wonders of the Buddha's Dhamma, and how he teaches the path of bliss and eternal happiness.

Finally he said, "Well, I've talked for long enough, you tell me about your life. What is your philosophy? Who is your teacher? What do you proclaim as the truth?" The Buddha started to speak, saying, "I will, in return for your narrative, unfold to you the doctrine of the Buddha." He described the Four Noble Truths: the truth of suffering, the origin of suffering, cessation of suffering and the Path; and he expounded on anicca, impermanence, and anatta, selflessness. As he began, Kamanita was looking quite interested and taking it all in, but after a while he began to think, "This guy is a bit of a sourpuss … this isn't the Master's teaching as I understand it. Well, never mind, he's got his rights to think like he does."

As the Buddha continued, Kamanita got more and more uncomfortable. All that this monk was saying to him seemed to hang together logically and it felt disturbingly right, but seemingly it had a horrible negative life-denying streak to it: all about extinction and cessation, and with no promise of "eternal and blessèd life" after death. His mind was still heavily programmed towards the idea of eternal happiness so, by the time the Buddha got on to anatta, Kamanita was decidedly agitated and did not know what to do. The monk's exposition was obviously flawless but Kamanita's heart was fixed on the fact that he must be wrong, so he thought, "What he is saying is all wrong! This is bad philosophy. The Buddha is the great teacher, he teaches absolute bliss for eternity. I am going to get the teaching directly from him. I should forget this guy, he really does not know what he is talking about." The Buddha finishes speaking and sees that Kamanita is a bit agitated.

Finally, in a subdued tone Kamanita asks him, "Have you heard all this from the mouth of the perfect Buddha himself?"

At this point a smile plays around the Master's lips.

"No, brother, I cannot say I have."

Greatly relieved to hear this, Kamanita reassures himself that they will be able to meet the Buddha in person soon and that this monk's mistaken and destructive conception of the Buddha's teaching will be set straight.

Kamanita never realises his mistake – not until much later anyway, but that's another story.… The Buddha, when asked about him, said, "Foolish as an unreasonable child was the pilgrim Kamanita, he took offence at the Teaching…"; in this lifetime his karmic obstructions were too dense to enable him to see what was right in front of him.

Ajahn Chah often said that this is a position that we find ourselves in – face to face with the Buddha, sharing a room together, spending hours and hours deep in conversation and not realising who this is. The truth of life is staring us in the face, but because we have already got programmed with something else that we want and expect, we are missing out on the lessons that life is actually able to teach us.

What we need to understand then, is what this knowledge was that the Buddha was pointing to. Firstly, it's necessary to understand what we mean by the word existence – clinging to existence and clinging to being or non-being. The word 'existence' actually means 'to stand out'; that which exists stands out, it protrudes, it is something which comes out, like a branch coming out of a tree. What the Buddha is pointing to is that, as long as we are talking in terms of existence or even non-existence (which is as if, instead of coming out of the front door we have just gone out of the back door), both are taking a fixed position about some solid thing – there is still a separate 'thingness' there. What the Buddha is pointing to is that which does not come forth, that which is Home, that which is the basis, the root. 'Existence' means that which is standing out, i.e. a condition of nature, mental or physical. What the Buddha is pointing to here is the Unconditioned, that which does not stand out, that which is not created, that which is not born or dying.

This is perhaps a bit hard to grasp but it is a very important point: as long as we are talking about something 'existing' it does not mean that that is the only reality. An experience is an excursion out from the Unconditioned through a pattern of events, back to the Unconditioned, like water rising from the sea, falling on the mountains, running down through the streams into the rivers and back to the sea. It is an excursion of existence; a lifetime is just an excursion, so is a thought – it is something which arises from the Unconditioned, from the space of the mind, and dissolves back into it again.

When something 'exists' it has a false independence, a false individuality, because at that time, it seems to be of a different and separate substance to all other things. When we believe in separate existence then we are giving solidity that which is actually transparent, ephermeral, merely an element of the infinite patterns of consciousness in the mind. So the Buddha is pointing to the Unconditioned as the basis for reality. The Buddha's enlightenment was awakening to this Unconditioned nature of the basis of life; this was the dimension, the position from which he was seeing.

In this respect then, those aspects of life like the material, manifest world that we celebrate and which are so important, they become the basis for the realisation of the Unconditioned; the conditioned is needed in order to realise the Unconditioned. Through the agency of a human life and a human body, the Unconditioned can be realised. This process is a ripening or a transition, a transformation of the life spirit, the life force – the *jivita*. The conditioned, the green, is infertile but becomes the basis for that which ripens into the gold, like a field of corn: the green of life ripens as the gold of wisdom, civilisation and true knowledge. The *lokiya* becoming the basis for the realisation of the *lokuttara*, these two always exist in relationship to each other and the transformation, the ripening of the one to allow the realisation of the other is what, in Buddhism, is called stream entry.

This is also called 'the change of lineage' – when we see through our attachment to the body, to the mind, to ourself and to the world, it's known as a change of lineage because, rather than looking upon our physical parents as our origin and the source of our being, we see that the true Origin of all is the Unconditioned mind. This is the source of all creation – as Thomas Merton puts it: "The living law that rules the universe is nothing but the secret gravitation that draws all things to God as to their centre. Since all true art lays bare the action of this same law in the depths of our own nature, it makes us alive to the tremendous mystery of being, in which we ourselves, together with all other living and existing things, come forth from the depths of God and return again to Him."[4]

So, rather than placing ultimate value in the products and activities of the manifest, existent world, we learn to see that the *saccadhamma* – the Ultimate Reality of our own nature – is the source of all true value. When the need arises, we act, but when there's no need we are still – and whether there is activity or not, the essential nature of the *saccadhamma* remains the same. It doesn't have to prove its worth by taking a certain form, or any form at all; the sea is still the sea whether it's rough or placid, gold still has the nature of gold whatever shape we make it. So, in this process of realisation we are affirming the very source of life – the Uncreated, Unconditioned – rather than making value judgements about waves or their absence on the surface. The source of our life is the source of the whole universe – the heart of the universe is your heart – so, far from the Buddha-Dhamma being a life-denying, negative philosophy, it is actually the most earth-shaking, silent roar of **YES!!!** – it is just avoiding making a fuss about the secondary details and attending to the essence instead. It is a philosophy of the ultimate aesthetic: "Truth is beauty – one who has arrived at Release truly knows what Beauty is."

---

[1]*Essays in Zen Buddhism I*, p. 75.
"This spirit of freedom, which is the power impelling Buddhism to break through its monastic shell and bringing forward the idea of Enlightenment ever more vigorously before the masses, is the life-impulse of the universe – everything that interferes with this unhampered activity of spirit is destined to be defeated. The history of Buddhism is thus also a history of freedom in one's spiritual, intellectual, and moral life. The

moral aristocracy and disciplinary formalism of primitive Buddhism could not bind our spirit for a very long period of time...."

[2]Ud. III. 10; as in *Life of the Buddha,* by Bhikkhu Ñanamoli, B.P.S., p. 32.

[3]"The Pilgrim Kamanita"; Karl Gjellerup, Trans. John E. Logie, Dutton, 1912; Matichon & Sathirakoses-Nagapradipa (1977) in Thailand. Based on the story of Pukkusati in the Dhatuvibhangha Sutta M.140

[4]From *Thomas Merton, Monk and Poet,* by George Woodcock

Ninety days in the Whole XII

The turning earth obscures the sun,
night comes over England.
Vixens bark,
badgers trundle out,
mother calls the children in.

A breath of sleep and then
a skyful of stars as dawn comes.
Wake! Again!! Begin!!!

Hollow-legged, blinking;
emergence from oblivion
and the strange dream-logic
wherein vague feelings
and half-remembered characters
balloon into huge reality
then fade
without a murmur.

Owl-calls echo through the woods;
dew drips,
clattering softly on chestnut leaves.
Pale violet, rose,
the sky fills with light,
amethystine.

Venus and the crescent moon
have given up their sparkle
to the dawn.

Colour and birdsong
wash through the hills,
the dark is over.

Chithurst, August 1988

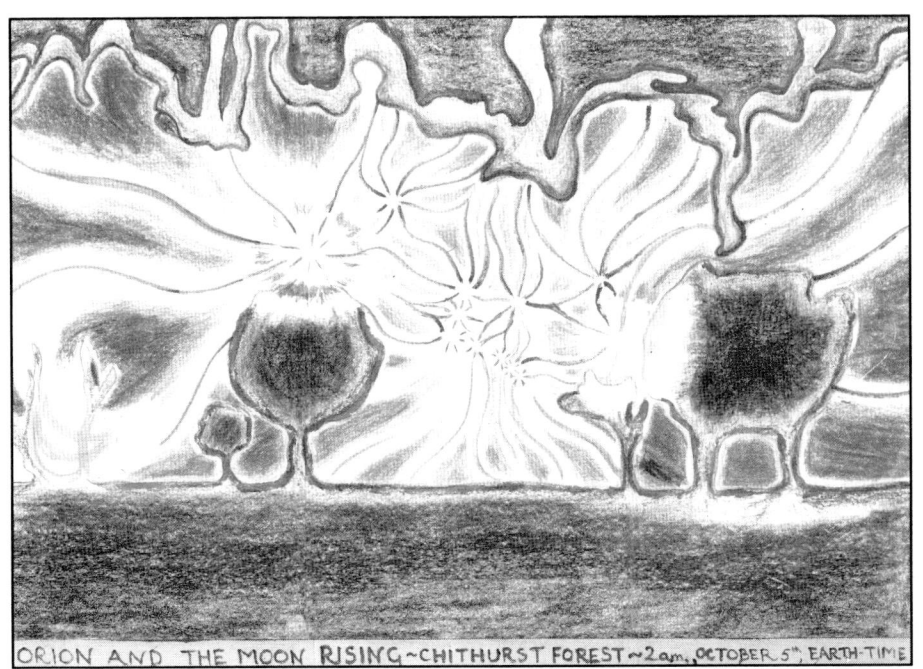

ORION AND THE MOON RISING ~CHITHURST FOREST ~2am, OCTOBER 5th EARTH-TIME

Wisdom

From a talk given on the winter retreat, Chithurst, January 1991

THIS HOUSE IS A PLACE OF REFUGE for us.
On a wild and stormy evening like this we are protected, we are safe here in this place, in this enclosure.

The teaching of the Buddha is, in the same way, always pointing us to that place which is comfortable, safe, secure; which is a protection from the storm; which is the still place, the centre of the cyclone; the place where everything rests: the place of enlightenment; the axis of the Dhamma-realm; this point of here and now. And it is directing us to take refuge in being awake.

Since Ajahn Kittisaro spoke so eloquently yesterday about compassion, I thought it would be suitable to talk about wisdom this evening. These two exist very much as the two wings of the Buddha's teaching.

In Tibetan, so I have heard, the word Lama means 'wisdom and compassion'. I'm not sure which one is which though – La means, I think, wisdom and Ma means compassion. The two go together. One who practises the Truth, one who lives according to the Way, is one who embodies wisdom and compassion.

Where compassion is the spirit of including – reaching out to and identification with all beings, feeling the life, the joys and sorrows, the fears and hopes of all beings as our own – wisdom is the recognition that there are in truth no beings, that all of this is not self. This is not who and what we are.

There is a line in the Gatha of the third Zen Patriach, which goes: "In this world of Suchness there is neither self nor other than self." This very beautifully illustrates the principle that, on the one hand, we have to entertain the reality that all beings are one: we are all of one nature. All things, all life, all existence is an intrinsically interconnected web of being. From the most dull matter to the highest, most sublime divine beings, and all states in between, this is one life, one substance. And on the other hand, "In this world of Suchness there is no self." Within each entity, there is nothing here which is absolutely me or mine, which can be taken as a true individuality. This is what the wisdom teachings are always pointing us to: the trap of identification that we make with the experiential world.

We take the body, the world, our internal life of thoughts and feelings, the things around us, the people that we live with, the events in the world, and we invest in them an absolute importance. Because of that we suffer.

We feel alienation, separation, lack of wholeness, we feel incomplete because if there is 'I', then there is 'you' and we are apart, there is distinction and there is separation. If we see through this and we dissolve the belief in an absolute separate existence, then the sense of separation naturally dissolves because it has no basis. There is a recognition of wholeness.

The Anatta-Lakkhana Sutta is the primary teaching on selflessness; you can see why this was the teaching that brought forth the first enlightened beings in this age. When teaching the Group of Five bhikkhus in the deer-park, there was this instruction on how to challenge and see through the identifications that we make with body and mind, and with the world. In challenging that sense of self, these people were able to penetrate, understand and break free of the bondage of habitual ways of seeing.

★ ★ ★

The principle of wisdom is something which is dynamic, it's a momentary experience. As we have all heard many times over, but it is probably worth reiterating, when we talk about the wisdom of the Buddha this is not speaking of an accumulation of knowledge. This is not the ability to see into the past or the future, to be able to be aware of the goings on in people's minds all around the world. It's not omniscience.

When we talk about Buddha-wisdom it means the wisdom of the pure mind, which is the same as the quality of wisdom which each of us is capable of drawing upon. It's the same wisdom. It can operate within a mind of Gotama Buddha, or all the enlightened sages, it can operate through the agency of **your** own body, **your** own thinking mind, **your** own senses. It is still the same wisdom, it's still the same quality. In the same way that the air we breathe is the same air that the Buddha breathed and that it is the same earth that we all walk upon.

That quality of wisdom is a pure Knowing, which arises as an attribute of Truth itself, of Dhamma. The primordial activity of Dhamma is that of Knowing. That which is the ultimate reality of all being, the *sacca-dhamma*, or the *paramattha-dhamma*, is not some kind of inert ethereal substance but is dynamic, alive, totally awake Knowing. Knowing is its primary attribute. That's why we say the Buddha arises from the Dhamma, is born of the Dhamma. That which knows arises from Suchness, the true Dhamma, which is the root of all being.

When we talk about Buddha-wisdom, we are talking about that Knowing quality which sees truly and clearly exactly how things are. This is not a memory of how things are, it's not an idea about it, but it's the way our mind can see, in this moment, how it is. What *is*. This is described in the phrase we hear over and over again in the scriptures: "When the eye of Dhamma opens," when someone awakens and sees the Path, then it is said that they see: "All that is subject to arising is subject to cessation." That is the basic liberating insight which is ennobling.

"All that arises passes away." It is very simple, but it's like a key for us. It's the key to the door of our prison of selfhood. Once we apply that and keep remembering to put the key in the lock and turn it, once this has been seen and we apply it through every aspect of our experience, then we discover freedom. We can open the door, because there is nothing whatsoever, of the entire fabric of our life or that of the world, that does not come under this formula. Everything which arises, passes away.

From a minuscule feeling to a whole universe, from the footstep of an ant, a leaf falling off a tree, to worlds coming into existence, colliding, vanishing. Every single thing in the whole sensory world follows this same law. All that arises passes away.

This is the fundamental insight which changes us from being a deluded living being into a Buddha. When the mind does not see clearly, then we are a living being, we are a separate independent entity, in the midst of an external world. In the moment of wisdom and clear seeing we are a buddha, a knower. There is buddhahood. This is maybe a very difficult principle to swallow and might seem like a great exaggeration but it's also very useful reflection to bear in mind. It helps to cut through our habitual negative opinions about ourselves as being somehow imperfect, or not of the same quality, capacity or potential as some great sage. We tend to feel that somehow their minds are intrinsically different, more powerful, more pure, more capable than our own.

The more that we learn to let go of our delusions about life – let go of identification with the body, with feelings, with perceptions, ideas – the more we allow wisdom to operate, then that becomes our way of relating to life. As we develop the use of wisdom we begin to see that wisdom is not a cold, clinical, dissection of experience, as if we were defusing life. It's not like draining the colour out of it and taking away its vigour or its substance. In fact it's just the opposite, because the more wisdom that we apply, the more light we experience within our life, the more truly alive, awake and vivid our life becomes; this is because the true nature of our mind is bright, radiant. There is a beautiful expression that the Buddha used, the *'pabhassara citta'* – the radiant mind, the mind of clear light. He pointed out very clearly that the mind's nature is inherently radiant. Its brightness is not something that we have to produce, rather it is the intrinsic nature of mind, the *citta*.

"*Cittaṁ pabhassaraṁ agantukehi kilesehi.*" "The nature of the mind is radiant, defilements are only visitors." The more we bring forth the quality of wisdom, which is non-conceptual and non-dualistic, then the more we experience the mind of light.

At first – because wisdom is aligned more with intellect, whereas compassion is more aligned with emotion and the qualities of the heart – the use of wisdom in bringing forth the questioning and analytical aspect of mind can create a cold, negating tone. This is only because one gets into the habit of saying, "No, I don't believe it," to all the different thoughts and feelings and experiences that we have, so we can develop a callous streak towards our experience. It is like thinking: "Don't touch it, don't believe it – it's just another pattern in your mind!"

When the clouds of ignorance start to dissipate and the sunlight of true wisdom starts to appear, then in the same way, we unconsciously shy away from, and become suspicious or negative towards the brightness of our own mind. We tend to shut that out, simply out of a habit of negating all things. When we don't have a habit of negating experiences or conditions of mind, however, and we allow the mind to relax and to fully Know, what is there when a condition of mind ends? We feel more and more clearly the purity and intrinsic radiance of the mind.

This is why in meditation we talk about realising emptiness. If our meditation is always about trying to **get** something, if it's always tied up with achieving, purifying or developing something, even though what we're trying to develop might be very wholesome and good, then we find that there is very little space in our mind. It might be very concentrated or very high but there is often a strong sense of self and a lot of 'doingness'; a lot of activity and no real quality of purity there. When we watch some thought or a feeling coming into existence, we feel its presence for a while and then we watch it fade. The tendency of the mind is then to immediately look for the next thing, or to want to do something – to create something wholesome or to get on to the next thing or to find another object and see its emptiness! Instead, if we are patient and we just allow the mind to watch, we notice that there is space there.

I felt at first that such space was a bit blank and empty, nondescript. I felt, "Come on, let's go on to something else, let's do something. What's next? Come on, let's get going." If you allow the mind to not follow that and to just rest in that space instead, then the veil which made the mind seemingly blank and nondescript dissolves. You see that very space broadening, lightening and becoming warm, vast, peaceful. We realise that which is not becoming, that which has always been there, the Unconditioned, the Mind Ground, pure, peaceful, timeless. That quality is something we don't usually see, because of our constantly zipping our attention from one thing to another, to another, to another.... If we just take the trouble to look through the cracks, then we find the vast and beautiful space of our own true nature here, on the other side.

It is very helpful to recognise that the bringing forth of this quality is always something that we can do. It's never beyond our reach. We are not trying to **become** wise; we are not trying to do something now to become wise in the future, to accumulate wisdom like some kind of commodity. It's much more useful to see it in terms of the fact that there is an infinite resource of wisdom which is part of our own intrinsic nature, which we can dip into any time. We can dip into the well. At first it can seem as though our store of wisdom is like a deep well stuffed up with straw and husks and is completely bunged up and inaccessible to us. The mind can play up and gripe and feel insufficient and imperfect. So sometimes we need to arouse our energies like the Buddha's *udana*, an ecstatic utterance, a gesture of determination to not be swayed by any kind of obstruction – for that which is blocking up, obscuring the wisdom of the mind to be just blasted out of the way by the power of faith and resolution. Then there is water everywhere!

★ ★ ★

We say that the Buddha is the archetype of wisdom and, both internally and externally, the Buddha is 'The One Who Knows'. But still we are not trying to identify with a particular quality like that, because if we take a single quality and make that our goal, or emphasise that too much, then we become fixated upon that individual thing. The whole point of the spiritual path, using compassion and wisdom, or devotion or whatever, is that these are all designed to take us to the goal, to Nibbana. These are all skilful means that suit different people's natures. Some people are faith types, other people are wisdom types, other people are energy types. There are many different methods and modes of liberation. One can be liberated through faith, concentration, energy or through wisdom, and some methods are quicker than others, some accord with our own characteristics more than others. The whole point of any form of approach or use of Buddhist principles is to take us to the Goal.

I remember, years ago I came across a very interesting little verse, it was in a biography of a Chinese monk, called Han Shan, who was told this verse by the Bodhisattva Maitreya in a visionary dream that he had. It was a very long and amazing dream; by the end of it, however, he was sitting at the feet of the Lord Maitreya. And what the Lord Maitreya said to him was:

> "Discrimination is consciousness,
> non-discrimination is wisdom.
> Clinging to consciousness causes defilement,
> wisdom ensures purity.
> Defilement causes birth and death,
> whereas purity leads to where there are no Buddhas."

I thought "That's a funny ending. I thought the ideal was to realise and know the Buddha mind. Isn't that the point of it?" Everything else in it seemed to be so correct and good. I thought, "What does that mean? 'Purity leads to where there are **no** Buddhas.'" I contemplated, "How did the Buddha talk about this?" He himself discouraged people from attaching to him as a person – making a big deal about the Tathagata as an entity present in the world was not the point, and not quite accurate anyway.

Once we see the Truth, we become 'independent in the Teacher's dispensation', as the phrase goes, which means there is no longer the need to look to an external source of wisdom or Truth. We no longer need to look to the Guru, the Sage, the Guide, the Saint, to be the one on whom our eyes are fixed. When the Truth is seen, then the idea of separate beings, of a Buddha in the world, or no Buddha in the world, becomes recognised as merely a relative truth, and is seen for what it is.

So, I took this verse to mean that the place where there are no Buddhas is the place where there is only Buddhahood. When there is Buddhahood, then there is no need for external Buddhas to appear. Buddhas appear in the world as external teachers for the sake of ignorant living beings but purity takes the mind to that place where everything is our teacher. There is a complete transcendence and unification, a complete oneness with all life, with all things. There is no separation into a you and I and independent beings. There is only Buddhahood, true understanding.

These two elements, of wisdom and compassion, transcendence and wholeness are also embodied in the word that the Buddha used to refer to himself: Tathagata. Scholars debate whether the word is really supposed to mean 'Tath-agata', 'thus come' or 'Tatha-gata', 'thus gone'. Which is the **real** meaning?

The Buddha was very fond of word-plays, however, and my suspicion is that he coined the word 'Tathagata' precisely because it implied both attributes: is that Buddha quality completely transcendent – utterly gone, or is it immanent – completely here, present now? The term is perfect in that it carries both these meanings and indicates that the two, immanence (or wholeness) and transcendence, do not exclude each other in any way.

Inner Landscapes

TRAVELS WITH THE TEACHER
AND THE GREEN MAN

The following is an account of a short 'tudong' walk through Lancashire and Cumbria, made by Ajahn Sumedho, Nick Scott and me in the summer of 1987.

Nick has a presence like the Green Man, the spirit of the woods himself: from head to foot clad in dark emerald waterproofs, a khaki pack, a chestnut face flowing into a russet beard occasionally speckled by bits of moss and tree bark. Slightly chaotic, son and agent of the Earth Mother – energised, practical, effulgent, urgent – leaping forward like the force of green growth itself. Fast mutable in mood – from sun to wind and lightning – and behind it all the endless ability to **rebound.**

With him, the Ajahn, a voice of the silence – well-equipped and present, the cause for the journey, but in country matters assuming second place. Nick, like the Old One himself, leads the way across the sodden bogs and crags. And the third one ... well, I am just the author....

I

WE SIT NOW by the churgling waters of a small river. It has run off the Bowland Fells, as have we, this dry and easy afternoon. The fire is dying and the Ajahn has gone to rest.

Local anglers greeted us as we trundled past them on our first afternoon, taking in the dragonflies, carpet moths and yellow flag as we went. We laughed as a mother-duck did her best to maintain her dignity as she and her little ones plunged into the river from the branches of an overhanging tree. We cut down to join the river Brock, followed a 'one-cow' track of delightful ease through woody banks, and halted for the night at a bend below a weir;

> water music
>   leaping
>   gurgling
>   hopping
>   churning.

Why does the run of a river make us feel so alive?

As we broke camp the next day the rain began as a warning to us – the Master, disciple and the Green Man – now rain-lashed as we ascended our first hill, up into the Bowland Fells.

Steep clumps of cranberry, heaving legs – not as strong as they used to be – heaving breath – "I will be all right in a minute" – low cloud water lashes the air.

We traverse across the bog-tops. Rich sphagnum and water, moss and lichens lie settled in thick easy pools; dense green, growing upon aeons of their forebears, from tussock to tussock we tread. The rain-clouds come heavily, more upon more – for a while we're at sea but, rounding the crown of the hill we find our valley.

Wild,
desolate, empty of human signs,
steep and rough but with a good track, even though it winds into shapeless nowhere. 'Langdon Castle' is our meeting point but of it there is no sign, not a trace…. "I wonder if…."

Suddenly the folk from Blackpool with whom we were to meet appeared upon the path ahead of us. The 'Castle' turned out to be a shepherd's bothy with Gothic windows and a good roof. They had prepared a warm welcome for us, having trekked in with fire-wood, food and friends, so we were blessed with shelter and good company. Six hours passed as we watched the rain, pouring in seamless sheets but, with a good fire and many questions to ask and answer, there was not much urgency to move.

The rain passed. We made our way down to a road and thence to the river Dunsop. The three of us then took the way into the woodlands further up the valley, glad of the easy track which ran by the river.

> hurgling water,
> liquid leaping frenzy,
> cavorting, tea-brown,
> boulder-bruising peat-soaked

We found a soft bend of river to camp by and even a heap of fire-wood awaiting us.

Morning came with a climb up Costy Clough: a steep narrow valley, a stair of fountained moss-gardens spread down the hillside as if by the stroke of some deft and cosmic calligrapher. Half a mile of Kyoto-temple gardens carefully cultivated by our earth & water-mother, shining green.

Over the hilltop we met up with a couple of friends from Lancaster University. After a meal they walked with us far down the Salter's Road: in mediaeval times this track had been a highway, a busy road that wound through the hills though now it was quite empty. I wondered if one day the motorways would become like this – abandoned ribbons frequented by rabbits and an isolated handful of wanderers? Even though there were many miles of fine clear track, a dry well-tested route, built by hand in days of muscle and sweat, we were quite alone.

We met briefly with birdwatcher and gamekeeper, feuders over which creatures should hold sway, and an inland colony of gulls filled the air with wheeling mewls and quarks. Down from the fells we came into Bowland Forest proper and camped by a river-bend there. Nick stopped by a cottage for water and the farmer kindly offered us a perfect meadow for the night.

Running music of water is in our ears, we are tired and footsore but it feels **so** good. Travels with the Teacher and the Green Man – with life so simple there is little to be said. As I watch and learn from the manner of response, I try to create no persona as we talk. As we walk along and handle all the things that happen, sometimes I feel like I am an oaf – but when 'I' vanishes something else takes over, then there is only beauty here.

II

We began our day by breakfasting on bantam eggs and jersey milk, courtesy of the farmer, by waters babbling along. As we made our way down to a spot where we could cross the river Lune, we happened by a small wooden shack, it blended in so well with the woodland around it that we had failed to see it when we first passed by. Nick could not resist knocking to ask the way – what kind of being would dwell in such a den, down in the woods by the river? A young basket-weaver named Stella appeared and was surprised and delighted to meet us. We talked for a long while and, even though there was the need to press on, the ancient woods kept calling us to a halt in awe. We stalled again and again; here a deer, now orchids and sedges, deep green gulleys carved in the layered shales. We rolled along, somehow empty of thought and feeling, making tracks for a rendezvous in Hornby.

The rain began again as we made the last half mile; we ducked beneath a great stone bridge once we had met up with the Leeds Buddhist group, who had gathered their forces for this day.

" What a blessing it is," the Ajahn reflected, "to offer the chance to meet
>The Ajahn
>The President
>The Abbot
with cow-shit on his boots, and to shelter beneath a road-bridge in the rain."

We feasted royally, and with as much dignity as could be mustered as we clustered there, surrounded by our gear.

"Excuse the informality," begged the Ajahn to our friends as he passed a loaf of bread, manoeuvring through the roughness with aplomb.

> On the tip of every blade of grass,
> a bead of rain –
> crystalline –
> no moment
> is devalued by its appearance.

The drizzle departed along with our friends and we spent the afternoon following the course of the river. The sun peeked through and we even paused for a while to cool our aching feet in the swirling waters. The brightness was not to be for long though; as we came up from the river, heading for Hutton Roof, the cloud lowered and rain began to pour. And it poured. We were soon drenched, and depressing feelings began to creep into the mind. There was a clandestine negativity, a **reasonable** hatred brewing for the rain but then, when I turned and looked into the leaves of the hedge beside me, they were lapping it up, luxuriating –

> and a slug curled,
> wrapped, enraptured
> around a bracken frond.
> Curl matching curl,
> luxuriating.

Who am I to judge the rain as not belonging here?

Who am I to curse it with bad feeling?

On Hutton Roof Crags that night we nestled around a fire of juniper and ash. The rain had gone and we sat high and cool, watching lights appear in the villages below us. Yggdrasil, the holy ash, has often roofed us from the rain, now it burns warm and bright, offers up its life and boils up our tea to end the day.

III

Rock-hewn bridges, human constructions, enter disuse and pursue their cycle of change. Now green fronds emerge from between the stones, ivy clambers and moss distends across the wall. This is not 'nature reclaiming' but our participation, the human element in the flow of change. Layers of sandstone now are split and swirling ferns appear. As yesterday, for a moment we were the Lune – no river apart – sediment formed upon our feet as tiny fishes explored our toes, while they were planted in the cool running water. The inner and outer landscapes we contemplate: complexity and stability are twinned in nature, and the stable heart is that which can accommodate all conditions in harmony.

"There is only one Mind –" as the Ajahn put it, "it is the ultimate simplicity which contains all complexity."

A day of nature reserves and conservation areas bring these thoughts to mind; conservation being the sustenance of the great complexity for the blessing and benefit of all.

Yesterday, as we headed down from Hutton Roof, we talked much of living with the wetness. "You can see the entry of self," the Ajahn said, " 'My sleeping bag is wet, my socks, my robes' – the worrying mind goes on and on. But this is simply the way things **are**, and when that is seen, then there is no suffering – water in a sleeping bag, so what?"

We met up with Arthur and some friends from Preston and then made our way to the Gaitbarrows Reserve. After a little search we found a yew-grotto and strung our tent up to make a silver awning. Like woodland creatures, forest bhikkhus in their element, we perched ourselves between the mossy rocks and spread out the mats to take our meal. Little was spoken; amidst the offerings of shelter and food there passed good feeling and the strength of kind support. We were damp and chill and were facing another long trek that afternoon.

> Rain upon
> rain
> upon rain

We beat through the bushes of Haweswater Reserve and arrived rainsoaked in Silverdale. There was a sad feeling brought on by the sight of narrow-minded human ways as we passed through some estates and farms around there. Nick described it as the '*If it isn't a sheep or a blade of grass, kill it*' attitude. Disease-free pig-pens, dead moles on a fence, a field of bullocks who rushed across to see us, all these brought a feeling of frustration and unfulfilment, of an unkindness put upon the earth.

We arrived at Silverdale train station and found shelter on the platform there. Being on the shores of Morecambe Bay by now, we had a river to cross in order to continue westwards – there was a pregnant moment as we found out that the next train across the estuary left far too late for us to reach the place we had planned to camp.

"I wonder what happens now?"

Nick disappeared to see if he could find the house of some friends of his who lived somewhere in the village. We waited....

Out of the silence of the pause, Arthur's voice suddenly arose – "A beautiful smell pervades your clothing – juniper – just like Tibetan incense."

Nick reappeared with the broad grin of success and we were invited into the home of the Clothier family. Four generations gathered round a fire in their sitting room on this Sunday afternoon. We apologised for our invasion and were presented in return with tea and warmth and commiserations about the rain. The rain!

At Roundsea Woods we made a quick circuit of a raised peat bog and met up with a green carpet-moth. A noctuid, it rested on Nick's leathered hand as it dried off from a rain-drop and revved for take-off:

> Fore-wings on –
> Under-wings on –
> Antennae for'ard –
> **Lift off.**
> Straight to its silver birch home.

Still in rain we reached the promontory and found a spot to camp – beneath little oaks, Chinese and gnarly, low cloud and drizzle on the bay. It rained all night but nonetheless we had to push to leave early. All the gear that the Ajahn and I had was waterlogged by now, the only dry item we had between the three of us was one pair of socks belonging to Nick. He shared these out and we borrowed the veranda of an empty cottage as a shelter while we brewed some tea and dried our boots. At that moment heaven was simply a few covered feet in which to shake out our tent and a dry place to sit and watch the rain. A breeze-block public toilet became a palace for a while as we paused to adjust our gear and rest our packs.

These are the ways the mind instinctively reacts to the rains but, looking closely, what is wetness anyway? A feeling in skin, unknown by the water, it has no name or expression for its own nature. Water on skin, in cloth, on the ground – in grey rain it is tolerated, in a hot shower it is loved, appreciated in laundry yet an invader in our boots. Water and life – aren't they strange?

As we have been journeying I have tried to attune to the ways of the Ajahn:

"I can't be bothered with trying to set the world straight – it's endless. You just have to go in the right direction yourself and there will be some who follow and some who don't."

In turning to the ways of the Teacher, personality is seen to arise and be highlighted by the emptiness of his mirror. The self emerges like a spare part accompanied by shadows of error and ineptitude. A moment of embarrassment dissolves, however, when the light is allowed to shine forth. The person has no owner, it appears for social convention only, a big red 'I' standing all alone.

We arrived at Mañjushri quite waterlogged. Nick is now busy masterminding the laundering of clothes – the tents are hanging, the Ajahn rests alone and we are in the dry and protective embrace of thoughtful welcome. Profound hospitality has met us here; Roy Tyson – the director – has been attentive, respectful, sensitive and sincere. He introduced us to the resident teacher, Geshe Konchog Tsewang, who greeted us warmly – no English but no problem.

At last the clouds have gone, the late sky has now dimmed to ultra-violet and aquamarine. It is late and this day has been long – time to put things down and let it end.

IV

By a rivulet feeding the Lickle we have lain down to sleep. The day has been fair, "Mañjushri did you proud, Tan Ajahn."

"Yes, indeed they did!"

Our clothes are dry and clean, rejuvenated as we have been by a night's sleep with clean linen and beneath a sturdy roof. Many came to the talk which was requested from the Ajahn. He extemporised at length on the themes of contentment with the lowest standards of living, the nature of the self, the complaining mind and the Beyond.

Later in the day we made our way out into the country north of Broughton-in-Furness, bearing much in the way of gifts and good wishes. We traced the lanes of this English Shangri-la, a land dreamed of and died for – verdant valleys and empty roads, a pair of monks with their guide.

Down the hill we swept into the midst of it all, then climbed steeply through the woods on the other side. We found a perfect camping spot by a bend in a farm-track and got our tents and gear sorted out fast. A week on the road has lent our hands a new dexterity, all is accomplished in silence without fuss. A sudden shower sent the foreshadow of another test but no … there will be no more rain for now. The sky is speckled with the new-born clouds that roll over us as they form beyond the hills. There is a crescent moon and below us the sound of the Lickle river runs on.

V

The weather was close and humid and, even though the day at Mañjushri had helped a lot, all of us felt a little weary. During the afternoon we took a path heading northwards, leading right into the heart of Lakeland country. We clambered along rock-falls, under beech and pine-woods, along mossy tracks far from human clamours. It was a grand bazaar of botanistic curiosities and both Nick and Angie, who was with us for the day, were in their element.

Angie left us in the late afternoon and we made a long descent into the valley below Hardknott. It was tough going for the Ajahn.…

"That was quite a workout!" – an innocent observation, but one which was somewhat ominous; both Nick and I had found the walking easy. After this there was a long and gentle climb following the swerves of the river Esk, the day was bright and the waters clear, but the Ajahn was plainly tired.

What to do?

I questioned myself, surveying the inner landscapes; again and again, as earlier in the day, he ushered me to go on ahead. Eventually I realised that there was nothing to get excited or concerned about, "He just needs to adjust to a slower pace – actually he is quite O.K."

It was a long haul but the weather was clearing and our raggedness had become a familiar feeling. My neck, which had become mysteriously swollen before the walk, was now being massaged regularly by the Ajahn. Despite this it was steadily getting worse – no real rest, too much strain – but it did not really seem to be a problem.

"How are *you* feeling, Tan Ajahn?"

"I can go on."

Life is so lovely when there is no complaint. It is strange how, so quickly, the importance of the rain has been replaced in our mythology by the effect of the slopes. Wetness is already a vague and forgotten inconsequence, the attention is grabbed instead by the mountain paths and the question of our ability to climb them. The desire mind claims – "This is a REAL problem!" – but the heart knows it is only what we make of it.

We camped up high by a bend in the river on a spread of even turf below some crags. In the morning a golden mountain, washed with early sunlight, met our vision and the mountain tops were clear. Scafell could be seen and handfuls of cloud rolled over the hill beside the river.

We ate early and were away, the Ajahn's pace was slow – there was not far to go, but two thousand feet of climbing. On top of Scafell (the highest point in England), as was predicted, "Everyone and their Granny" were there.

"Soon you will be the highest bhikkhu in England, Tan Ajahn. Maybe you could add that to your list of titles?"

"What? – 'Your Highness'?" he replied and we choked on our Mars bars with laughter, perched on some rocks below the peak. We retreated, after we had reached the top, to a sheltered point some hundred yards away which looked out over the whole valley we had just ascended. Silent, still and clear, away from the day-glo horde (everyone, their Granny **and** the dog) which now crowded around the top-most cairn.

Eventually we left the peak and carried on with the journey – it was a long, long day's hike.

Down – we scoot around Great Gable, all of us on our last legs, constantly checking for the Ajahn's progress. He has to go slowly, unsure of his foot-holds and there is a constant effort to help him move around – still, he never slips, always goes on undaunted. Evening is now falling and Nick had said that we would camp on the far side of the lake, over the brow of the next hill.

Up – we reach the crest – "Is that where we're going?" the Ajahn innocently asks in a pale voice, pointing beyond the end of the huge lake, Ennerdale Water, far below us – at least 15 or 20 miles away.

"No no, Tan Ajahn" (this man really knows how to surrender!) "just down here," said Nick, indicating the little tarn a hundred yards away. It has been the hardest day for walking so far, mountain paths are not a joke with all this weight. We are all very weary but the eve is bright and still, and abundant heather gives us a boiling billy within minutes. After taking a very welcome cup of tea we are ready for an early night.

Tomorrow will begin with a descent to Honister Pass. Tomorrow night we should be in Chithurst … it is hard to believe that we could return again to that other world. It is so easy to become absorbed in the path you are upon – fire-wood hunts, weakening legs, leaky boots, fire fanning and rain threats, broad views and spring-water moss – these have become the sum total of our world – tent, mat, pack, hill, valley, an easy path or hard – a web of values and expecta-tions all of its own. When the mind leaves hold of it, though, action follows its natural course and leaves the heart silent, still and warm, unbounded.

VI

The Ajahn – zinc oxide pallor, three-day stubble and the weariness of having been stretched far past his limitations – he looks so old this morning, crumpled after heavy sleep, pouched and stooped – what have we done to him?

We refreshed ourselves with a shave, a good wash and some breakfast, and had an easy morning's walk down to the pass. As we went along we talked of the weariness we had experienced the day before: the Ajahn had not wanted to hold 'the young bucks' back, negotiating with the faltering of the body as it reached middle-age; so he had just dropped himself into a lower gear. Instinctively and unconsciously I had found myself, despite all attempts to hold back, repeatedly at his heels up the hill rock-trails – the bodies' paces so different from each other. On the physical level, age surrenders to youth, as is eventually the way with all things in nature. Youth in turn defers to the wisdom of age and follows it in matters of the spirit. The art of life is to slide gracefully into these respective rôles when the time is right. The sounds of vaulting ambition, humiliation, self-criticism or self-aggrandisement, these voices sound like long-imprisoned demons released as the doors are beaten open. This wandering life does a lot to stretch us, and does a good job of getting the voices to speak up…!

Having left our packs in a friend's car at the pass, we strode along like prisoners released on feet of wind. It was hard to believe how quickly and completely things had changed again – only a day before, every step had been a torture – and now we fly.

We lingered long at mid-day, settled on a hill-crest, eventually setting off down the long green ridge leading into the grey stone town of Keswick. The sun was bright, shaded now and then by a sprinkling of clouds – it was hard to believe a few days before we had been so wet. At High Spy cairn a woman who recognised Ajahn Sumedho stopped and chatted with us for a while, a kilted man greeted us with his palms together in *añjali* as he passed by and finally, when we reached the town, we met a young man who came from North-east Thailand: we had emerged back into the other world.

Kalyanasiri, a good friend from down south, had driven all the way up to collect us. We were a bit late but eventually we found each other. We asked forgiveness and bade farewell as evergreen Nick went off back to Northumberland. We loaded up our things, settled into our seats and then, letting the road and the wheels carry us, we rode – far into the night....

★ ★ ★

"How beautiful upon the mountains are the feet of them that publisheth peace and bring glad tidings of good things."

Isaiah Ch.52 v.7

All Things Have Their Beauty

From a talk given on the Easter retreat, Amaravati, 1992

IN THE MORNING we hear the bird song. Every morning, every dawn, the birds sing. What is in the mind of the bird when it sings? What is it saying? This we don't know.

Many wonderful stories are told about the reason why birds sing at dawn or why the sea is salt, why the world is the way it is; but in many ways it remains a great mystery to us. Mythical explanations, scientific explanations – when it comes down to it, all we can really know is that this is how it is: at dawn the birds sing. What you can be sure of about the mind of the bird is just this much – it knows when the light comes, it wakes up, it's time to sing and it just sings its own song. It does what it is supposed to do. A starling doesn't sing a blackbird's song, a blackbird doesn't sing a thrush's song. They all do their own thing, they all have their own pattern. In just the same way we human beings each have our own pattern, our own character, and the Path opens up before us when we learn to live simply, when we learn to be natural.

The simplicity of a bird singing in the morning, of water flowing along in a stream, a cloud moving across the sky: if we can live this naturally, this easily, then we can find true contentment. We struggle so much because we try to be what we are not. We try to compare the way we are to some ideal form. Much of our spiritual practice is based around acknowledging the way we are and simply using that as our means of activity and our means of communication. Each pattern, each character has its own beauty: introvert, extrovert, emotional, intellectual, naïve, cynical, male, female, old, young. Every single configuration of characteristics that we have has its own perfection. When we are truly wise, we return to the simplicity of that natural activity. We often say that the mind of a sage is like the mind of a child; it has that innocence, that purity, that simplicity. Yet it is a simplicity and purity that is born of wisdom, not of naïveté – the cycle of learning has been completed.

We often feel intimidated, or jealous of the way other people seem to be, because we feel so imperfect in our selves. But it helps to be able to generate a quality of acceptance and affection towards the way we are, rather than always to be comparing ourselves with other people. To trust, or even just to suggest, that the way we are is okay.

There is a story in the scriptures of Sariputta and Mogallana, who were the Buddha's two chief disciples. Sariputta was the wise one, a great sage who had developed a lot of deep states of meditation and analytical insight. Mogallana was the one with powerful psychic abilities, he could fly through the air, walk through walls, multiply his body, go up into heaven and down into the hells – all those kind of things.

One day Sariputta and Mogallana were sitting in the forest meditating; this was in the night-time and Sariputta was sitting, with a freshly shaven head, under the moonlight, out in the open. Two yakkhas, celestial demons, were flying southwards and one of them noticed Sariputta sitting there with his invitingly shaven head and said, "I am going to clobber this monk." The other yakkha said, "Friend, it would not be wise to strike that monk, he is the disciple of the Tathagata, and surely some dreadful fate will befall you if you attack him." But the first yakkha considered this and said, "Well … I'm going to clobber him anyway." So he took his club, approached Sariputta and gave him a blow on his head "that would have felled a mighty elephant". But far from Sariputta being knocked over, he just sat there completely still; the yakkha scratched his thorny head, unable to believe his eyes, and then went off a bit disgruntled. A little further along the way, the ground opened up and he was swallowed in a sheet of flame into the pits of hell.

All this time Mogallana was sitting watching this scene with total amazement. After a while Sariputta came out of his meditation and Mogallana said to him, "Are you all right, friend?" "Yes. Why do you ask?" "Well, I just was concerned about you, are you feeling okay? Are you in pain, or are you in any discomfort at all?" "Well, I do have a slight headache." "A slight headache! This is incredible, this is indeed marvellous, this is miraculous; just a little while ago this enormous yakkha came up to you and hit you on the head with a blow that would have felled a mighty elephant, and yet Sariputta the great, the marvellous disciple of the Tathagata, says that he merely has a slight headache: this is indeed miraculous!!"

Then Sariputta said, "Well, it may be so Mogallana, but I feel that it is equally miraculous that you are able to see these things; I am so devoid of any such psychic powers that I cannot even see so much as a mud-sprite let alone anything more refined. It is a wonderful and marvellous thing that the venerable Mogallana is capable of witnessing these extraordinary events on other planes of existence." The two of them patted each other on the back and each decided that the other was highly eminent and worthy.

This is supposed to be a true story, but even if it is not, it is a good illustration of how we can be deeply impressed by the abilities of our friends and quite neglectful or dismissive of our own faculties. But if Mogallana had spent his life being miserable and jealous of Sariputta's wisdom and if Sariputta had spent his life being envious of Mogallana's psychic powers, both of them would have led a lot less fruitful existence, their lives would have been a poor example for us to follow. Instead they were able to use the abilities and the talents that they each had, to offer what they had in their own way and to have joy – *mudita* – in each other's success, leaving that attitude as a legacy to the people around them and to the world.

★ ★ ★

It is of fundamental importance to be able to arouse the attitude of benevolence towards ourselves, no matter where we happen to be, or whatever state of mind happens to be there. If we have no kindness towards ourselves, then it is almost as if we can't even start. The beginning of freedom is to acknowledge and to cherish in our hearts our own character with all its talents and all its faults, with all its beauty and all its ugliness, with all its mediocrity. To embrace it all in our hearts and to acknowledge that, right or wrong, beautiful or ugly, this is the way I am and this is the way life actually is. From that starting point, all good things flow. When we are able to harmonise our inner world in this way then we are more able to harmonise with those around us.

Today there is a great gathering taking place;* this is something that the Buddha placed great importance upon, for our own spiritual development and for the welfare of all beings. As long as we meet often and in large numbers, as long as we meet in concord, carry on our business together in concord, depart in concord; as long as we revere the elders and leaders of our tribe; as long as we maintain the established decorum, as long as we relate respectfully towards each other – then our group, our society will prosper and not decline.

On a day of such a gathering like today we exercise a quality of openness – free exchange between ourselves and other people. Meeting each other, talking, all gathered together in one large group – even though this may not seem to be related to meditation, stillness, silence and non-attachment – surrounded by hundreds of people, involved in contact and social activity – it is all part of the same system.

To learn to give ourselves to a communal spirit, to surrender my own particular point of view and my preferences, to live as one member of a unified whole, to recognise our existence as a part of a greater universe, this provides the context of our meditation practice. So long as meditation is based around 'me and my practice', as long as it is something that I am doing just for my own salvation, then I am forgetting half of the picture. We forget a large part of our life and find ourselves adrift from reality. One comes across a lot of people in the monastic world and in the world of Buddhist meditation retreats who are very dedicated, earnest and sincere about their practice. But it is very much **my** practice, "I have got to have this for **my** practice," "I've got to have this environment," "I've got to be away from this, that and the other influence – otherwise my practice will be disturbed."

Well, if we are so concerned with **my** practice, and we see the world only in terms of being beneficial for my practice, or harmful for my practice,

_____

*The 100th day after the passing away of Ven. Ajahn Chah

and that is the only way we judge it, we become incredibly self-centred and self-concerned. Everything in the world seems to be related to that one person-based activity. So one finds people who are ideologically very committed towards Buddha-Dhamma and realisation of Truth, but the actuality of the way they steer their lives is one of great selfishness – they find they are a cause of discord.

Ajahn Chah realised this when, as a young monk, he found himself getting angry with all the not-so-diligent monks around him, because they would upset his practice – they would do things that would annoy him, they would disappoint him. His commitment to goodness thus went awry and became a cause for destructiveness.

Certainly we need to put effort into our own enlightenment. Our life is the one that we work on most directly, this is our field of activity where our personal choices are most centred. But we also exist as part of the human race, part of the whole web of living beings, and if we try to ignore that, or assume that "my life is more significant than yours", then we throw the whole thing into disharmony. We need to acknowledge our existence as a social being as well as an individual.

So to be able to be alone and to commit ourselves to energetic solitary practice, but to also give ourselves to others, to communicate, these are two aspects of the one art that we are developing here, these are all part of our training.

★ ★ ★

People ask: "Should I adopt this practice and be very strict? Or should I be more easygoing and go with the flow? If you set yourself a task to do, should you stick to it? Or should you just be ready to adapt to conditions?" We love to have a formula to follow, a simple pattern that we can always obey that tells us we should be like this or be like that, but in many ways we need to be like a tree: a tree has both hardness, firmness and it also has flexibility. If a tree has just firmness, then when the fierce winds blow the tree will break, the branches will snap. If the tree has just flexibility and no rigidity at all then it can't stand up, it has no resilience, it will bend too easily. So in the same way, our practice uses both these qualities: being resolute and independent within ourselves, staying with that which we have committed ourselves to, and at the same time being ready to bend, move and shift according to the time, place and situation. These qualities are not conflicting; like in a tree, we don't think of the soft curves of a tall tree and the way it moves in the wind as being something disharmonious or ugly. We don't see its hardness and softness fighting against each other.

In our own minds we can imagine our own strength and our own flexibility arguing with each other, worrying about which one is right – "Should I be this or should I be that?" The more we develop the quality of mindfulness, the mind full of the present moment, we find these different qualities of our own being operate together quite naturally. Strength and flexibility operate side by side all the time, just like the different aspects of the tree. The whole intellectual, idealistic approach of, "Should I? Shouldn't I? What is right? What is wrong?" is an overlaid description, just a verbal way of conceptualising what is going on. But if we really listen to our hearts, our heart knows what to do. Just like in the meditation, when the body is out of kilter, when there is some kind of stiffness or some imbalance in the body, if we simply bring awareness to that and let go from our very heart, then we find that the body knows how to adapt, it straightens the right amount, it moves just as much as it needs to without any volitional interference on the part of the thinking mind. The world responds.

There is a saying by a T'ai Chi Master called Al Huang that goes, "When we move our little finger, the universe adjusts." We can let our whole life adjust and let our judgement be guided by awareness, by Nature, by awakening to that fundamental reality. This is our basic guide. The verbal teachings are just a backup to embellish it; our hearts know what is the right thing and we can trust that.

★ ★ ★

The retreat has gone by. We've travelled through all sorts of inner land-scapes: beautiful, terrible, warring, strange, dreary. We travelled as a group through this time together. We arrive at today, and say to ourselves, "This is the last day." Every end has a beginning, however; the way we look at things is very subjective. The end conditions the beginning, the beginning conditions the end. The retreat came together, we all arrived at this place, put ourselves into this situation, lived as a group for this period of time, and now we disperse. Just like an inhalation and an exhalation. The Retreat Centre breathed us in, we cir-culated around its lungs for a little while and now it breathes us out again. Just a different kind of breath.

Just as in using the breath as a meditation object: first of all, we can't hold it in our attention at all, then we can hold it occasionally, then hold it more consistently. Then we are able to start noticing the space between breaths, the pause after the exhalation before the next inhalation begins. The pause after the inhalation, the moment before the exhalation. We notice these spots of still-ness. Then we notice the stillness that pervades the whole breath, the stillness the breath moves through, the stillness of the mind which is the context for all activity. This is the silence out of which all sound arises, the silence into which it dissolves, the silence which sits behind, permeates, surrounds all experience, all vibration. This is a wordless realisation that we touch upon more and more consistently. This is what our meditation has been guiding us towards – touch-ing this unified field of experience, the mind ground, the ground of being, the Unconditioned mind, Original Mind, or whatever one wants to call it.

To know this, to awaken to this unifying principle of our own being, this is the substance of growing up. This is our process of maturation, our in-itiation. One who is an initiate of truth is one who sees this reality and is awake to its fundamental principle. If you are familiar with the deck of tarot cards, you know that the Initiate is the final card of the major arcana. The first card is that of the Fool, Zero. This is where we begin; the fool is always depicted dancing merrily at the edge of a cliff with his dog playing around his heels. This image came to mind the other day when we were talking about absorbing into wonderful passions; it is wonderful to dance, but it is also folly not to notice there is a cliff two inches away from our right heel and it's a long, long way down.

That in us which is foolish seizes hold of the ups in life, seizes hold of the pleasant, seizes hold of success, praise, comfort, physical security, affirmation from people around us, seizes hold of youth and strength, attractiveness, seizes hold of Spring and the upwards swinging part of the cycle. The Fool is that which invests in the pleasure principle, the arising, and neglects the ceasing, the falling; because as we seize hold of the wheel at the point of Spring, at the point of success, praise, health and prosperity, then we are still holding the wheel as it swings around and it goes down into Winter, into criticism, into failure, into illness, into rejection. This is what we mean by 'Samsara'. That in us which clings on to the rim of the wheel and swings around and around, trying to get past the grim bits to find the next experience of arising.

I hope that during this time we have learned to see the painfulness of holding the wheel, the painfulness of swinging around and around, identifying with our swings of mood and the events of the day. I hope that we have learned more to take refuge in that which knows the wheel and its turning, that which knows success and failure, praise and criticism, night and day, spring and winter.

This knowing is our home, this is our basis, this is where we belong, if you like. This is the home where our heart is. We take this wherever we go, although we may neglect it, forget it very often. This is why we as monastics take homelessness as our basic style of living. We try not to depend upon houses or our own physical place to live, in order to encourage us to dwell instead in our *real* home, in the liberated heart, the mind which is awake.

Queen Mary's Rose Garden

A circle within a circle
a rose within a rose
within a rose.
Gentle blossom,
the indestructible
in the heart of the inferno –
the nucleus of worldly powers,
earthly powers.

The garden –
nature tamed or rather
guided by humankind;
crystallised arranged,
sprinkled into patterns
of golden scarlet,
rose –
circles of rose,
layer upon layer
lapping on each other,
fragrance and colour
fill the city air.
The garden –
the gesture of the wakened
and the bright.

A circle of light
shines in the city heart –
the garden of a queen, Maria,
bearer of an ocean of compassion,
cradles rows,
spirals of rose,
safe in the heart
of the city.

Shape and colour,
line and fragrance,
in subtle counterpoints;
flame and blush
of peace and passion
lead us into knowledge:
"We are in the midst
of a great miracle."
We **are**
a great miracle.
Vision and knowledge
celebrate the light;
the life that sparkles
silent, opalescent
in the pinks of petal-flesh
ranged in perfect patterns
all around.

At the heart,
all-subsuming
frames of crystal light
emanate, permeate,
suffuse every city street
with perfume and pattern,
symmetry and colour;

and every urgent line
on every haggard face
rolls by
as a wave
of the Miracle.

(*Regent's Park, London, 1989*)

Perfect Proof

From a talk given on the winter retreat, Chithurst, January 1991

SOMETHING WHICH COMES UP REGULARLY in dealing with the question of spiritual practice and spiritual authority in the scriptures is: How do we know anything is true? So I thought to speak this evening about proof, about how something comes to be proven.

I remember reading somewhere that the definition of proof is that it is a shrine in front of which pure mathematicians immolate themselves. The quest for certainty, absolute knowledge, is something which has been very strong in our culture, particularly in the last few hundred years. So much of our thought and our style of life has been based around rationalism and certainty, that this has given a whole tone to our society. The sense of wanting to be able to prove everything is very strong, and this quest for certainty is based on the understanding that, when we have everything proven, then everything will be all right....

Up until the turn of the last century, people in the scientific world felt that we were getting through the problems bit by bit and that soon we would have the whole material, natural world understood – there was even the hope that psychology was going to become a mathematical science. At Harvard University, in the 1890s I believe, they closed the post-graduate section of the physics department because they thought that there was nothing left to discover. There were just two slightly strange effects that they needed to figure out: one was radioactivity and the other was why hot bodies emit light in the way that they do. The belief was that once they got those two little things figured out, then all knowledge about the physical world would be complete.

So they shut the post-graduate department. Unfortunately, Max Planck and Albert Einstein came along a few years later and blew the whole thing to pieces with their insights and discoveries about the nature of matter, energy and the sub-atomic world. This kind of hubris within us is very strong – the rational mind feels that somehow it can get everything tied up, and that we can establish absolute knowledge within the realm of thought.

Also around the turn of the century in England, a couple of philosophical mathematicians, Bertrand Russell and Alfred North Whitehead, set about trying to prove from first principles all of the most important theorems and aspects of mathematics, starting out with the absolute basics – no assumptions whatsoever. They spent about fifteen years doing this and they published, I think in 1913, their massive masterpiece, *The Principia Mathematica*. They had the whole thing tied up – "There's nothing more to be done here, this is it, we've got it, it's all fixed, WE KNOW."

A few years later another person came along with an insight that I feel is extremely important for the philosophy of our age. From a background also of rationalism and logic, which our society worships and looks up to as its great idol, this man came up with an insight, a proof that turned the whole thing on its head. And, for humanity at this time, an inroad into the realisation that the absolute cannot be established in terms of the relative is very important.

This man's name was Kurt Gödel. In 1931 – when he was quite a young man – he produced a proof whereby he showed that any formal system, any logical form whatsoever, any mathematical system has to be either incomplete or imperfect. Paraphrased, it reads something like: "All consistent axiomatic formulations of number theory include undecidable propositions."[1] In this way he came up with a very straightforward and ingenious proof that shows one can't establish absolute certainty in relative terms. It is intrinsically impossible. It cannot be done. It is like a camera – it can take pictures of everything in the world except for itself, there is always something that has to be left out of the picture. You either have to generalise things and leave things inaccurate or there is something left out, there is a piece missing. And he proved that no matter how hard you try and work it, no matter how you try to get around it, intrinsic in every single proposition, every single idea or proof, there is this quality of incompleteness, the lack of absolute certainty.

In a way this was an insight into the First Noble Truth, it was a recognition of dukkha in its subtler sense. This was displaying, from a very logical standpoint, the same insight that the Buddha had: that any thing whatsoever, by its very thing-ness, by its very existence, has imperfection or insubstantiality or change or unsatisfactoriness intrinsically embodied in it. It has to be there. There is no way around it.

Now this rather deflated poor Bertrand Russell, even though young Gödel didn't really trust the strength of his own insight; when he published it, he published it as "Part One", sure that people were going to come along and shoot holes in it – but they didn't. There was nothing wrong with it. There was no "Part Two". He had captured it in one simple expression, a clear act of understanding that still stands up today. Its verity is unshaken and it's proving to be more and more of a significant factor in the understanding our own nature as conscious interdependent beings. It's having more and more of an effect on the philosophical climate. Interestingly enough, Whitehead seemed to get the message, adapted his line of thinking in his later work and it is his name behind much of today's liveliest and most viable thinking in the academic world.[2]

The Buddha used the term *sankhara-dukkha* to refer to this same kind of imperfection, which is not saying there is something bad about the world of things and ideas but that, in the very nature of the apparent independence or particular individuality of things, there is dukkha bound up with them. There is not the vision of wholeness.

A way to look at this and understand it is to think in terms of the arising of the material and mental realities that we experience from the scientific point of view. From a Buddhist point of view we describe *namarupa*, mind and body, as arising from consciousness, and originally arising out of the *sacca-dhamma*, the fundamental, ultimate reality which is the ground, the basis for all things. In scientific terms, some have called this *sacca-dhamma* the 'sea of potential'; that energetic vacuum which is the basis of all physical and mental reality, and out of which all things emerge.

The body and the mind – atoms and molecules, protons, neutrons, electrons and everything that forms our material world and the consciousness that arises also – they all arise from the same place. They arise from that same basic, fundamental reality. They are two aspects of the same fundamental reality that spring forth into being. And one can reflect that atoms and molecules and the forces between them exist in very much the same way that we as individual people and the relationships between us exist. The wave-like and particle-like nature of matter is mirrored in the material and mental aspects of our own life; *namarupa* is like an expanded version of the wave- and particle-like nature of matter, of reality at its most basic level; *rupa* being the particular and *nama* being somewhat wavey.

So, springing out of this sea of potential, this ground of being, are our physical being, our mental world, our thoughts and feelings and the whole universe. These spring forth and then return to that same sea, as the Buddha said, "All conditions arise from the Unconditioned and they return to the Unconditioned"; "All conditions merge in the Deathless."

This is a pattern for our whole experience of existence. We see that the Unconditioned in itself can be uninteresting. One analogy often used is that the Unconditioned is like space, like the space of this room. It doesn't catch our attention – the bodies, the pictures, the light, the colours in the room do. So in that sense the Unconditioned is not 'interesting'. It has no features, it has no characteristics. When the mind opens to it its nature becomes more vivid and understood, more real. But at first glance it seems as though there's nothing there. The potential that is there can perhaps only know itself through the fluctuations or excitations that occur within it.

Our thoughts arise out of the Unconditioned. They come into being and become interesting, then the attention fixes on them and so they start to seem very real but they purchase that reality, that substance at the cost of separation from the ground of being, from the Unconditioned. So this is where the experience of dukkha or alienation, imperfection arises, and trying to know or to understand the Unconditioned in terms of the conditioned will always bring us a sense of lack, a sense of incompleteness.

In Buddhist terms, this is what we talk about as the arising of *sankhara* – that bringing forth of a whole material/mental world and the attendant dukkha that arises within it. But, when that is seen with knowledge and vision, when the mind is awake, then this is the ending of dukkha, the ending of illusory separation; we understand clearly the origin and nature of things.

In a way this is also what is represented by the Fall, in the Biblical sense – that separation which is eventually the source of knowledge, bought at the price of leaving the total fusion and wholeness of the Unconditioned, life in Eden. Our journey through life and our evolution as human beings is an evolution through this sense of separation to the quality of knowledge clarified, to where we realise the true nature of things. We find our way back to Eden, back to the peace of the Original Mind, that was always there but we felt we'd lost it only because our eyes were closed, our vision was absent and we didn't see it. It's like becoming so enraptured with all of the objects in this room or so worried about all the people, liking this one and not liking that one, becoming so caught up in the web of relationships that we feel there is no space in this place, "I need more space, I need more space, there's just things and people and activity and...." The place is full of space, there's nothing but space, but we just fail to see it.

The Unconditioned, the bliss of the mind's own nature, is here right in our own hearts, it's always right here behind every thought, behind every sound, inside every colour, every feeling, every mood; if we penetrate to the heart of it that same purity, radiance, peacefulness is right there, **right here**, if only we take the trouble to look for it.

This is pointing to the fact that in order to deal with the Fall, to deal with suffering and the inability that we have to establish certainty and completeness on the sensory level – or in terms of what we think, what we do and what we have – we can solve this simply through being awake. We solve the riddle through the true understanding and penetration of the sensory world; by the complete relinquishing of any illusion that wholeness can come from any thought, from words, from achievements or from possessions. It's only through the true awakening in our own hearts to the fundamental nature of things – which is not just a clear idea but an actual transmutation of our vision of life right here within us – a breaking of the habit of self-identification that divides reality into subject and object, self and other – it's only through this that we come to recognise absoluteness, we come to recognise certainty, we come to perfect proof, to completeness.[3]

★ ★ ★

In terms of Dhamma, spiritual teachings, we often talk about non-duality; this is because there is something in us which knows that wholeness is true, that is to say that any kind of apparent separation or fragmentation is somehow a mistake, an error. There's something in our gut level feelings that tells us, "This just isn't right"; there's a longing for completeness, and this takes shape as desire. Desire is a sense of having something missing, so we look for an object of desire to fill that gap: longing for home, like Ulysses longing to return to Ithaca, that feeling driving him on and on through all the terrors and trials of a ten-year journey – being pulled home.

With any kind of desire that we experience, we feel that there is something missing and that, if only we could just get that thing – "If I could only achieve this or acquire that or get to this place then everything will be all right." We want to be whole, we don't want to be two, we want to be one. So *tanha, upadana, bhava* – craving, clinging, becoming – these, in a sense, come from the same drive that pulls us towards that realisation of wholeness, the Unconditioned. In the moment of becoming, that thrill of, "At last I've got it, this is it, I have it," that thrill is like an echo that comes from the thrill of wholeness, the satisfaction of knowing there's not two, there is one.

It's because that thrill doesn't and cannot last that we experience dukkha, so the spiritual path is always pointing to the place where we can really find completion, where we won't be disappointed, where that sense of wholeness and satisfaction won't be conditional, temporary and fragile. The Buddha taught the Four Noble Truths based on the letting go of desire, arriving at non-duality. He said: first of all, stop looking for wholeness in terms of sense objects. This is where we really cause problems for ourselves. He also said, "Ignorance is the cause of suffering" but this is perhaps a bit too subtle for most of our minds to grasp. Desire is the place where we can see the problem most easily, most readily. We can spot the mistake happening. So he taught us to see desire, notice desire but to not follow it. Just let desire pass through the mind like a wave. Let it come through the mind. Let it dissolve back into the silence, into the Unconditioned. Let desires end, relinquish, abandon them.

The Buddha uses a beautiful sequence of terms: "*viveka, viraga, nirodha, vossagga*". This means seclusion or separation – this is *viveka;* then *viraga,* detatchment; *nirodha* cessation; *vossagga,* surrender or abandonment – this is the putting down, leaving alone of desire. It's like putting down something in your hand which is burning hot, leaving it alone, walking away from it, not looking back, we let go of desire in this way.

The problem is that we don't recognise that desire **is** desire. Often it can seem to be very reasonable: putting one's mind onto a task and getting down to it. In spiritual practice there's a lot of emphasis on making effort and using energy but often this is particularly difficult to be clear about. It so easily slips into the desire to become: that effort, doing the right thing, very easily overreaches itself and becomes a yearning, a racing ahead, a blind trying. Particularly if we are engaged in spiritual practice, what we want to become is something that has got all the right credentials. We want to become a good person, we want to become wise, compassionate, loving, unselfish and so on and so on. The objects of desire are all very wholesome and praiseworthy, but that very trying can be that which blocks the mind.

I had a very revealing experience a year or so ago, when I was on retreat in the forest here at Chithurst. I'd been about two weeks on retreat and my mind was very energised and concentrated. I came in to spend an all-night sitting on the new-moon day here in the house. I was very awake and found myself without any trouble sitting up all night long. I was sitting there full of energy with a mind concentrated and clear but all the time there was a feeling of adjusting and pushing and shoving: "Just a little bit more of this and a little bit less of that and, oh yes, nearly there, and oh, right, doing well here, yes, this is it, **this** is what I like, yes, oh no, no, gone, oh it's slipped away, oops, O.K., what am I doing, yes, go back to what I was doing five minutes ago, right, O.K., a bit more of this, ah, right, yes, yes, getting there, nearly, that's it, steady, steady, right," and all night long this was going on. There was a nagging feeling of discontent, restless becoming, going on all the time. When the night was over and I was walking back to my hut in the forest, I felt a deep sense of irritation and disappointment, sadness that somehow I was getting it all wrong. The breakthrough into perfect peace had seemed so close, yet so veiled all night long; like pressing at a thin curtain, tantalisingly unable to get through.

It was just after dawn when I got back to the little hut. I lay down in this same kind of mood, fell asleep for about half an hour and then woke up. I was really energised, my body was still charged up from the night's meditation and so I thought, "Oh, no. I can't even go to sleep. This is really unfair!" So I shoved my bedding into an untidy heap in the corner and decided to forget the whole thing. "I'm not going to meditate. I'll just lie here in a crumpled lump," so I flopped down and just let go of everything – the result of this was that my mind instantaneously went into an absolutely clear, peaceful balanced state. It was as if I could hear the voice of Wisdom saying, "At last! I was wondering when you were going to stop all that mucking about. It was getting quite exhausting there."

As I half sat, half lay there I experienced a wonderful, transcendent peacefulness and clarity. The mind seemed light, empty and void of personality. It was a tremendously liberating and wonderful experience. It was very clear that, all the way along, the trying was what had been obscuring the Truth; that bashing, thrashing effort in the mind, trying to get something and become something. Even though what I wanted to become was very reasonable, it was 'I' that was doing it and that was what was creating all the problems.

The following afternoon, just by way of reiterating the predicament, I found myself sitting in the doorway of my hut, as I often did. The door was open but there was an insect, a bee, bashing away on the glass trying to get out. Over and over again it kept flying into the glass and bashing into it to escape, even though the door was open. I began to look at the poor thing, thinking, "Let me help you get out." I got a little card and tried to get the card behind it to scoop it out around the window frame and release it, "Look, friend, all you've got to do is just go around this way, it's right here, just let me help you."

But the more I tried to help it the more frantic and frustrated it became, the harder it flapped its wings and the harder it bashed itself against the glass. I kept saying, "No, no, no, it's all right, don't worry, just sit still and I'll help you to get out." Then I began to notice a distinct similarity between my own mind states of the previous night and this insect bashing away on the glass. So I thought perhaps I'd better leave it alone; and in exactly the same way, once I stopped trying to help it, after a little while the insect calmed down, it eventually got to the edge of the window frame and then, by just waiting for the right moment, with one quick move and a little flick with a piece of card, the insect was away. I thought, "How wonderful! This is exactly what was happening during the previous night: there I was, bashing away at the glass, longing for the Light – I could see the Light and was flying at it but kept colliding with time and the sense of self – resulting in: frustration. All that it had needed was a moment of inconsequential calm, when the fury and flurry had abated, patience, observation for when the time was ripe and then BOP! Freedom at last – the open door.

The state of freedom, wholeness, carefree peace is our Original Nature and we only appear to depart from it and feel the need for something to replace it because of *avijja* – not knowing, in its most profound sense. Space, light, selflessness these are all words pointing to that inexpressible pure heart that is the centre of everything. It is from that wholeness or suchness, that the sense of self and other arises – the arising of '*sankhara*' is the division between self and other, subject and object, the sense of 'I' and 'the world'. This sense of self is the most basic illusion so, even if one is breaking the chain of Dependent Origination at 'desire', there is still the unconscious creation of the sense of 'I' and 'the world' or even 'I' seeing the 'Truth'.

In one of his teachings (the Pañcattaya Sutta) the Buddha points out how, if some person is meditating and has developed a lot of insight and peacefulness, they might arrive at a blissful state of mind where there is clarity and knowledge; then the thought arises in them, "I am at peace, I am without clinging, I have attained Nibbana." Then that very thought proclaims the clinging which is still there. Even if there is just a sense of "I seeing the Truth" then there's still a subtle sense of division, there's still *sankhara* there, subtly being created and producing the feeling of separateness and therefore imperfection.

Our goal is to break through even that, to be able to remain at the root, to go right back to the Source and break through even that sense of there being an observer. Just to let the mind dissolve in the ground of its own being so that there is no sense of 'me' seeing the 'Truth', an observer and an observed, there's only peacefulness, clarity and the sense of wholeness. The world of 'things' is not formulated and therefore any idea that there could be certainty or 'decidability' is without a basis – there is no **thing** there to be decidable or not – this is true completeness, proof of the Real. In knowing such completion, no shadow of imperfection of any sort at all can remain.

---

[1]Technically it reads like this: "To every ω-consistent recursive class κ of *formulae* there correspond recursive *class-signs* r, such that neither v Gen r nor Neg(v Gen r) belongs to Flg (κ) (where v is the free variable of r)"!!!

[2]His magnum opus is called *Process and Reality,* published by McMillan.

[3]The Cistercian monk, Brother David Steindl-Rast, phrases this point very beautifully: "At the peak of our Peak Experience everything suddenly makes sense. Your heart is

touched and there is peace. Not that suddenly you found answers to all your questions. Not that all contradictions are suddenly reconciled. Not even your problems are solved. But you have hit upon something deeper than questions; more comprehensive than all contradictions; something that can support all problems without need for solutions. How strange. We usually think that we must trace our questions to the ultimate question to arrive at the ultimate answer. We are convinced that we must work our way through contradiction after contradiction to arrive at an ultimate reconciliation; struggle with problem after problem to find the ultimate solution. Yet, what happened here is something entirely different. For one split second we were distracted from our preoccupations with problems, questions, and contradictions. That child catching minnows in a tidepool, that line of a melody, that flash in our lover's eyes, did it. For one split second we dropped the load of our preoccupations and the super-solution, the super-answer is suddenly ours, in one great super-reconciliation of everything.

"What paradox! When I drop the question, there's the answer. In fact, we might begin to suspect that the answer is there all the time, trying to get through to us, while we are too preoccupied with our questions. But what disproportion between cause and effect. Why should one moment of true looking or listening yield what no amount of grappling with problems can wrestle from life? Our experience itself suggests an answer to this question. When we watch carefully, we notice that the child, the music, the loving glance, teased us for a moment into saying "Yes" to reality, a very special "Yes." We were caught off guard. Our heart went out to this tiny fragment of reality and burst into an unconditional "Yes." But having said this kind of "Yes" to the humblest fringe of reality, we have implicitly affirmed all there is. By drinking deeply from the stream we have said "Yes" to the Source. That is why our humble encounter is truly mystical, truly an experience of communion with Ultimate Reality. And since Ultimate Reality is the very "coincidence of opposites," we should not be surprised if we experience this communion as paradoxical."

(Brother David Steindl-Rast, *A Listening Heart*, p. 39, Crossroads)

Primaveritas

unfathomable the Buddha the heart of inconceivable sparkling colours Thought that shrinks from the brink a well of silence autumn summer winter the flickering change mandala of awakening the light good earth treading the lotus spring light the slenderbone electric spaces transparent mother of pearl little of wing Buddha mind from the eye's corner half discerns shimmer jewel of the ocean cracks limitless silent power pivot at here and now the if it moves it is beginning and I said to my soul be still and darkness and now the uncounted galaxies without space without time true awakening joy nowhere light and no here E

Chithurst, April 1982

Emptiness and Pure Awareness

or

What happened when Scarlett met Rhett…?

From a talk given on the winter retreat, Chithurst, February 1991

OTAMA BUDDHA SAID, when he was an old man, "This body is like an old cart, held together by straps; this body only keeps going by makeshift repairs. The only way I can feel comfortable is to absorb my mind into signless concentration."

For all of us, the Buddha included, we are faced with the inevitable presence of dissatisfaction and physical discomfort. Ever present is the danger of pain and disease, because we are born. Because there is a physical birth, there must be physical decay, the two have to go together, they are one thing. Thus our only true refuge is the Deathless, that which is not subject to disease, not subject to defilement, not subject to time or to limitation, that which is unsupported. In this way, returning to our source, the Deathless, is our only way to *cure* disease, the only way to pass beyond it.

This returning to the Source, or realising the Deathless, is the sense of coming to know the source of our life, the origin of our life. Because it is the very fabric of our life, the basis of our existence, it is something that has been exerting a power of attraction on us all through our life, the attraction of Truth, of the Real, the completely satisfying, the completely safe.

When we are children we function on the instinctual level, and so that spiritual attraction becomes focussed on/sublimated by food and warmth, comfort and toys. Then, later on, that satisfaction is found with people, with activities, relationships, machines, ambitions, the doings of worldly existence. All along, however, that pull has fundamentally been a spiritual motivation.

It gets sidetracked by the search for wealth, for material security, for permanent happy relationships. But one sees the reason why these things don't complete the picture: they are not really sustainable as our support because they are impermanent, and also because the heart knows it has not gone the whole way, one has taken a side road. If you are trying to make a journey to a distant place and you take a detour, you get caught up in interesting things along the way. But it is only when you get to your destination that there is feeling of, "Ahh, now we are home, now we are safe, now everything is okay."

Even when you are sidetracked, there is a feeling lingering in your heart, "Well, there is a bit further to go." Or, "This is all very interesting, but, mmm, there is something missing here, there is something not quite right, not quite true, not quite final here."

The attraction towards Truth is fundamental. It is attraction towards reality, the basic fabric of all being. This is the primary natural law; it's the living law that rules the universe. The gravitation which draws all things to Truth, drawing everything to the centre, this is the basic law of life. So once we are attuned to this pull and have realised its spiritual nature, and have picked up the idea that life is fundamentally and completely a spiritual activity, once we have got that clear in our mind, the task is much easier, and the realisation of the Goal becomes inevitable. The tendency to get sidetracked becomes diminished, the knowing of the true nature of the Goal calls us on, encourages and inspires us to keep going.

★ ★ ★

When we talk about the Deathless, or the Absolute, or the Goal, or the Other Shore, the mind goes a little bit blank trying to get a hold of it. Even in the way we speak about 'Nibbana' – 'cooling down', 'coolness' – we don't use any dramatic or emotive term, it's all a bit bland, non-descriptive. We talk about 'emptiness': the realisation of Absolute Truth, of our true nature, the realisation of the non-conceptual pure mind, we describe as 'the ultimate emptiness'.

We use that kind of terminology not because there is nothing there, but because when the conceptual mind tries to grasp ultimate reality, since it can't be formed into a pattern, it finds that there is no *thing* there. It is like picking up a book in Chinese; if you can't read Chinese you are picking up a book in a foreign language. Here is a book, perhaps full of profound and wonderful teachings and pure truths, but you can't read the script, so it's meaningless. This is like the conceptual mind trying to grasp Ultimate Truth, the nature of the Godhead. The thinking mind says, "Well what is it"? "How do you describe it?" "Where is it?" "Am I it?" "Am I not it?" It gropes for some kind of handle. In the same way, the thinking mind falls flat, as when trying to read a book in Chinese or Devanagari or whatever when it only knows English.

So, because to the conceptual mind the experience of Ultimate Truth has no form, it can be described as 'emptiness'. But to the non-conceptual wisdom-mind, the realisation of Truth is like the Truth seeing itself. Pure Mind, aware of its own nature. When the mind is completely unattached, when there is no identification, no sense of self whatsoever, the mind rests pure and still, simply aware of its own nature. The Dhamma aware of its own nature. There is a realisation that everything is Dhamma, but that realisation is non-verbal, non-conceptual, so the conceptual mind calls it empty. But to itself, its real nature is apparent, it is understood, it is clear.

★ ★ ★

This is the source of our life, the basis of our reality. Our world of people and things, of doing this and of doing that, this is what we call the world of manifestation, the conditioned or sensory world. The Buddha taught in terms of the relationship between these two, the Unconditioned and the conditioned, the ultimate and the relative, the *samutti sacca* and *paramattha sacca*, conventional truth and ultimate truth. A lot of Buddhist practice is about learning to understand the relationship between these two aspects of what is.

When we see clearly, when we have a realisation of the Unconditioned, what flows forth is harmonious, beautiful, and that which is beautiful and harmonious helps to lead the mind back to the Uncreated. All religious acts, teachings, works of art, these are designed to be harmonious and pure forms which draw the mind back to recognise the silence, stillness, that purity which lies behind all things. As in the chanting that we do: even though the sound itself is quite beautiful, its real importance is that it leads the mind to an apprehension of the silence of Ultimate Truth which lies behind the sound, permeates the sound. This is why certain pieces of music or works of art stop the mind, or fill the heart with warmth and light and a feeling of blessèdness and beauty. It's a religious experience. All true art is a religious experience. That is what it is for.

One witnesses the same thing with relationships: if we try to find happiness simply on the level of personality, try to find a completely satisfying and perfect relationship just on the external level, then all we get is an outpouring of selfhood. We get our projections of how the other person should behave, or what they should be like to make me happy.

This is something that one sees not just in romantic relationships, but also in monastic life as well, particularly within the relationship between someone and their teacher. You find that if you have got very fixed ideas about the teacher – what they should be like, what they should say, what they shouldn't say, what they should do and what they shouldn't do – it is very much divided up into 'me and them'. Then you end up feeling terribly pleased and enthusiastic about being connected with this person when they say all the things that you like and when they pat you on the head and compliment you. And you also get filled with terrible irritation and disappointment, hurt feelings and anger when they don't do the things that you like, they upset your image of them or they don't fit into your projections about them. Intense devotion and affection very easily goes into intense violence and destruction.

In the Greek myths, Aphrodite and Aries were lovers, even though they were the goddess of love and the god of war. This is very indicative of the human condition, in that passion easily goes into either attraction or aversion. When there is blindness there, it will go easily either way. They say that 90% of all murders have some kind of sexual aspect to them, which is a pretty astonishing statistic. But you can see why. You can see why, when we have very definite expectations or feelings about each other, and it remains stuck on a personal level, then we *have* to end up in dissatisfaction of some sort. It *has* to be that way, because true satisfaction can only come by seeing that which is beyond personality, beyond the sense of 'me' and 'you'.

Devotion to a teacher, to a guru, or being in love, these are in a sense all religious experiences. The devotional practices we do generate a sense of love, because in that sense of love we lose identity, we lose the sense of 'me'. In romantic love we forget ourselves because we are completely absorbed in the Other. The Other becomes supremely important and the sense of 'I' vanishes. The blissful feeling of being in love is almost religious, there is no sense of self, there is perfect happiness.

That happiness is conditioned because it depends on the presence of the other, their affection, or their abiding interest or whatever. But at the moment of pure romantic contact the sense of self vanishes, and there is bliss. In 'Gone with the Wind', the moment that Scarlett O'Hara and Rhett Butler kiss is very interesting; it is described something like this: "All she knew was everything vanished: the world vanished, he and she vanished, all there was was total bliss and a great sound roaring in her ears." Which is a very common description of mystical experiences! So one sees that, on the level of personal relationship, when there is a complete abandonment of the sense of 'I', it takes us, at least momentarily, to that place of unification, wholeness, contentment, of perfection.

The Religious Path is a way of taking this possibility of realising perfect happiness, fullness of being, and making that an ever-present actuality that doesn't depend on the presence of the teacher or the presence of the belovèd, or a kind word or good health or *anything*. It is founded completely on mindfulness, wisdom and purity of heart; it is not just an ecstatic experience through drugs or romantic union, or through an experience of a wonderful piece of music or work of art. It is only when that experience is founded on spiritual qualities, and is independent of the sensory world that we experience unshakeability. Otherwise, even though that experience is there, and for a moment there is complete transportation, it inevitably has a pale shadow of, "This isn't going to last. This is wonderful now but I have to go home after the concert, I have to leave, have to separate, have to go to work, have to pay...."

That is why this is a difficult path. To establish the unshakeable happiness means we have to be ready to leave all of the 'secondary' happinesses on one side. We have to grow out of our old skins, like a reptile, or an insect grows out of its old skins and leaves them behind. In our life we have to keep sustaining this sense of being ready to leave behind the old. Not hanging on to our old skins, our old identities, our old achievements and attachments. For an insect or a reptile, when they leave that skin behind, for that moment they are very fragile, vulnerable; their new skin is soft, very delicate. It takes time for it to harden and become strong. So in our own spiritual development, when we leave something behind, when we let something go, there is a feeling of relief: "Oh, glad I'm out of that one." But then there is a sense of vulnerability, being open to the way life actually is, with laying down the protection of our 'self'.

We are making ourselves open, sensitive to the entire vast nature of our life, the universe or whatever can be experienced by us. So we can feel fear or hesitation: "I think I'll just climb back into my old skin – it doesn't fit and it's falling to bits but at least I can *try* and climb back in there, I'll be covered up a little bit, protected a little bit." But we realise in our hearts we can't do this, you can't get back into the clothes that you wore when you were five years old, no way. There might be one or two things, like a scarf or a little bracelet or something that we had, but we realise that it's impossible to keep dragging along all our old identities, our loves and our attachments and our problems, our trials and our pains, our mistreatments.

It is hard for us to leave behind the things that we like but sometimes being parted from the things that make us suffer is even more difficult. A wise teacher once said, "You can take away anything from people except for their suffering, they will cling onto that until death." We realise that in actuality we have to let everything go, no matter how reasonable it is to long for something, or to bemoan something, to feel pain over something. We have to leave it all behind. We can't go back to it. As we grow up we learn that the best thing, the only real way to go, is to face that sense of vulnerability, being open to the unknown. The unknown is frightening: when we don't know, when the thinking mind can't get itself around an experience, when it can't describe, or name, or pigeonhole what's happening, then we experience fear – because of the sense of self.

The unknown is frightening as long as there is the sense of self. When we face the unknown and abandon selfhood, then the unknown changes from being frightening to being mysterious, full of wonder. The mind is left in a state of wonderment, rather than terror. This is the transmutation that frees, it liberates, it is our path.

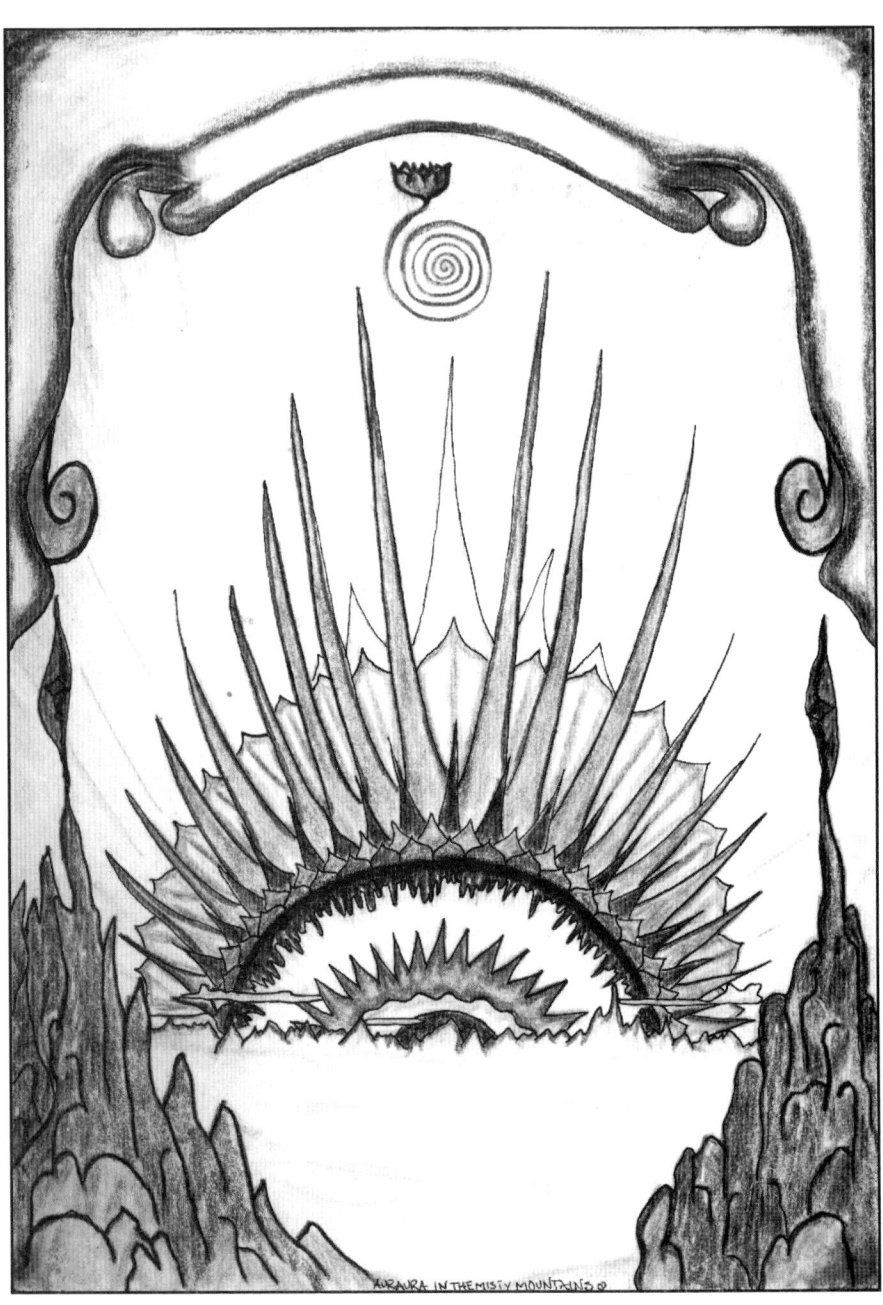

AURAURA IN THE MISTY MOUNTAINS ©

A Meeting with Holiness

PART ONE

This is a record of a visit made to India in March of 1993, to participate in a conference of 24 Western Buddhist teachers with H.H. the Dalai Lama.

So, A NIGHT FALLS on India and the rich clangour of Delhi merges into the hazy tones of a March sky. Dogs, car horns, fragmented bars of nautch songs and the sparkling of 10,000 lakh of lights as the city flows on into the dark. A great dreadnought of humanity and a buzzing, wailing, whimpering, swooping flotilla of living beings around it.

And here we are – strangely perched, watching the cruisers below from a hotelic eyrie, up on the 10th floor, ironically resonant of countless non-descript hotel rooms around the world, complete with TV and armchair. I had expected to find myself in one of those dingy, serviceable, user-testing, cockroach-friendly small hotels that abound in these parts, but the car from the airport, for better or for worse, carried us here. I thought we were doing a tour of the city to admire some posh buildings in the financial district, but suddenly our chugging Morris Oxford look-alike swung into the forecourt of the Park Hotel. Chandeliers, dignified Brahmins, gaily swathed tourists with that air that Westerners have when, to the best of their ability, they try to work some leverage on the impact of their Asian surroundings. So here we are, with liveried room service, dakhinis drifting about in gold-strung saris yet, ho ho, no friends or, of course, money to provide any food or drink. Mother India had produced already, however; on the plane someone passed on to me a whole bagful of dried fruit and energy bars as we had touched down that morning:

"I don't know if you'll be able to make use of this."

"Thank you very much – I am supposed to be met here, but you never know what's going to happen."

Silent, alone – no-one knows me here – waiting but not waiting; tomorrow others should come – Surya Das, the organiser of the conference, is due to arrive and the whole venture will roll into motion. Here, now is that pregnant and delicious moment where we live on the brink of purpose, definition and action – that moment of truly undefined existence. Is-ness without being, before the flames leap forth or the dam breaks, acres of vacant hours ahead, a sole human pausing at the moment in and out of time.

The Delhi night ignites – fully real and dense with the comic and the tragic,

133

with pathos and glory – here it is, yet there is also the cocoon of presence, the glowing, golden act of balancing itself. The stars are out, the full moon risen, but the vigour of the seething night does not entice – the place of silence pleases, once you settle and snuggle into the great armchair of the Way. Bells, dogs, cars, the twinklings in the mysterious dark like the eye of the Belovèd – yes, it's real, but its true beauty lies in its transparency.

★ ★ ★

The city slowly creaking, waking, I go with my bowl wandering on busy thoroughfares, by bus stations and scruffy lanes. Everywhere a familiar stranger: the still numb figures squatting on the sides, knowing their own purpose, going nowhere; vendors, their bikes laden with newspapers and bananas, wind their ways around; vigorous, well-dressed and in the mode of students everywhere, clutching files and papers to their chests, bright ladies converge on the Young Women's Technical Academy; an ancient figure, bent double, leads his tiny wide-eyed companion along – their heads at equal height but the elder stooped so low his eyes bear only on the pavement.

As much in Delhi as in New York or anywhere, warm human contact comes much more easily among the poor than on the streets full of traffic and the haves. My alms-food for the day consisted of a small glass of chai, offered by a young man (he was drinking it at the time) as I passed a small patch of brick-built shanties. He and a young friend stopped me as I moved along, I was shy to intrude or beg, cautious of improprieties and half-embarrassed, half-amused by the fact that I was a *sannyasin* living on alms, yet staying in a hotel the cost of a room in which for one night would probably feed a whole family for weeks. But here we are – this strange white wave across the earth – dwellers in many worlds, homeless ones who live on faith and bear their light wherever their feet take them.

★ ★ ★

Pastel clouds merge softly with the grey-blue haze that is the abiding presence over the land here. Below, a couple of new homes have been set up on the vacant, sewagey lot between the back of the hotel compound and a temple with its cluster of buildings across the way. All around the greenness of earth rims the ramshackle structures, trees abundant and strong-boned, suffering from the air no doubt, but still poised to let us know that, when the humans have done with this patch of land, green Mother Kali will devour it all again.

Temples, office buildings, public housing, all places are fringed by tiny dwellings, shacks and shanties – on rooftops, in backyards, betwixt, between, above, below, behind – every place the human seed could find a foothold, like an all-pervasive lichen, we have carved a niche and made it into home. How vast and commodious is the embrace of Mother India – allowing, bending, endlessly accommodating as she does!

Lama Surya Das, Sylvia Wetzel of the German Buddhist Union, and Lila Wheeler arrived yesterday, Ursi and Fred von Allmen have come too; some of the lamas, Stephen and Martine Batchelor also appear. The afternoon passes –

hours of talk, picking up the personalities and centre-pieces of the conference.

By the evening's end Surya Das and I are left alone – he is wilting and yet to me, not having eaten much for the last three days, the night seems charged and young. Later, lying in the warm dark mothering of the night, sleep is not interested in coming. Hours go by and dawn soon unveils herself again. Jack Kornfield and I spent a long while over breakfast, dunking our croissants and soaking up the details of the past year – Ajahn Chah's funeral and the rest.

Gathering slowly, the organism formulates itself and fleshes out – where is the conference but here, where the inner and outer meet and are resolved, that point wider than the skies of India, pure and simple, yet multifarious as the crowded street – here we meet, the place of no abiding. We gather, not to achieve anything, but to realise what we already are.

(Are we such Maharajas of Dharma, though, that we choose to spend our gifts on the comforts of the Park Hotel – are we really so delicate? Patient endurance is the supreme austerity, after all.... We regret not reaching minorities, yet we choose to live like the rest of the white middle classes of Brooklyn, Marin and Berkhamsted. What kind of Dharma are we teaching? Are we putting the Buddha's children into the rôle of precious princelings and princesses?)

★ ★ ★

Teeming, gleaming, steaming, grinning, flashing, rushing to avoid the rain. Lightning bolts illuminate the night sky with blue. Outside of the realms of the elite; seething, glittering, grimacing, the life of Delhi's night swarms and clusters. Strange smells fill the nostrils; billboards flash. Old Delhi station, brimming with the movement of beings: be-turbanned Sikhs clutching hockey sticks and scimitars, their rainbow-coloured consorts hugging their goodbyes; a crowd of withered, low-tech sadhus swish and totter in their oranges, on walking sticks. We lose each other amid this sublime chaos. Yes, I could spend my life here – it'd be easier than in Acton.

★ ★ ★

"One half hour to Pathan Khot, please Sirs...."

★ ★ ★

Now, the late afternoon sun breaks through the heavy storm clouds that have shed their contents on Dharamsala throughout the day. The streams of maroon and multi-coloured pilgrims flow on, ascending the hill for today's initiations, picking their way around the rivulets of rainwater, robes wrapped around bristly and plaited heads – to-ing and fro-ing on the road far below my window. A pipe drips nearby and the sun picks off the wisps of mist wrapping themselves in amongst the folds and roof-tops of the glass-green hill across the way.

The air is chill – rhododendrons in scarlet and small fruit trees blooming white. The vast valley sprawls below like bolts of green and silver cloth unrolled, displayed for us by grand, invisible vendors. The group gathers and makes its introductions. The Kagyu lamas, Edie Irwin from Samye Ling, the

Batchelors, Robert Thurman – a huge, golden, shambling whirlwind of a man – Kulananda of the FWBO and others whose names I haven't caught yet. All of us came here up the winding trail from the plains. Vehicles picking their way through empty army posts, lagoons and roadworks. Our driver – a Tibetan as leathery and sure of himself as any weathered warrior – carried us safely but declined to use the windscreen wipers on the way, until we stopped for a chai break, that was. The ten of our party nestled beneath the funky, rag-tag sheets of roofing of the little stall; the water for the chai collecting in a bowl beneath a trickle coming down over the rocks forming the edge of the café – what a contrast to the palatial nervousness of the Park Hotel! We munch spicy potatoes joyfully and sip our chai from small, well-used glasses.

Our driver bashes the horn as we make our way through the rain and pilgrims. Broad, timeless faces scowl and grin – we are jumping into a stream here: just another thing for the Dalai Lama to give himself to; now, initiations, in a day or two, the conference, then away again to – who knows where? So we prepare ourselves to join the flow of his life for a while, to share time together and decorate, enrich each other's worlds. Stepping into this river, anticipatory of … what? A big chill, intense streams of energy; to be refreshed, buoyed up, cleansed or carried away? Who knows?

★ ★ ★

On the first evening, after hours of talk and introductions, a huge electric storm bursts over and all around us. Blue fire bolting back and forth across the sky, wild thunder crashing, smashing hail and hard rain on the windows. For hours and hours the sky is alive with the roaring and raging of the gods – fierce, dark and bitter cold. From inside the warm, the idea of ramshackle, leaky dwellings suddenly seems less romantic, but who knows – often in the midst of difficulty we feel our greatest humour and know our greatest peace. We shall see….

★ ★ ★

The uncertainties of looking after the two Theravadan bhikkhus amongst the group bring a little wrinkle or two into the air – do people find us for breakfast? Do we make ourselves visible? There was much arranging and watchchecking as the morning session of introductions and biographies evolved. We passed 11.30 and Olande Ananda was very concerned to stay within the circle of discussion. The anxiety of our carers was rising, however, so we ducked out to take our meal as the others continued. Hmmm. Ananda felt quite uncomfortable about being different from everyone; this left little 'me' somewhat on the spot – do I stick to my form (which would have its own message about the need to bend to the orthodoxy) – or should I go along with the wishes of the elder bhikkhu? Hmmm…. So we left it that I would just go with the others, trusting (on the side) that maybe they will make efforts to make it easy for us. It had to happen, I guess, but right here we have the strict classical style meeting with the urge for uniformity/concord/convenience. It is a point reflecting something of the substance of the whole conference: since most of the others have adopted a lay form (of some description) – yet are looking at this like an-

other Sangha Council à la Rajgir – does it behoove one to bow to the patriarchs of old and say "**Niet**" to a late meal, does one politely fast, ask all the
others to bend to the ancient way, or write a new set of standards to fit the
time? The monks and nuns of the Tibetan tradition, plus the Zen shaven
ones, all are tucking into supper quite merrily, so the 'Theravadan two' are the
only monastics following this form.

To be faithful is good, but – faithful to the form you know? faithful to the
group style? or faithful to Truth? Here is a good question....

★ ★ ★

The afternoon discussions were around the question "What is your greatest
struggle/challenge of the moment?" Most of the group spoke, some obviously
keener to hold the floor than others. Some displayed great ease and honesty,
some egos performed loudly. Largely, it was a feeling out of the substance of
the group: who has what character? What issues are burning? What way do we
want to steer our energies?

One feels a strong sense of wanting to perform well, to not misrepresent one's
tradition and yet to sympathise with and include all outlooks in one's comments. I feel my heart beat strongly when something to say arises. Glad at nods
of approval and notes of one's words being taken, anxious at faces turned to the
carpet or the window – how strange the whole process is! In a day or two, we
will have lived in each other's pockets long enough not to care – it's like the
first day in a new town. Veils of self-consciousness and uncertainty abound.

★ ★ ★

After the great storm, the morning was washed bright and clear. Snowy
mountain ranges were suddenly visible to our north, the sky was blue and
specked with crows and wheeling hawks. As evening draws in, dense greyness
washes over us again, sheets of rain sweep across the pines and muddy lanes.
Outside my window, a nameless hill rises, dotted with coloured houses, temples, flags and trails – what is over there? Who lives there? Just like the politics
and machinations within the Zen and Tibetan groups, the mind is blissfully
unknowing of it. Suspended in consciousness, known but unknown, un-
involved in the glories, strains and clashes, names and meanings of the forms
that meet the senses. How close to the primal state – hovering before attention
gives birth to interest, to conceptual formations, to self and other, good and
bad and the whole Samsaric drama. Like the feeling that was there when I first
arrived at the International Forest Monastery in Thailand – before I knew anything about Buddhism or had heard of other teachers, traditions and meditations – "Cherish this moment and, in peace, watch a world come into being."

Turning the Wheel in the West

PART ONE

An interview conducted with me, by the Forest Sangha Newsletter,
on the Conference of Western Buddhist teachers held at Dharamsala
with H.H. the Dalai Lama, March 1993.

Question: *What were the aims of the Conference, and why was it held?*

Answer: There were a variety of reasons. One was to bring together people from all the different Buddhist traditions who were involved in teaching Buddha-Dharma in the West to learn from each other. There were a number of issues in the air – particularly around the ethical conduct of people teaching Buddhism in the West. For many there was a need to establish clear ethical guidelines. There were also individuals' questions concerning problems that were unique to their own situation – such as being very isolated or being set up as a teacher by other people, then being left to fend for themselves. Also, there were the problems entailed in shifting from one tradition to another.

The number of different issues raised was quite remarkable. There were others who had benefitted from psychotherapy and felt that vast areas of their lives did not seem to be addressed within traditional Buddha-Dharma. They had found that psychotherapy, for example, did help address these areas. So they had questions.

Another common theme was that of transposing the essence of the teaching from the East to the West into a form which is suitable for the Western psyche.

Did you find that the various teachers were experiencing similar problems in conveying the teachings to people in the West? Do you think that this made the differences between the different traditions less obvious?

There was so much accord between us all that the differences were hardly remarked on. Discord or disparity was not created with regard to the tra-

138

ditional patterns in which the teachings are expressed, but more associated with the vehemence with which one believed in one's own particular pattern. The real differences were not to do with whether you were a Theravadan, Tibetan or Zen, but how prone you were to being self-righteous. The only polarity was to do with attachment to views.

We had all come up through the same cultural milieu: we all went to the same movies and we all did the same things through the sixties and seventies. I was the youngest of the delegates there at thirty-six. Most of the others had been practising for fifteen to thirty years or more. The group was very much practice-oriented rather than academics or 'traditional Buddhists' – none of us had grown up in Buddhist cultures. Our practice centred around our own cultural conditioning – too much conceptualisation, too much self-obsession, too much drink and drugs, too much self-hatred. All of us have grown up and worked with this stuff. So whether you're dealing with it as *Nirmanakaya-Sambhogakaya-Dharmakaya,* or whether you're using a koan or anicca-dukkha-anatta – the particular formulation seemed to be secondary. One area of distinction, however, was between those who were still living as monastics and those who weren't. Naturally, there are particular problems, questions and attributes of living as a monastic. I noticed that during meal times and free time together often there would be a separate monastic cluster – a little group of shaven-headed ones would form itself. Most people, though, were very self-effacing about their own traditions and there wasn't even a hint of "My Path is better than yours."

So it was remarkably free of the historical distinctions and stratifications that have been given to the Buddhist world. His Holiness helped with this and made it very clear that he regarded kindness and compassion as primary and Buddhism as secondary: that we had to base our understanding around ordinary human values and tangible human qualities, not around ideological principles.

Can you talk about the perspectives on Sangha that were expressed there?

Most people had their own 'community' and 'congregation' which weren't necessarily monastic, so they too had a sense of Sangha. The teachers at this conference were like the nuclei of their own particular community or at least significant figures within them. In terms of Sangha, the lay-people didn't view the monastics as separate from themselves – just as having a different way of doing the same thing. There was a universal recognition that 'spiritual community' is a crucial element and that there are many different ways of doing that. So the monastics were viewed as having a more formalised rendition of that same quality of commitment to spiritual community which everyone agreed was essential. Conversation was more centred around what to do when that goes sour.

There seemed to be a variety of relationships between the monastics and the lay teachers. With some you could see that there was a sincere respect and admiration for the monastic life and its discipline. Others were obviously indifferent, or having been monastics, felt that they were now living more truly to the Teachings outside of that form. Sometimes amongst monastics there can be a tacit assumption that if you're not a monk or a nun you don't really mean business. Or having left the Sangha you somehow fall back in the training. If you hang on to those views then you find yourself taking on monasticism as an identity – which is precisely what it's not for. On the other hand, lay teachers can be friendly and polite but within themselves be dismissive of the monastic life, perhaps from a need to justify their decision to leave monasticism for lay life. Sometimes this can be coming from a bias to defend an individual's choice – which is okay, but it can colour the relationships between the monastics and the lay community. Because those attending had been selected in view of their common commitment towards Buddhist practice, I didn't experience this very strongly at the Conference. There was generally a wonderful mutual respect not born out of tradition but coming from a sincere, friendly attitude of "You choose to do it your way, I choose to do it mine."

His Holiness expressed support for all forms of practice, but what I interpreted from his words was that the Vinaya and monastic form is a *sine qua non* of the health of the dispensation of the Buddha's teaching; that the representation of the Teaching revolves around the presence of those committed to renunciation as exemplified by the Buddha himself. That's our reference point.

Once he was asked: "How can you tell if the Buddha-Dharma is truly established in a country?" His initial response was: "When there is the presence of the Four-Fold Assembly – monks, nuns, lay women and laymen." He pointed out on another occasion that, as the more essential teachings of compassion, dependent origination and emptiness were developed, this would lead to a greater understanding of the process of rebirth, and the more that you understand rebirth the more you see the possibility of the realisation of Nirvana, and this leads naturally to an inclination towards the renunciant life of monk or a nun. Q.E.D.

How did the Dalai Lama reflect upon Western lay and ordained teachers who claim to have insight and yet are unable even to keep the Five Precepts, as we have seen of late in the West?

He pointed out that if there is a true realisation of emptiness it has to include getting beyond afflictive emotions or *kilesas*. The two are intrinsically connected – the realisation of emptiness and the realisation of causality has to affect your behaviour – through understanding the relationship between desire and suffering. For instance, that action born out of ignorance and desire leads to suffering. Therefore the response to understanding emptiness can only be compassionate action, and well-ordered moral behaviour. He said that perhaps the insights of these people weren't as profound or complete as they thought, for if they were, they would not be capable of acting in the way that they do – being alcoholic or using the bodies of their disciples in a very gratuitous way. Many examples were raised of various characters from the Tibetan and Zen traditions that behaved in these ways whilst also apparently being great 'Maha Siddhas' or realised yogis who had made the final breakthrough. People love these stories – they're far more spicy than stories about the virtuous monk who sits on a cushion all day meditating. His Holiness, however, pointed out that in the Tibetan tradition anyone who had developed to the level where those were really valid activities would make a dramatic display of psychic power. For instance, they would float up into the air and transform themselves into a cosmic Buddha, as sign to indicate that they were not just an old lecher but demonstrating that "I am a master of the Path and I know what I'm doing."

He also remarked on those who wish to practise one of the Tantras which entailed engaging in sexual intercourse as a means of potentiating the mind for enlightenment. He said that the traditional way of finding out whether or not someone is ready for that is if they can drink alcohol, eat human flesh, drink urine and eat faeces – and that the tastes are all exactly the same. So if you can do that, then you're ready! Later, when he was pressed on the point of whether he knew anyone who was capable of Tantric practice at this level, he couldn't name a single person. It was a powerful moment in the Conference because these things are often spoken about in a theoretical sense and yet the Dalai Lama, who knows some extraordinary yogis and meditators, didn't know anyone who could get beyond such conventional morality. When he said this, the room went very quiet. As the conversion carried on, he suggested that it is probably best to avoid the whole thing.

With so many representatives of the different traditions in the West, who were obviously having to adapt in their own way to the situations they find themselves in, did you find that the examples that you heard from the Dalai Lama's comments confirmed things that we had been experimenting with here in England, or did it seem as though we were going off on the wrong track?

Although it seems that we're very much an institution at Amaravati, there is obviously a high degree of openness and willingness to learn from other traditions and other ways. Even though the Thai Forest tradition is quite strong in form, there is still a liberality of practice on the internal level, and people here are encouraged to find out what really helps them and works for them. Many people at the Conference seemed to have a narrow view of what

Vipassana meditation was. I talked with people about Ajahn Sumedho's usage of Vipassana, and how the practice is based much more around using the body as a reference point, rather than the avoidance of experience or feeling; that he emphasised developing the practice around feeling life completely. People were quite surprised at this almost psychological approach. In fact, it's all right there in the Satipatthana Sutta. This is the original thing the Buddha was describing – opening the mind.

Perhaps less formalised?

Yes. To me the Satipatthana Sutta, particularly *cittanupassana*, is very much what Ajahn Sumedho teaches. Knowing the angry mind as angry, the expanded mind as expanded, and the contracted mind as contracted. Just knowing what's happening and being open to it, rather than strictly controlling things. One feels that Vipassana has been misinterpreted: people seemed quite surprised that we weren't just concentrating fiercely on a particular sensation, or 'noting' everything.

The majority of the Conference dwelt on questions that didn't affect us very deeply. In a way the whole ethical question wasn't something that our community had suffered a great deal from – having teachers who were alcoholic or profligate with their students. But in terms of adaptations of the Teachings or translation, it was amazing how all the different people had developed in a similar pattern – apart from the Zen people who had not studied under Japanese teachers. But the Tibetans and the Theravadans for the most part all had the same kind of experiences of trying to work with terms and meaning and translation.

And with the adaptations of traditional forms that they used, were there also similar experiences in that field?

Yes. There were a number of adaptations by the Tibetans that were suggested, or that they had made, or things that were proposed at the Conference that we had already either noticed or thought about. For instance, the whole issue of helping to bring the women of the community into a more egalitarian format with the men. Many of the same questions had come up concerning changes within a tradition. I think that we're closer to our Orthodoxy in some ways than the Tibetans who are in a diaspora state without a massive national tradition still available for them to refer to. Many of the Tibetan lamas are simply trying to sustain the old traditions and to keep alive the forms which they are accustomed to. But there's a sort of cultural terror of being wiped out, which obviously makes any kind of adaptation more resisted.

A Meeting with Holiness

PART TWO

A DAY GOES BY – heavy, heavy rain and hail all afternoon, all evening. The people at the initiations with the Dalai Lama mostly sit outdoors and are content that the hours of rain, thunder and lightning are products/correlates of the powerful deities and practices being invoked.

During the afternoon some of us went off for a walk beyond the tiny compaction of muddy streets of McLeod Ganj, up the hillside beyond the Tushita Retreat Centre. As we waited for some of the others to arrive before setting off, a small Shaivite, with glistening beard, caparisoned with trident, orange turban and purple tilak, came up to me with empty tin and a hungry look. He had obviously taken a fancy to the fawn-coloured wrap I had acquired in England and of which I had become inordinately fond. It was a sticky moment – he rubbed the tattered counterpart across his shoulders, and muttered some phrases that I couldn't follow but guessed the meaning of with a sinking heart. I have often said that I do not ever want to own anything that I wouldn't give away when asked; when the moment comes, however, the desire mind would rather escape. I gave him the best blank, uncomprehending look I could muster, but obviously I have yet to master these arts. He was a beautiful little fellow – eventually my heart melted and I placed it respectfully over his head. He then took the trouble to coax a few rupees out of Surya Das – these guys certainly have the system worked out – still, I hoped he would be kept a little warmer for a while.

The morning's talk had been in small groups – picking up particular themes from the long list of topics suggested for the four days. It covered a huge range of items, reflecting the various slants, positions and conventions that we all come from.

The conference is becoming such a highly charged blizzard of words that, when one escapes from the group for a while, there is a mixture of serene inertness and iridescent, magical activity. That afternoon Jack suggested a visualisation of how we each might see the world when the Dharma was spread all over it in the future. What was revealing was how many envisaged and looked forward to the disappearance of Buddha-Dharma altogether – "How grand it will be when we're all just spiritual beings, living in harmony and needing no religious institutions at all...." This came from maybe 70% of the group (my figure), which was quite astonishing in itself; the other 30% of us proposed a presence of monasteries or temples, or at least some vestige of traditional Buddhism. It seemed as though all those who were disillusioned themselves with the Sangha institution, had become fed up with their teacher, Asian ways, the monastic life or needed an excuse no longer to be a nun or a monk, pitched for this strange option of a world filled with goodness yet having no need for the means to generate it.

This is the Saha world (in some sense) so don't we need to realise that, while, say, delighting in being on this hillside, in this sacred little town, surrounded by lush forest, shouldn't we at least acknowledge the money, time and effort spent in building and flying the planes, staffing and paying for the plush hotels, the roads, the railway (and Lord Dalhousie who engineered it)? Don't we need at least to acknowledge and preserve those vehicles and means of moving and being? It's fine that we got here, but what of those who come after? How can we expect the Teaching to persist in the world if there are no structures to sustain and protect it? For a room full of Mahayanist minds, this seems a little strange....

Perhaps it is just a great poverty amongst us that our own resentment of sacrifice and self-surrender gets projected as a philosophy for all. When the gesture is made with a full heart, the result is liberation at its richest – not defeat or capitulation.

Later that afternoon, I talked on this subject with Bob Thurman at some length – or rather, I listened to him expound. Having heard him refer to monasticism as the only bastion against the military machine of the materialistic culture, I wondered what he made of all the 'non-Buddhist Buddha-Dharma'. His response was: "Extraordinarily naïve! How do they think the teaching will survive without such a container and, more importantly, why are they so afraid of the monastic institution?"

Surya Das asked the question of Alex Berzin, a man whose knowledge of Dharma and Buddhist history was vast: "In countries where Buddhism adapted strongly to the native culture, how did it survive?" This was predicated on his impressions of the afternoon where so many seemed so eager to trash the monasteries, the teaching structures, and all. Alex covered the point by saying basically that it didn't last at all well: Indonesian and Indian post-Brahmanic civilisation (i.e. Buddha as an incarnation of Vishnu) being used as an example. It's an interesting point and we'll see how and if it pops up again – I am also eager to hear His Holiness speak on the subject. How much do we have to adapt and what is essential to keep?

That evening Bob Thurman 'declined' to give a talk but then launched into the most powerful **RA**!!! for the centrality of monastic life and the Vinaya – all were hooting with laughter and touched by his erudition and feeling, he struck home very deeply. Some easily modified his impact by labelling him a "wounded ex-monk, trying to recompense for his own shortcomings," but ... he made his points very well, pushing *dana* and the 'Peace Warrior' as his main theme and begging to see us all establish at least one 'free lunch' monastery within the West, i.e. a place where one could simply 'go forth' and commit oneself to Buddhist practice without being asked to pay for anything or being expected to teach or serve in some way. As an aside, and a comment on the gulf between the academic and contemplative worlds, it was astonishing that he had never heard of Ajahn Sumedho or all the 'free lunch monasteries' that he has established in the West over the last 18 years.

★ ★ ★

Today was the first day with His Holiness (the words roll off the tongue without a thought now). We gathered at the 'palace' under a bright sun, and four great hawks, marking the corners of a perfect square, wheeled around the hilltop in immaculate cycles. The whole day was bright and still; the wild Yamantaka (Death Destroyer) initiations were over and the local biosphere seemed to have settled down again.

The interview room is broad and spacious, the walls hung – as Bob Thurman gleefully pointed out – with beautiful *thankas* depicting sixteen Arahats and with Shakyamuni Buddha at the centre. When His Holiness came all the previous impressions of a humble, loving man with a razor-sharp wit were amplified and illuminated by his being so close and giving his attention to such a small group of us. He chuckles, he mutters with the translators, he frowns and pierces with his mind all the points and problems of the day. Effortlessly delighting, sorrowing at the horror stories, moving easily between learning and advising.

At the end of the afternoon, he said his farewells; I had been on the last panel of four presenters and as he took my hands he joined brows with me. Our contact in the meeting had been very clear and open, direct and warm.

As the days go by, we become more and more known to each other, our little strolls and chats, cups of tea here and there together, all serve to bind us tighter and deeper as a tribe. At the dinner time, Bob came over to chat and flesh out my understanding of Tantrayana; we launched into a long discussion on it in relationship to the first *parajika* – the rule against sexual intercourse. He did say that if a monk needed to "use the female in the flesh", he would leave the monastic life – even though the practice depended on total relinquishment of ordinary sense-consciousness and cannot be considered (by the participants!) as ordinary sexual intercourse. I had pointed out during the day that, despite the purest of intentions of those involved, a passer-by might easily think: "That monk and nun are having sex." His Holiness responded by saying that, to cover himself, such a monk would display some supernormal powers to indicate his accomplishment

★ ★ ★

After a long day we were all tired, but the evening discussion caught fire around 'naming names' to His Holiness (he had asked to know who, amongst Buddhist teachers, was misbehaving). There was also much concern about publicising a code of ethics and how to get the message through to some of the incorrigibles.

Some well-known teachers came in for a lot of flak, but people were generally afraid of turning this gathering into a Buddhist Inquisition. All was left hanging, pending further thought etc., but it was a momentous evening – bringing to heart and bringing home many strong feelings, and creating bonds of friendship between these powerhouses of an intensity that I feel surprises even them.

★ ★ ★

The days have run themselves so close together it's hard to keep any track of passing time. Dark and light punctuate our hours but the flow of the group energy is such as to render the surroundings little more than a theatre backdrop.

This is hard to credit, and in those brief spaces when there is a pause in the verbal world and its buzzing concerns, the mind stops and opens to the ethereal grandeur and grubby wonder of this town, brimming with devotion, draped in maroon and gold and perched precariously on the hills at the edge of India. Below us, the gulley of McLeod Ganj sweeps down in a broad arc to the south and east – green steeps speckled with the multicoloured buildings of the orphan village and dominated by strings of army barracks. The valley then takes a twist to the right and opens out, in diminishing ripples, into the broad plains below. A blue haze, still and light-filled, veils the whole scene; at the edge of our vision's rim the broad spread of a reservoir creates a silvery band, weaving in and out of the tucks and lumps which form its basin. All is pure from this height – distance has a way of unifying all diversity into a congruent whole. The sky is sun-drenched – glaring bright all day.

In the early morning the light illuminates the ranges of green stacking up behind us – slopes and ridges climb to the skyline – losing their colour into the slate grey rockiness, then transforming suddenly into brilliant white, as if overcome with excitement as they rise to the great blue consummation of sky. Shimmering on azure, specks of brown hawk wheel and bend the air in lazy circles – wingtips stretched to feather and balance on the shifting airs. Below and above, like past and future, stretch away from us and yet they rest – idealised, purified by their remoteness. The present, like the street we stand on, remains gloriously mundane, shabby, fragmented, totally alive; filled with hope, devotion and fear. Faces worn by care and weather, self-discipline, laughter, pain and tears.

We pause, only a moment, as our party makes its way along to the palace. Talk and mentation ceases, the eyes draw wide, the feet stop still – a moment of transfigured wonder and then … and then the momentum of our mission carries us on, the talk subtly altered, hushed a tad or two – a point in time to be a reference for all others.

★ ★ ★

To-ing and fro-ing between the palace and the hotel, we built up a great friendship with the local lepers who beg each day along the roadside. Junpo Sensei stopped once and turned back to hand a 50-rupee note to one of them, saying, "It's hard to work when you've got no fingers." I felt repeatedly helpless and unkind in professing "No money" (*padme hum*) and it was only later that I had the inspiration to hand out biscuits instead. Now we smile to each other as I place a few each day in their cupped and mutilated hands.

★ ★ ★

Another night of lightning bolts, pounding thunder and rain – with the morning the air is cool and still again, the nearby hilltops are snow-bedecked and the only sounds are the rumbling generators, dripping pipes and the cries and chirrups of local bird-life at the opening of their day.

His Holiness's way of being reminds me more and more of Ajahn Chah in action. Chuckling endlessly, totally amused and pained by the absurdity and tragedy of it all. Stern, direct, hopelessly full of glee, bubbling with kindness and laughter all day long – pronouncing on this, poking fun at that, making 'heretical' statements about rebirth or referring to Jesus as a Bodhisattva; stressing the Buddha's party line, encouraging Vinaya, dispensing with false appearances and titles. The experience is that of feasting on holy wisdom's diamond light as if it were a rainbow-sweet ambrosia.

The sun goes down, oval and orange, most of us opt for an early evening – too many words in our eagerness to get it all right. The enthusiasm for our venture burns bright.

Turning the Wheel in the West

PART TWO

Question: *Did you feel that there was any similarity between the way the Dalai Lama and Ajahn Chah related to Westerners?*

Answer: I didn't really spend that much time with Ajahn Chah. But from what I remember from being around him, his whole manner and mode of response was very similar to that of the Dalai Lama.

For instance, people would make statements and he would just pause and take things in. You could see that he wasn't just reacting to ideas. Sometimes he would make no reply, or just ask a question back.

Sometimes he would just un-pick the question. He seemed to be coming from an empty and loving place – totally attuned to the people around him. Pushing and yielding as and when needed. I felt an immediate and tremendous similarity – it was like the same man in a different robe. But rather than saying that Ajahn Chah had a unique understanding of Westerners, I think both of them had a very profound understanding of human nature.

Which goes beyond conditions and culture?

Yes, although the Dalai Lama is also aware of the particular agendas that Westerners have. He could see where certain questions were coming from, and knew what lay behind them. If someone was making a point, he would politely side-step things sometimes, not just pick up on some line that he was being fed. He was extraordinarily perceptive and very sharp. One could imagine that someone in his position – a monarch as well as a religious leader – could just be a figurehead but it was apparent that the Dalai Lama is very different from that.

His mental acuity – even if he wasn't the Dalai Lama – would be impressive. He would remember things that had been said a day or two before, and remember who said them. He could pick up a point that had been talked about before and carry on, or use that to illustrate something else. In the same way that Ajahn Chah had developed the human potential to its limit the Dalai

Lama could also be very sensitive, unafraid to feel emotion, and at the same time be fierce if he needed to.

Did he directly address the question about how much to stick with Dhamma-Vinaya to deal with the problems of our conditioning and how much to use techniques outside the Dhamma-Vinaya?

The discussion that I remember most clearly was around the subject of psychotherapy. There were some delegates who expressed the view that our present conditioning is such that people do not have the same 'mind-set' today in the Western world as they did in the time of the Buddha. The other position was that the complete practice is already found in the Buddha-Dharma, we just don't know how to use it.

His Holiness was very impressed with people's reports on the use of psychotherapy. But he felt that it was an exaggeration to think psychotherapy was something that is a necessity for all people. He said that it would be a mistake to assume a sense of uniqueness as Westerners – even though our Western materialism, de-spiritualised society, and high-speed environment are somewhat unique.

Even though he agreed that psychotherapy could help certain people, he felt it should be looked upon in terms of not knowing how to use what is there in the Buddha-Dharma in a way that is helpful. His point was that the mind is extraordinarily complex and that is why the Buddha presented the Dharma in a very complex way. It has many facets, many layers, and to think that you can deal with all of the complexities of the mind with one simple practice or instrument is expecting too much.

His Holiness concluded by saying, "The Buddha-Dharma is sufficient for realising Buddhahood, so it should be enough."

It was one of those moments when everything stopped and we felt: Yes, of course, if it wasn't sufficient for Buddhahood it wouldn't be Buddha-Dharma. But there was a sense that there are good things to learn from Western psychotherapy; in fact, the Dalai Lama thought that it would be good if some of the lamas studied this. He makes a point of educating himself in Western psychology and science.

The other issue, which seems to be one of the most important ones for the monastic Buddhist communities in the West, is the whole question about the position of women in the Sangha, and women in the context of the Buddhist world. How was this topic discussed at the Conference and what kind of impression did you come back with?

There was a universal agreement – amongst the group I was with, anyway – that a totally egalitarian system should be established. That's the reason, I think, why many women have never entered the Sangha, or have left – because of the male dominance of the whole picture and the way that the women are very much shunted into the background. This is certainly how it is in the Asian system – all the leading rôles historically and contemporaneously being filled by men. For some it was a much stronger issue than others, although there was a certain sympathy for monastic orders who are trying to adapt traditional formats.

People took it for granted that you would set things up in a totally egalitarian way if you could. It was remarkable in its absoluteness. Martine Batchelor had just come back from touring in Asia, doing a book about Buddhist nuns. She'd been to Korea, Taiwan, Thailand and Burma interviewing nuns and women in the Buddhist world. She had a very practical approach to it. Others had a much more idealised approach from the feminist viewpoint. I think everyone had a lot of sympathy for those voices, but one also felt that people didn't want to make it a political issue. It was recognised that beyond a certain point, it gets destructive. It destroys its own potential through becoming a position that you're taking rather than something that you're seeing as supportive to the practice of Buddha-Dharma. The general feeling was that we should aim towards egalitarianism in every way possible.

It was interesting that by the end of the conference I'd fallen into the rôle of representing the old orthodoxy. I happened to be sitting next to one of the keenest feminist voices on the final evening and we were all giving a little account of our impressions. She finished her talk by saying, "I really look forward to seeing a Buddhism which is free from the patriarchy." That afternoon I'd been visiting people and happened to have visited a nunnery where they had given me some white scarves as a greeting. So I had a number of these in my bag which I thought I would give away in the evening. I had considered giving one of these to this woman as a peace offering, but had thought better of it as it would have been too condescending. So I didn't, but they happened to be sitting in my bag, and after she'd made her dramatic point for an end to patriarchy I realised the moment had come. I picked up one of the white scarves and put it around her neck as a gesture of friendship saying that even though the old order might seem to be something to contend with or leave behind, there is also that which conserves and is respectful to the past. Furthermore, that tradition can be respectful towards the agents of reform. I realised that this might look a bit out of order but it seemed important to make that kind of gesture – on the one level, not going along with that line of thinking, but on another level, supporting another's right to hold a different opinion. Differences should not interrupt our communion as Buddhists. It was a poignant moment which received gales of applause.

While the whole monastic/non-monastic, male/female, patriarchy/nonpatriarchy issues weren't always contentious, they were there. The gesture seemed to bring a release of tension. It was a way of uniting her efforts with ours. Whether we like it or not, we're tied to each other. We're in the same boat. However much people may want to renovate everything and get beyond Buddhism as an 'ism', still Buddhism is tied to the Buddha, and the orthodoxy. Also, no matter how much you want to sustain the purity of the old order, you've got to be sensitive and open to change. It's unavoidable.

Do you feel that there was a sense of how the two approaches to practice could start to work in a more harmonious way together in the Teaching?

Certainly. Because if we're actually practising it's an inevitable outcome. I think that we come into Buddhist practice full of our own fervour and inspiration, perhaps thinking: Tibetan Buddhism is IT, or that lay practice, or monastic life is IT. After a while you realise that that's not 'it', that's the way to get to 'it'. Naturally your whole perception broadens and you see that maybe you were inspired by this because it was the first thing you saw. If you're drowning, any lump of wood to hang on to is very special to you. It's only when you're up on your bit of driftwood that you see other bits of driftwood around. The first thing you grab can seem very important to you. So you can relate to different traditions or teachers or styles of practice with a frantic enthusiasm. But what I saw within this group, and in the Buddhist world generally, is less frantic. After twenty years of Buddhism in the Western world, it's settling down with a mutuality of respect. Why should we all be the same? I choose to do it *this* way but I don't want to judge too quickly where people are at because of the label that they wear or the style in which they choose to practise.

Within an egalitarian Western mentality, having men always first and women second is an oddity. But if such a convention is really that intolerable to you then you can leave your 'family' and go and live somewhere else. If you can see that individuals within that community aren't so bad etc., then maybe you can come to terms with that aspect of it. Because of the mutual respect at this meeting, I felt that it boded very well for the future.

A Meeting with Holiness

PART THREE

THE CONFERENCE HAS DRAWN into the final bend of the course and the finish now comes into view. Today was our last day with His Holiness and a very poignant one – after Ani Tenzin Palmo, who has been a nun for thirty years, described the lot of Western monastics and the nuns in particular, and specifically the low regard in which they were held and their lack of support, His Holiness was lost for words, then put his head in his hands and wept for a few minutes. He promised he would do all he could to help. Thubten Chodron, an American nun, put a packet of tissues by his seat – just in case he needed them again.

The feeling amongst the group has become closer, warmer and more unitary in purpose as the days have gone by, yet already the talk of travel plans begins. Last night, and the night before, 'Dharma crowns' were awarded to Lama Drubgyu and Junpo Sensei for extraordinary courage in raising personal and pointed issues with His Holiness. And profound admiration was expressed to Sylvia Wetzel who, it was noted, was probably the first woman in fourteen incarnations to teach a visualisation practice to the Dalai Lama. Her experiment was to imagine replacing all the male figures of a Dharma centre or monastery (i.e. the lama, the lineage holders, the arahats and even Shakyamuni Buddha) with female figures and envisaging the response of a male neophyte to the invitation of the (lady) lama to take up the wonderful and meritorious opportunity to become a *'dakha'* or consort of hers – HOW WOULD IT FEEL?!? This is probably now branded into the mythology of the Western Buddhist world for the duration of the aeon.

I suspect that I will mostly be remembered for my remarks after His Holiness asked me, "Bhikshu – what do you think about birth control?" "I think it's a very good idea," I replied – "I'm doing my bit!" Then I paused and said, "Actually, Your Holiness, I have heard it said that one could look upon the whole Buddha-Dharma as **re**birth control." *(Laughter!)*

★ ★ ★

In the early morning, I awaken as if bathed all night in some celestial balm, steeped in the holiness of these days. Strange dreams, full of symbol and phantasm – every night a show of kaleidoscopic grandeur – like the satisfaction that comes at the end of a long journey, a job well done or a banquet consumed: the feeling of being tired, enriched but very full – washed, permeated, transmuted into the blessing of holiness itself.

Over these days a strange transmutation has taken place: at the start of the meetings the words "His Holiness", "Your Holiness" meant no more to me than "Dear Sir" at the top of a letter; now, when I speak to him or of him, I feel as though I am more talking of holiness itself – addressing the quality of holiness embodied rather than a person. The title has transformed itself into a recognition of the presence of transcendent Truth.

★ ★ ★

As our friendships have deepened and familiarity and mutual respectfulness grown, the group slowly loses energy and disperses – one here, one there. Jack flew out this morning, Robert and Nena Thurman a day or two ago; talk turns more and more to our plans for departure, sprinkled in amongst the last subjects to be discussed: hurt students and teachers, livelihood, the subcommittees of other conferences, publishing, etc. Like the fourth movement of a symphony, we make our way inexorably towards our crescendo and coda – our fingers and feet well-used by now to the spirit and colour of the piece, comfortable in the accomplishment of what has been done so far; relaxed and steady, the anxieties over, we guide ourselves into our final ending.

A few of us spent the sun-drenched morning circumambulating the palace on the 'Mani trail', a narrow path following the lower contours of the conical hill on which the Dalai Lama resides. Now and again we would be passed by local devotees, their faces a woven picture of deep wrinkles carved in tawny arcs, peppered with gold and turquoise in grins and earrings, braids and bands. Prayer wheels are whirled gently as they move, passing the neat heaps of slate and local rock, carved with strings of holy phrases, proclaiming "*OM MANI PADME HUM*" and who knows what other power-words.

On our way down to Bhagsu, a little settlement clustered around a stream which winds its way somehow to join the Ganges, Hindu pilgrims pass us by as we take some chai at the café; beyond us, on the spread of rocks below the waterfall, the laundry of a score of monks, plus multicoloured wraps and saris form a brilliant explosion of maroon and gold, greens as bright as flashing parakeets, patchworks and deep blues – shades deep as midnight – shimmering, picked out in rectangles upon the dull grey ground. Up in the cluster of houses some raving Western sage – his brows decorated with fierce and sweeping curves like Yamantaka or Vajrapani when terribly upset – sits perched in the upstairs of a restaurant, exclaiming the truth that is his own to the beat of his ghetto-blaster and the indifferent bemusement of the other patrons.

The afternoon and evening filled themselves with endless hours of talk – picking through the last few subjects and sketching out our future plans – diminuendo. When it came to discussing livelihood, there came that familiar reaction of, "Well, it's all right for you monks to call yourself 'penniless' – you've got a massive support system behind you." It often gets forgotten why that support is there and one picks up a sense of negativity towards the supposed double standard.

Ani Tenzin Palmo again won everybody's heart by professing her vow to live on faith and not solicit or take up offers in any way. Strange that while she uses money yet lives on total trust, we never touch it, but are perceived as hypocritical pseudo-aristocrats – this might be an exaggeration, but that view is in the air.... Anyway, such issues are the norm for the human realm and the years have taught that it is wiser to relish the opportunity of being misunderstood. This attitude always helps to clarify the true refuge and to dispel any pride or self-view that may be around; besides, "Those who justify themselves do not convince...." (Lao-Tzu)

★ ★ ★

Jutima, a nun from New Zealand – now Sanghye Chötso – came by at lunch and brought some gifts and letters for England, including some local seeds for my mother whom she had met and chatted with before. She returned at 5 p.m. and hauled me off for a welcome walk and took me to visit the nuns at Jamyang Choeling. This place was a collection of long, low, rough buildings, slate-roofed, bearing a few patches of plastic, no running water or toilet but with the wonder of electricity. Inside we visited the room of one of the young sisters. Sanghye Chötso knew them all by name and the province that they came from – Zanskar, Arunachal Pradesh, Ladakh or Spiti – this being a *kamzen*, or vihara of all the non-Tibetan nuns. Shy and smiling, strangely self-assured, we sat and shared a glass of tea as, one by one, they dropped in. The tiniest were two who claimed to be thirteen years old, but it was hard to believe that they were more than nine; the petitest fingers, comely smiles, bright eyes full of life and coyness.

The three or four buildings had been commandeered for these women by an American nun, Sangye Khadro. Their life was obviously somewhat rough but they had the joy of Dharma and each other, and were learning texts never before taught to any women. A long history of patriarchy had laid down certain forms and only now were such polarised opportunities being dissolved.

The evening was filled with our final business and resolutions for the future. Closing with a round of testimonials from us all (even though one is always at least politely enthusiastic on such occasions), a true, deep and heartfelt appreciation was expressed – for some, indeed, it had been a major point in their Dharma life.

I must admit that my heart sank a little when, amidst the energy and enthusiasm of the evening, I saw some of the participants of the conference sharing a few bottles of beer together. Oh well ... you would have thought that after all the talk, all the hours of concern and debate ... still, sometimes people feel the need to prove a point – to themselves or to everyone else. Yes indeed, this path is rough and thorny.

Turning the Wheel in the West

PART THREE

Question: *Was there general agreement on the doctrine within all the differences of the traditions?*

Answer: There were no doctrinal differences at all. But there were differences of interpretation on the ethical values. Some people have different interpretations of the third and the fifth Precepts – there were a variety of renderings – "What the Buddha really meant, of course, is that you shouldn't get drunk rather than total abstinence." When this was brought up His Holiness mentioned that in the Tibetan tradition the limit is set as not more alcohol than will sit on the tip of a blade of *kusa* grass (i.e. not very much!). Everyone agreed that keeping the Five Precepts was a standard that anyone who is teaching the Buddha-Dharma should adhere to as a minimum requirement. If you can't keep the Five Precepts, what kind of a Buddhist are you really?

Did you find that there's always been an understanding between the people who are practising but that the arguments and debates are more by scholars and academics?

Yes. The more you meditate the less these differences can have any real substance. The delegates were all meditation teachers – meditation is the basis of their Buddhist practice. So the natural result was that they were far less likely to hold on blindly to views. It was very encouraging to see that if you don't just talk about Dhamma but actually *do* it then the conflicts resolve themselves.

The other thing which comes to mind is the question of how Westerners practise with devotion and faith.

It wasn't discussed very much. I think that devotion takes different forms, one of these being commitment to what you're doing. We don't behold Buddha as a God – the practice is around one's own psyche. It's not externalised. There was some discussion of moving away from the position of regarding the teacher as a guru – and training yourself to see instead. For West-

157

erners I think there's a long road ahead before we hit the point where we just see an image of the Buddha and tears come to our eyes. If there is a reaction to a Buddha image it usually has more to do with the aesthetics of it. I think our devotion is demonstrated more in the amount of dedication and will that you exert in giving yourself to what you're doing.

At the end of this Conference what discussions were there on how understanding and co-operation could be developed?

Many were extremely enthusiastic about the results of the Conference and had high hopes that it would not be an isolated event. Many of these people had come from an anti-institutional background but inexorably, amidst some cries of despair, the group moved towards formulating itself as an organisation. The name 'The Network for Western Buddhists Teachers' was chosen. Various people undertook to help organise similar events in America. They would like to have a conference with either His Holiness – who is very keen to do it again – or someone of similar stature every year, or at least every other year. There were also ideas about smaller local conferences amongst teachers including a wider field of people.

There were thoughts of having a newsletter once or twice a year just to update people on the various meetings and what's in the air. An immediate result of the Conference was that about ten people undertook to write articles either for their own journals or other Buddhist, New Age and local magazines, as well as some in-house journals such as our own Newsletter. They are also planning to produce a small booklet and then a full-length book about the Conference.

There were also undertakings to help His Holiness set up a training programme for Tibetan lamas to go to the West, and to offer guidance and help in setting up a nunnery for Western women.

There was talk of having a four- or five-day retreat together instead of a conference. So I volunteered Amaravati as a venue for that, either for the whole group or just for the people in Europe.

Could you sum up what you think the historical significance of this meeting is?

I'm not saying that it was wrinkle-free – I had unpleasant moments, as I'm sure many others did. However, despite the extremes of viewpoints – in the FWBO, ourselves, and the Zen tradition, for example, and the range of characters and orientations – it was incredibly civilised. I wouldn't equate it with the level of a Great Council but it was certainly significant how harmonious it was. So, on that level I think it was a wonderful sign for the global Buddhist community. As Buddhism gradually reformulates itself out of the cultural trappings of its countries of origin, it bodes well that we met in this way. In centuries to come they may find it hard to believe that we were all able to speak to each other and get along. Right now the prospect is very healthy. With the general turbulence of the world, and the difficulties of holding on to monastic precepts and sustaining a commitment to the Triple Gem, it is always going to take a lot of work to hold everything together, but there was an example here of tremendous cohesiveness and energy. Who knows where it will lead to? The last words of the Dalai Lama at the conference were: "The past is the past. The future is ours. We must make **every** effort. But if we fail … it doesn't matter." There's all this potential for goodness and you can work like crazy to bring it about and make it happen, but if you all get caught into a tidal wave – LET GO!

How did this experience affect you in terms of your monastic life?

It's both deepened my commitment to living as a monk and deepened my appreciation of all the other ways that you can do it. I certainly didn't feel envious of what anybody else had got, but I didn't feel that they were getting it wrong, either.

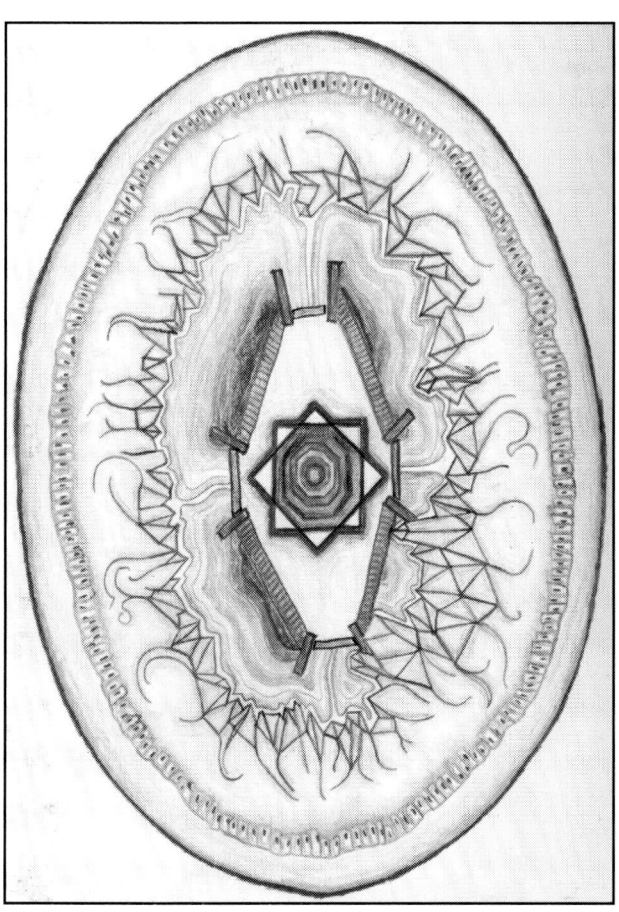

A Meeting with Holiness

PART FOUR

ANOTHER CIRCLE completes itself – once again, the strange face of a shaven-headed, bare-chested figure stares out at me from the large mirrored surfaces of a room high in Delhi's Park Hotel. Outside, the blaring of Indian streets and the wheeling of eagles (yes!) in the endless, hazy blue-lace agate sky. The hours are empty, the talk is over. The entity that drew itself into being has now dispersed and only a few breaths of the present incarnation yet remain – dissolution and the empty theatre. As with all things, however, the effect of this gathering will ripple throughout all time; the deeds done and connections made creating a momentum that will choose to incarnate again, now here, now there, subtly resonant of the old, unique and awake to the new. Having lived for the past two weeks amongst the assumptions, politics and myths of the Tibetan world, one now thinks easily in terms of Buddha Dharma as a map of the nature of our lives in the form of a multi-dimensional web of labyrinths, smeared out over the entirety of space and time. Nothing is really what it seems.

★ ★ ★

It seemed a great shame to have come all this way, to be in the heart of the Tibetan Buddhist world, and to have spent 99% of the time with the great middle-class white crowd. My last morning in Dharamsala was therefore built around a walk to visit some of the special places and to meet some of the great Tibetan lamas around here. My guides were Richard and Carol Weingarten, an American couple who had done a lot to help the Tibetan people and whom the Dalai Lama asked to be guardians and tutors of Ling Rimpoche (a seven year-old lama who, apparently, has always been the tutor of the Dalai Lamas over the centuries).

Once we had met up we made our way outside the village to a church built by the Brits in the days of the Raj. St John of the Wilderness, a classic English village church, sat perched amongst the pines, like a Grand Duke of the Empire, utterly self-possessed and confident of its authority, oblivious to the alien-ness of its presence here. Beside it, along the hillside, exquisitely landscaped among the curves of stone conduits bringing the streams down along their appointed pathways, a graveyard full of stories lay spread. Each headstone told its tale: Capt. Jack, killed by a bear; Mary Louisa, aged 24, gone to join the Lord; tiny Charlotte, aged just one, asleep forever, away in the sunny country. They must have loved this place, yet it was savage too – you can see why Mother Kali, un-squeamish devourer, is the patron deity of this noble land.

We headed off to the monastery of the Nechung Kuten. The Nechung is the State Oracle and does not have a human body; the Kuten is the form he utilises to communicate with the human world. I had expected the Kuten to be a wild-eyed shaman, decked with silver, coral and turquoise, streaming coloured ribbons and bearing strange accoutrements. Instead, he turned out to be the most ordinary young bhikshu, soft, bright and gentle in his manner. The story goes that the Chinese killed the previous Kuten in Tibet and that the Tibetan leaders were very worried that the Oracle was gone or wouldn't come to India. He is a powerful spirit, tamed by Padmasambhava, and sworn to protect the Tibetan people. About six years ago, he returned and entered the body of this young monk, at which the people here were ecstatic. The Nechung is said to be the only true spiritual friend of His Holiness, whose cosmic form is the thousand-armed Avalokiteshvara, and it is in these cosmic forms that they commune.

All major decisions are taken only after the Oracle has been consulted, so it was a great relief to have him back again. When a reading is needed, the Kuten dons the 200-pound head-dress (unliftable by an average person) and the Nechung takes over. The body swells by about six inches all over and takes on a terrifying aspect. He swirls around, dancing with ease under the massive re-galia, speaking in a strange tongue, comprehensible to only a few. The process is naturally very draining – the Kuten blacks out when it's all over – and the strain is such that they do not live very long.

In the shrine room of his monastery, upon each sitting mat, identical robes sat folded like reposing monks, stooped in earnest prayer – almost as if the robes carried on the sacred observances whilst their owners went about their business around the monastery.

★ ★ ★

In such a short time, one feels greatly at home in this rich little fellowship begotten by tragedy. A seasoned people with demeanour and faces of such beauty: that blend of self-assurance and modesty that is one of humanity's profoundest charms. Eyes and smiles that fill the heart with peace and delight: agèd traveller or wizened crone, from whose mouths occasionally a pink and shining tongue would slide out (to show they had not the black one of a demon) or the young and strong, freshly bloomed, whose loveliness and grace could make the vajra crown of a delinquent lama take off and fly several laps of the Dharma-Hall.

★ ★ ★

Our last visit of the morning was to an old lama, Druptok Rinpoche, whom Richard and Carol had met a few times before. We had heard he was off in Tilopa's cave and were disappointed for a while until the Kuten told us, "Oh, he's right here! He arrived yesterday," pointing to the next room. One of the great yogis, he is largely unknown and has no students, although he is revered by many as a 'living Buddha' – an appellation very rarely offered by the Tibet-ans. He was the picture of the ancient sage: a huge pile of hair, wound into a grey mountain, nine or ten inches thick from top to bottom; his eyes blinked regularly but I could hardly see his face, both because of the light coming through the window behind him and because of the light he himself exuded. From the total warmth of his presence and the other-worldly air that surrounded him, one understood why he was regarded as one 'Thus come' and 'Thus gone'.

The blinking, I was told, was the result of having lived in a dark cave for 16 years, surviving only on water and tsampa (barley gruel). He asked me about the conference (despite the fact that none of us had mentioned it to him) and I told him of the themes we had followed: the problems of sustaining essence and adaptation to the Western environment, the question of immoral behaviour in teachers, the styles of practice and the dangers of sectarianism and empire-building and the wealth of guidance and encouragement that His Holiness was able to give us.

The Rinpoche, not surprisingly, said that he would pray that the pure Dharma be established around the world for the benefit of all beings. The whole exchange lasted less than ten minutes and in one way was utterly unremarkable; on another level one felt a quiet blessing was being generated and a true friendship being formed: four or five bodies in a dim room, together for a moment – what is it? Nothing much. But, as he had earlier pointed out to Carol and Richard, "Mind is everything, everything is mind, mind is everything, everything is mind." So maybe one should say, "Nothing – Much!"

★ ★ ★

We set off on our return, winding our way down from the hills following the Kangra valley until we drew into Pathan Khot a few hours later. All along the highway roadworks were going on, much of the heavy labour, as in McLeod Ganj, being done by women young and old. It's a strange and painful sight to see such rock-breaking and mud-carrying by poised and upright people clad in full but grubby saris. The men – as one unfortunately might have expected – are more often than not squatting nearby directing operations, just watching the women work or, at best, doing the lighter, easier parts of the operation. How they see it themselves I do not know – they are probably glad just to get a few rupees a day in any way they can – and one is aware of seeing the situation through Western eyes; still, without being condescending, the picture is one that pains the heart. Perhaps the supposed mythological defamation of women in the Buddhist world stems from the same deep current as this; it certainly has much the same result.

Arriving at the train station, I am repeatedly informed by a wild local yogi – tall, dishevelled, grey ringlets floating, eyes flashing – "You are the supreme power of Pathan Khot! Two rupees only for a cup of tea...." My assertions that I am penniless are made a little watery by the Yves St.Laurent travel wallet that I am clutching in my hand. Eventually, the young Tibetan girl with us fends him off with a rupee and then the crowd that has gathered to watch the scene – and provide some protection it seems – disperses, satisfied that justice has been done and savagery averted.

It had been a full day, but it was not yet over: through the dingy archway, leading past the ticket office (over the windows the hopeful injunction "courtesy begets courtesy") onto the platform we go; dirt poor beggars come by, dull and dusty, wrapped in old sacking. A frightfully well-spoken old *sanyasin* catches my eye, tugs on his snowy goat-beard, "You are from Thailand, ah yes...." His tiny eyes a-sparkle behind well-worn spectacles, orange turban, bidee stamped out under naked foot, "Ah yes, the world is beautiful, if you are happy, the world is beautiful, everyone is beautiful.... Ah yes, everyone is beautiful. Jai Ram, Hari Ram, I go to Rishikesh, ah yes.... Safe journey! I go...."

There is some confusion on the train as to where we sleep; I open the door to one couchette and a stern man in a dressing-gown looks up, apparently a little cross. Later on, when I find myself back in there, having been shunted around a little, he breaks the ice after an hour or so by offering me a Sai Baba magazine. It turns out he is a brigadier in the Advocate General's office, responsible for courts martial in the Jammu and Kashmir districts. In one week, he will retire and is now looking more and more to his spiritual life. Far from having been annoyed by my appearance at his door, he confessed he had been disappointed when I went away. When we spoke, his slightly stern appearance melted and the smile of a child broke through – or of one who feels naughty for having wasted the last 30 years obsessively chasing only money and a livelihood.

For a day full of remarkable meetings, it was a wonderful conclusion – when we started to talk he asked me of my life and what I had been doing – I told him I was returning from Dharamsala. He replied that he too had gone to try and see His Holiness whilst he was in the area on duty, saying his last good-byes, but that he was told His Holiness was in a conference with some Westerners (!) and had had no free time. He deduced that my karma was **much** better than his, but that if not in this life then in some future one, if he kept trying, he would meet His Holiness sooner or later. How humble and lovely a man! When he asked me about meditation, I began to describe sitting posture and mindfulness of breathing – he was quite tickled when, while telling me that he could sit in lotus posture for half an hour, I observed that it was highly unlikely that any senior (or junior, for that matter) British officer would be able to do the same.

What a land this is! I feel that India is leaving me with such an aftertaste of goodness that, in the future, it will be hard to stay away....

Oracle Spring

His heart is open as the sky,
the Master sees things as they are
– *wind sound and moonlight wear away* –
stop trying to control,
the Master stays behind.

Express yourself completely
– *strange birds circling my eaves with twigs and grass* –
and everything will fall into place,
everyone knows this is true;
let them go their own way
then trust your natural responses,
allow things to come & go –
the Valley Spirit never dies.

The Master views all parts with compassion
– *Yin & Yang have turned my mind to snow* –
empty yet inexhaustible,
they give birth to infinite worlds
in harmony with the Way;
right and wrong don't enter the clouds,
the soft overcomes the hard
yet mystery and manifestation
arise from the same source –
it is named the Mysterious Feminine.

Content with the way things are
the gentle overcomes the rigid,
it is the base from which sprang earth & heaven,
this source is called Darkness –
being still.

The earth is solid and full
– *I've scanned the whole world & seen* –
divine and unifying,
the sky is clear and spacious.
Tree shadows drink in a stream,
that is why she is one with them –
the latent power of the Way.
A pond in spring rippling green,
water and earth in greeting.
Late autumn rain drives down,
things pass through.
Nothing in the world
is as soft and yielding as water:
she is detached from all things
because she has let go of herself.

His constant practice is humility –
draw upon it as you will,
free from desire you realise the mystery;
he is perfectly fulfilled
but lets himself be shaped by the Way.
A hundred years slip by when you're free…
therefore you keep quiet.

Without trying to control
the world will govern itself.
The gateway to all understanding
never can be closed,
open yourself to the Way
but trust the inner vision –
let go.

Nothing in mind,
the moon through space
– *my door stays open when spring days get long* –
everything's growth
depends on old roots,
everything fades
and resides at the centre of the circle.

Centred,
the Master observes the world,
she understands the whole –
caught in desire
you see only manifestations.

All creatures flourish together,
the Master doesn't glitter like a jewel –
head for the mountains and choose any tree,
let go of fixed plans and concepts
IT is there with us always.
The Way is called the Great Mother,
that is why she is ahead:
Darkness within Darkness,
yet for dissolving the hard and inflexible
I sit by a window gazing at mountains.

One layer then another,
as rugged and common as stone,
nothing can surpass it:
sea
emptiness
no mind anywhere
– *the wind through the trees* –
earth water fire and wind
listen:
the sound of spring…

Amaravati, February 1993;
courtesy of
Lao-Tzu & Stephen Mitchell, Stonehouse & Red Pine

The Ring of Fire

Dependent Origination

"Circles can be peaceful,
but they can also be vicious"

Ajahn Sucitto

A talk given in Diamond Heights, San Francisco, May 1993

★

And what, monks, is the Noble Truth of the Arising of Suffering?

Dependent on ignorance arise formations; dependent on formations, consciousness; dependent on consciousness, mind and body; dependent on mind and body, the six senses; dependent on the six senses, contact; dependent on contact, feeling; dependent on feeling, desire; dependent on desire, clinging; dependent on clinging, the process of becoming; dependent on the process of becoming, birth; dependent on birth, ageing and death, sorrow, lamentation, pain, grief and despair come to pass. Thus does the whole mass of suffering arise.

This, monks, is called the Noble Truth of the Arising of Suffering.

And what, monks, is the Noble Truth of the Cessation of Suffering?

Through the entire cessation of ignorance, formations cease; through the cessation of formations, consciousness; through the cessation of consciousness, mind and body; through the cessation of mind and body, the six senses; through the cessation of the six senses, contact; through the cessation of contact, feeling; through the cessation of feeling, desire; through the cessation of desire, clinging; through the cessation of clinging, the process of becoming; through the cessation of the process of becoming, birth; through the cessation of birth, ageing and death, sorrow, lamentation, pain, grief and despair all cease. Thus there is the cessation of the whole mass of suffering.

This, monks, is called the Noble Truth of the Cessation of Suffering.

Anguttara Nikaya III 61

ALITTLE WHILE AGO when we were passing through Soquel I was slightly surprised by a notice-board by the side of the road which simply said, "eschew obfuscation". Which means, "Don't be difficult to understand." I couldn't figure out why it was there but it was the most literary road sign I have seen in the whole United States! I realise that we are entering a somewhat technical subject this evening so you must forgive me if I get too obfuscatory and difficult to follow; I will try and keep things fairly clear, though, and give you symbols, explanations and imagery that is easy to follow.

Apart from being translated as Dependent Origination, this subject also has been rendered as 'Conditioned Genesis' or 'The Cycle of Subjective Captivity'. As well as in other places, this pattern of insight is contained in a number of the descriptions of the Buddha's enlightenment. A week after the great Awakening, when he emerged from his absorption in the bliss of release, his first night was spent contemplating this. It is described that during the first two hours of the night, he followed it going in the forward order, 'with the grain', from ignorance through to birth, old age, sickness and death. In the second watch of the night he contemplated it in the order 'against the grain', with the cessation of ignorance through to the cessation of old age, suffering and death. Then in the last watch of the night he contemplated it forwards and backwards, in both forward and reverse order. His enlightenment was actually the process of understanding this simple pattern; so this is mighty stuff, these are the essentials of the Teaching. If we look we can see that it's an analysis of the Second and the Third Noble Truth: the Second Truth being the cause of the arising of dukkha, of dissatisfaction, and the Third Truth being the ending, cessation, the fading away of dukkha.

Other descriptions of the enlightenment are in terms of insight into the Four Noble Truths and the Three True Knowledges, but obviously these are just different ways of looking at the same thing. What we have in this simple pattern of arising and the ceasing described here is the journey from the Second to the Third Truth: from what causes us to experience dissatisfaction, alienation and so on, to what brings about its cessation, its transcendence.

The Buddha said, "Rather than trying to figure out a metaphysical structure for time, life, the universe and the mind, just put attention onto the essential elements of this vast subject, because this is what is significant." If we can figure out what causes us to experience suffering and we can see what enables us to transcend suffering, then we are doing the best we can with human life. If we pick up information on how the whole machine works or came into existence, then that is fine, but it is an extra; because even if we can't understand the nature of the universe conceptually, if we are in harmony with it, where's the problem??? There isn't one!

★ ★ ★

The traditional presentation of this teaching can be read in a couple of different ways: on the one level, the external, we are talking about the arrival in the world of a human being, the arising of dissatisfaction and its effects; the other approach is to regard it as a pattern referring to the psychological domain – a pattern we are experiencing within ourselves on a momentary basis. The first one is what you find in most of the classical scriptures and commentaries, they talk about this very much in an external way. But more recently some, particularly Ajahn Buddhadasa and Ajahn Chah in Thailand, have taken this formulation and pointed out, "Well, if we talk about this just as how suffering arises due to causes before this life, this doesn't give us a very good tool for meditation or for transcending dukkha right here and now."

Ajahn Buddhadasa spent many years analysing this and explaining how one can regard this same process as occurring in a momentary pattern. He gives a very clear description of how our experience arises and how it can turn into suffering – and how we can break that cycle of recurring habits and transcend the suffering that we create. He has received quite a bit of flak for this from more 'orthodox' quarters but Ajahn Chah was very much taken by this approach towards understanding and using Dependent Origination, and this is what he used to teach himself.

The first type of interpretation is referred to as the 'Three Life Theory', described as taking place over three life spans. The other is described as the 'momentary'. Ajahn Chah was very keen on the usefulness of it as a description of our momentary experience because, if one uses it in that way, it is a very immediate and powerful tool for working on our life and it shows us that our destiny, if you like, is not out of our grip. The first one tends to be more of a fatalistic interpretation.

The first one is described in the way the Buddha arrived at it during the night of enlightenment where he sat down and considered, "Why is there suffering?" This rendition is from 'Oriental Mythology' by Joseph Campbell:

"Where there is birth, there is inevitably old age, disease and death.
Where there has been attachment, then there is birth.
Where there is desire, there is then attachment.
Where a perception, there desire.
Where a contact, there perception.
Where there are organs of sense, that gives rise to the contact.
Where there is an organism, that is where the organs of sense arise from.
Where there is incipient consciousness, there, there is an organism.
Where there are inclinations derived from acts, there, there is created incipient consciousness.
And where there is ignorance, that creates these inclinations.
Therefore ignorance must be declared to be the root."

So this means that, because of past actions, unrealised biases are carried on from a previous life. When a being dies, the momentum of karma, attachment to 'fear of that', 'desire for this', 'aversion to that', this is what is called 'inclinations derived from acts', the habits that we have built up over a life time. So that when a person or any being dies, the unfinished business and habits of a lifetime are like the momentum of a flywheel, they carry on, and when the body dies, there is still the momentum of karma. This is the first life.

This gives rise to incipient consciousness. This means that that momentum gathers together as some form of consciousness. Once the body has died, then of course there is a large part missing from your world! Because of the enormous attachment to the body for most people, when the body dies, then one of the major inclinations is "Find me a body! Give me a body." Then that inclination is pulled towards a place of rebirth, either in the human world, the animal world, or heavenly world or wherever. (For the sake of simplicity we can just talk about the human world.) Then, having gravitated to the human world, we have the six sense organs. The process of contact and perception then proceeds, then desire, attachment and becoming – end of second life – and then birth again. Then, after this second birth we carry on into the future, living this life into old age, sickness and death again – end of life the third – phew!

Incidentally, the main propounder of this theory, Acarya Buddhaghosa, when he gets to the end of his explanation says something like, "Quite frankly, I don't really understand this, but this is the best I can do with what I can figure out from the scriptures." I remember when I read this for the first time, I thought, "Well ... it kind of hangs together, but of what real use is this to me? This insight is supposed to have been what liberated the Buddha?? It's a neat little puzzle that you can fit together (just), but so what!" Then in later times, when I came across the descriptions by Ajahn Chah and Ajahn Buddhadasa, it made a lot more sense because it is talking about something a lot more experiential and immediate. It's talking about the effect of ignorance here and now.

★ ★ ★

To begin with, when considering the 'momentary' approach, it's important to talk about the fundamental nature of mind, Original Mind. To describe this one uses terms like 'Suchness', *tathata*, but there are other descriptions also: this is from a Tibetan teacher, Kenpo Tsultrim Gyamtso Rimpoche:

"This luminous, self-aware non-conceptual mind, that is experienced in meditation, is Absolute Reality and not a *viññana* (partial, fragmented knowing). When the luminous Wisdom Mind is realised there is no seeing and seen aspect to that realisation. This is the non-conceptual non-dual Wisdom mind itself, the Clear Light Nature of Mind, the *Pabhassara Citta*, it is also called the *Dharmata* and the *Tathagatagarbha*."

Tathagatagarbha means 'the womb of the Tathagatas', which means the origin of the mind, the origin of awareness.

When we talk about ignorance, therefore, we are not talking about it as the basic nature of reality, but rather that ignorance is something which arises from Original Mind, which is the mother and father of everything, as Ajahn Chah's teacher Ajahn Mun liked to put it. Ignorance, and all perceptions of everything, arise out of that basic ground. Dependent Origination is thus talking about the arising of illusion out of reality.

In this respect we have a way of looking at what happens when the natural awareness of mind is clouded. When there is ignorance the mind doesn't see clearly – often ignorance is represented by the blind leading the blind.

When we lose our mindfulness this gives rise to *sankhara*. *Sankhara* means 'divided', 'particular' or that which is compounded; it means the arising of self and other, any kind of polarity. So that, out of this mind which recognises Suchness, we start to drift off to the sense of self and other. *Sankhara* also means 'thing-ness', the 'world of things' – the illusion of solid independent entities starts to arise. What we then have before us is a process of crystallisation or complexifying, so that basic sense of division into this and that becomes strengthened and becomes *viññana,* which means discriminative consciousness. The mind is not only just dividing 'this from that' and 'self from other', but is starting to be able to conceive a whole variety of different elements, different things within the sphere of attention.

Viññana leads on to *nama-rupa* – customarily we translate this as 'mind and body'. It's a more concerted diversification of consciousness into the physical body and into all the different ranges of physical and mental activity. It's a solidification – the mind is drifting off into a sense of separateness – then there is this body and there is this mind and the two are apart from each other. That leads on to the six senses, which means we are giving more reality to a greater field of perceptions. The whole world of sight and sound and flavour and smell and taste and touch comes alive and becomes far more real.

So the process is growing from a basic simple root, like a tree slowly branching, branching and branching, getting more and more complicated and multifarious, spread out and involved. A verse in the Tao Te Ching says:

> The Way gives rise to the One,
> the One gives rise to the Two,
> Two gives rise to Three,
> from the Three arise all 10,000 things.

Out of the Way, out of Suchness, there arises oneness then twoness then threeness, and once you've got three then you have got the ten thousand things.

As the mind absorbs into perception of a form then life appears more and more complex. Once we have a belief in the reality of the sense world, then all the feelings of pleasure and pain, like and dislike start to arise and become stronger, more interesting and compelling.

The process then describes how a feeling turns into a desire, some kind of self-centred craving; then how that desire around one particular sight or sound leads onto grasping: if an interest arises, the mind latches onto it, we see something, that produces a feeling of "That's beautiful", then the eye is attracted towards it and it says, "I wouldn't mind having one of those." Then the absorption goes further, to grasping, "Well I **really** would like to have that, it's a really beautiful thing." This is grasping. Then the decision to act on that, "Well, no-one is looking; here it is, a nice little fruit just hanging off the tree. After all, it's only going to drop to the ground and go to waste."

This is *upadana*: grasping means going after something, taking hold of it. *Bhava* comes next: this is a word translated as 'becoming'. It is a word that befuddled me for years and years – "Becoming, becoming, becoming what?

What is becoming? What is this talking about?" It took me a long time to realise that 'becoming' means the thrill of getting what you want. Becoming then leads to *jati*, which means 'birth'; this refers to suddenly realising, "Oh dear, this wasn't really mine to take," or "Well, one of them tasted good but I've just finished my fourteenth, I can feel indigestion coming on." 'Birth' is not necessarily talking about physical birth, but rather the point of no return where we have created karma and there is no going back. Once a child is born there is no turning back. Once that situation has been born we have to live through the whole life-span of its legacy, whatever that entails. And any condition that has been invested in goes towards *soka parideva* etc. – grief, sorrow and despair – ego-death in other words.

★ ★ ★

There are different patterns that one can use to illustrate this. It struck me some years ago how the early part of this pattern very much matches the structure of the material world. Physicists talk about the basis of matter and energy as a unified field, they use terms like, 'the sea of potential' or 'the well of being' (there are quite poetic people in these laboratories!). An undifferentiated field which is neither matter nor energy but which is universal, timeless – and all matter, all energy is spun forth out of this. One can actually watch a particle appear out of nowhere and disappear into nowhere. This makes it a very clear correlate for the quality of Suchness or the Unconditioned mind, the Unborn – in a way it is unborn energy or matter.

We use the Unborn, the Unoriginated, the Unconditioned, as terms for the pure mind. Matter arises from this same field, formulating itself into subatomic particles, atoms and molecules. Nowadays more and more physicists are having to bring consciousness into the equations of their understanding. They are coming to the conclusion that all matter has some kind of rudimentary form of consciousness. They now actually have conferences around subjects like 'Can electrons think?' They are also coming up with ideas for virtual particles called psychons which are reputed to be the conveyors of consciousness.

The scientific world is thus getting on to realising that as soon as there is any organisation of energy, there will be some rudimentary form of consciousness there. With each shift beyond a certain level of complexity then the level of consciousness will go up a step. They are now making studies of how life comes into existence; they see certain arrangements of molecules will start to produce life-like behaviour, consciousness-like properties that we would recognise. So in the same way, out of this ultimate field, prior to matter and energy, this Suchness, there is the basic act of formulation, things coming together. From that formulation, basic and rudimentary forms of consciousness arise until you get little creatures. The smallest living creatures are things like viruses, which are sometimes no more than a few strands of DNA.

As soon as you have even these tiniest organisms, then the organism needs ways of getting information about its environment. It needs to know, when it encounters an object, "Can I eat it? Can I mate with it? Is it going to kill me?" Even the tiniest, most basic of living creatures picks up this information. They have a consciousness, a physical form, the sense bases arise and they have a sense of their environment. As soon as the sense bases are there, then it's, "Oo, food! Chase!!" Or "Oo, enemy! Escape!" Desire arises, desire leads to clinging, clinging leads to becoming, becoming leads to birth, ageing and death, and so forth.

★ ★ ★

There is also a reason why it is called a cycle: maybe we follow some desire and we feel wretched about having done that – having eaten too much or yelled at someone – then we feel remorse afterwards. We may think, "So what, it was a painful thing, but it doesn't matter." But the whole process of rebirth hinges around the fact that having done that, having followed that impulse and not having understood it, then there is that momentum of habit whereby we are likely to do the same thing again even though the results were painful. The habit is created because we don't understand the pattern; we find ourselves likely to pursue the same thing again.

Say a similar situation arises – we are attracted towards seizing that thing or getting angry again. We think, "No, no, no, I shouldn't do this, the last time I did this the result was really bad. I made a terrible mistake, I shouldn't do it. I mustn't get angry, I mustn't say anything," and we try to hold it down. But in that very act of suppression we are empowering the habit and we have created that as an issue in our world, we have given it life. That potential for action is still there, so as soon as our grip slips and we are not in control, then ZOOM up it comes, we do the same thing again, and again, and so it goes on.

Even if we don't try and suppress it, and we have got a very good rationalising mind and we think, "Well, I've just got a problem with guilt, that's all; I should be able to do what I want to do and not look back. I've just got a heavy suppression problem." Then we do the same thing again and we think, "You know this really does hurt; I guess I've really got a bad problem with guilt, I definitely need to learn how to never look back!" We overpower our sense of shame.

However we do it, suffice to say this is why it's called cycle of rebirth – it's a vicious circle. Those very habits that we are still attached to by loving them, by hating them, by not understanding them, we tend to repeat them and so create cycles of fear and desire – the Ring of Fire – and we go round and around and around. This is Samsara; and this is not something that is remote, or tied up with stars in the sky or anything far away from us, it is right here in the very innards of our own world.

★ ★ ★

The way out is the whole *nirodha* aspect. With meditation, one is trying to witness the arising of ignorance, or to become aware of what causes the mind to cloud – to see the drifting of mindfulness. However, because our minds tend to be so busy we have to work our way down the scale; that is to say, when we start practising meditation we start at the level of just witnessing the results of what we have been doing, all the pleasurable and painful results of our actions. Slowly we begin to see that difficulty comes into being because of our following of fear and desire.

We try to recognise the feeling of clinging; then learn to be able to catch the mind as we grasp at something; then to respond by letting that thing go. The more that we refine the practice, the more we will find we can catch the process at the level before desire turns into clinging, when there is just a pull towards something: "Oh that looks nice!" The wisdom mind then says, "Wait a minute, remember – remember where this goes to." By developing this, the place where desire turns into clinging becomes a bit more visible. If one then refines the practice more, to be able to simply witness feeling, say the feeling of pleasure, then that is something delightful: there is innocence, just as is represented by the mythical image of the original couple in the Garden of Eden – joy and innocence.

It is a very important thing to recognise that we can feel innocent pleasure; it is not a crime for something to be delightful. Sometimes people get the impression that Buddhists are not supposed to enjoy anything, but the art of being able to enjoy things skilfully is a lot of what we are about: to be able to enjoy and be with life as it is, at that level of having the senses wide open, alert and awake to the whole world, yet not turning into desire, aversion, or to fear. The more we can establish things at that level then the more natural peace of mind we will know.

On a more fundamental level, in meditation, we begin to be aware of the Unconditioned, the primordial nature of mind, Original Mind – where there is no identification or grasping at all, where the mind just has the experience of Suchness. We can observe the patterns of *sankhara* arising when the attention drifts, we can watch the sense of self and other, here and there, coming into being. This is something that we can do, this is not out of our reach. It is something we can directly develop in meditation. Ajahn Sumedho would often give whole Dhamma talks on this one subject, summarising it as "Ignorance complicates everything". When the mind is clear, when there is an open view of things, there is a seeing of that complicating process. When there is no discrimination, when there is a realisation of Suchness, then a world can be watched coming into being. The sense of 'self and other', 'this and that', through the act of awareness and being alert to it, we can let it all go.

This is where we can really witness the strength of karmic formations, the underlying tendencies and habits that we have. What is it that most rapidly pulls our mind away from any kind of recognition of Suchness into the world of diversity? What are the benign things that we can live with easily? What sucks our eyes right out? We get to know these because these habitual tendencies of the mind are what empower the very processes of ignorance. A lot of what we are doing is becoming familiar with what is deluding, defrauding and compelling to us. What are our favourite delusions? What is your flavour – pistachio or lemon sorbet!?

It might seem like this is very remote and impossible to do, but I wouldn't be talking about it if it was; anyway, this is the only way we can fulfil our life as a human being. In this very act of letting go of division and, in so doing, recognising what it is that continues to blind us and create obstructions to awareness, we can awaken to what we are, to our true nature. We are not trying to become something different or special, we are simply removing the obscurations from what we already are so that we can recognise the truth of our own and everything else's nature that much more directly. This is the only way our life can be consummated.

To some of you who are new to Buddhism and meditation, this might all sound totally bizarre and utterly meaningless. If that is the case, then I am quite happy to take the consequences: we live for so many years in a world of seemingly solid people and things, which we see all as normal and good, so this kind of talk is ... "What on earth is all this about? What does this mean? Has this got anything to do with me at all? What has this got to do with real life?"

I would like to suggest that we can look at what we call real life with much more of an objective eye. To contemplate, "What is really going on here? What is this experience of being a separate person? What is the fabric of our world that we know? What has been going on for my whole life?" Through examining the process of experience itself we are confronted with many questions.

I came across an interesting exchange between a Western student and an old Tibetan master: His Holiness Dudjom Rimpoche (who was actually the first Buddhist teacher I ever met when I was a student in London University, years ago). Somebody asked him, "If everything is actually intrinsically perfect from the beginning, and it all happens within the context of the Great Perfection, then how did all of this happen?" Dudjom Rimpoche looked at him and asked, "Did it?"

That gives a pretty awesome perspective on the whole thing! Although I'm not entirely happy saying that it's all an illusion, because we then tend to misinterpret that idea. It's better simply to have an enquiring attitude: "What is really happening here?" "Is the world of people and things, and time and space, presidents and governments, cars and freeways, gas stations and Taco Bells – is that the real world?" "Even the world of friends and trees and skies and rivers, pure water and love songs – is that the real world?" "Meditation retreats, Dhamma teachings, life on the cushion – is that the real world?" One can keep shedding the layers. After a certain point we start to get a little bit quivery! That's why this word *nirodha* is good to contemplate; it comes from the root 'Rud' which means to check or restrain. If you are riding a horse you keep a tension on the reins, it's a check, everything is held in check – everything is **here**. When the world happens here – when we see that the world happens within our mind – then, in a way, the world ceases – it is held in check, it's in its context. "When all the world ceases to exist only the Wonderful remains." What that means is not that there is the sudden Zooop! of a nuclear explosion, and then we don't see or feel or hear or smell or taste or touch – the ending of the world doesn't mean a wipe-out of experience. The ending of the world means it all happens here, within the mind, and is the experience of wonderful existence within true emptiness. It exists, but it doesn't exist; it's empty but it's true. This is our abiding place.

When we contemplate the cessation of things and see it in this way, their apparent reality is punctured. One is seeing all things: births, human life, relationships, the stars, the planet, the ground, everything that we are and live with; if we see it all in context, allowing it to cease means that we realise that it all happens here within the mind. Then only the Wonderful remains.

> Life is truly a dream,
> all of its troubles I alone create
> when I stop creating, the trouble stops.
> With a single mind, with an unbounded heart
> we can wake up to the Wonderful Existence
> within True Emptiness
> that we are in the middle of right now.
> When all the world ceases to exist,
> only the Wonderful remains.

Bhikshu Heng Chau

★ ★ ★

One image that I like, one that I have used most often, is to think of the process like this: We are an eye in the sky, way, way, above the earth. Awareness and the infinite blue. Everything is O.K. Then our attention is caught by some movement in the blueness down below, the eye peers down and ponders, "I wonder what that is?" The attention starts to focus and draws close like a telescope on the surface of the sea. This is *sankhara*, self having interest in the other. *Viññana* is then the patterns on the water, the different shapes of the waves. We think, "That's interesting – beautiful waves!" Then that complexifies and diversifies into different kinds of consciousness, into perceptions, thought, feeling, body, the six senses; we've drawn closer and closer, now hopping from wave to wave, dodging from this one to that one, having a great time. Different types of waves: sound waves, colour waves, smell waves, touch waves, thought waves – all very nice. Then suddenly there's one we find **really** interesting; desire arises, "This is a great wave!" Desire turns into clinging and we think, "This one is ridable." Suddenly as if by magic a surfboard appears and we are away! Clinging turns into becoming – surfing, riding the crest of a great wave is the perfect image for becoming.

A couple of years ago I was down by Huntington Beach. They have a beautiful sculpture by the roadway, a big bronze of a youth, a teenage boy perched on top of his board riding high on the curl of the perfect wave. The heart of Southern Californian beach life seems to be the desire to become, epitomised by the riding of the crest. *Bhava* is the thrill of getting what we want – we are riding our wave and we're right in the teeth of it – TOTAL THRILL. Then *bhava* turns into *jati* which means either, "I've run out of wave" or "This wave is taking me to the rocks" or suchlike. Suddenly the wave collapses, we are thrown through mid-air, do a few somersaults, mouthfuls of sea water, don't know which way is up or down. Splat!! We're choking and spluttering and have been thoroughly dumped by the whole thing. So what do we do? Go looking for another wave, of course!

★ ★ ★

In the ignorance that implies impression that knits knowledge that finds the nameform that whets the wits that convey contacts that sweeten sensation that drives desire that adheres to attachment that dogs death that bitches birth that entails the ensuance of existentiality.

James Joyce
Finnegans Wake

Drops of Milk and Honey

Excerpts from a journal made of a teaching tour in Switzerland in the spring of 1986.

The promised land of the Israelites was a beautiful place, "Flowing with milk and honey". This can be taken to refer to a paradisaical country of material plenitude and comfort; in a symbolic way, however, it can also refer to 'The promised land' of spiritual practice. 'Israelite', in its wider sense, simply means 'religious seeker', and the Promised Land, the place of perfect ease and comfort, correspondingly refers to the awakened mind.

★ ★ ★

Sister Cittapala, Roberto and I flew into Switzerland a few days before our first retreat was due to begin. We thus had a chance to take our bearings in Bern and acquaint ourselves with the Swiss way of life.

Rainy days, up here in the attic of Ursula Sturzenegger's flat. Regularly grey skies drop their load on the impossible jumble of roofs and chimneys, red umber tiles, gutters, skylights, pitches and angles, but on Sunday morning, when it was quite fine, we went on our alms-round down to the river, Roberto, Cittapala and I. It is fast and green, aquamarine, cold and fresh from the mountains. Shaking the earth, the bridges and air, it surges, melt-water from the crags and hollows of the Eiger and the other Alps above Thunersee. A heaving, icy, crystal torrent, it is called the Aare and it is also the goal of many suicides from the high bridges over it. This city, though, is so quiet: it is true it is a Sunday morning, but the people seem so few, so restrained, not making waves: such control and neatness abounds, pure lines of silver birch at achingly equal intervals, even a stack of scaffolding and acrow-props arranged with impeccable taste. So neat and tidy, so clear-cut and well-groomed but, like the spirit of Truth, this electrifying alp-essence pours through it all un-bridled. This holy water hurtles on vital, anarchic, following naught but its own nature right through the heart of the spotless, the spick and span.

The day ends with the chimes of midnight – Bernese clock-towers mingle with the rain and the roaring ocean of Mind. I gaze at the face of Hui Neng, tucked in behind the cover of Finnegans Wake – that blether of images, life's mystery played out, mysterious and fine, bewildering and magnificent, I try to pick the sense out of foreign words – you can only get so much, the thinking mind strains and cracks but then ... what does it really matter? For that face, so still, the utter silence, precedes, pre-empts, surmounts and says it all.

★ ★ ★

We left Bern after these few days and journeyed to the retreat house at Staffelalp. This was situated about 20km from the town amongst the rich pastures of the valley-side, new spring flowers were scattered all around us.

Next to the retreat house was a small farm track which led to the forest which fills the further part of this hillside. Old and tall it was; unlike the pine-woods of England I have been in, it hummed gently with the life of bird-calls, mosses and mushrooms, lichens like tendrilous cabbages. We stopped for a while on the path, merging slowly and letting go of the rough boundaries of identity – where does the visitor end and the forest begin?

The retreat flowed on through the changing phases of day and night. We managed to pass through the heavy period, the initial confrontation with the walls of negativity, habitual selecting and discriminating patterns, by the end of the first full day. From being quite misty, the weather became continuously clearer and the shining sun helped tremendously to lift up everybody's hearts. Most of those on the retreat had done a lot of sitting before, so I felt inclined to keep the pressure up a bit. Just to create enough heat to do a decent job of extracting the golden ore from the raw rocks of our cluttered consciousness. It is difficult on a short retreat to keep it strong enough so people really learn something but yet light enough so that they feel uplifted and refreshed. Usually on a longer retreat it is only after the third day that the clouds begin to clear and people start to mellow and brighten up a bit. So I tried to emphasise the use of the mind's reflective power, the presence of the body and simple earthy things to help us climb down from our busy mental realms. The natural world, our common sense, will take the mind to silence if we let it: the shimmer of an even-sunlit spider's web, the way a dew-drop changes colour as you pass it, the breathing body, the ringing silence; serene reflection takes us to completeness.

By Saturday the sky had cleared completely and Friday night's eerie river of shimmering lights was revealed as Thun and the scattered settlements thick in this green valley all around it. Staffelalp is a thousand metres up on the northern side and, from this vantage point now, the Eiger, Mönch and Jungfrau could be seen draped in their threadbare whites. The ground is thick with spring grass with sprinklings of wild anemones, all about are clouds of something yellow, halfway between an oxslip and a primrose. Come the evening, up from the valley, well the haunting carillons of church-bells; during Sunday morning they mingle with the sounds of the local army practising on their firing ranges, sometimes the cannons, sometimes machine guns – the sounds of a nation trying to protect itself. The bells to announce defense for the heart, the guns defense for the body, but somehow their loudness seems to betray a sense of abiding fear.

"These are OUR perfect valleys, OUR neat and secure lives and the winds of change are never going to move us" – this despite the fact that the Chernobyl reactor had just exploded, sending its poison rains all across Europe.

★ ★ ★

The retreat came to a gentle close with the sounds of our chanted blessings. The people dispersed and we returned to Bern for a few more days before we set off for Zürich. This gave us more time to be with the Bernese Buddhists and eventually to make contact with a long-time student of Ajahn Sumedho's whom we knew would be pleased to hear we were around.

We left the broad rolling greens of the countryside behind and returned to the sanctity of 'the Ashram' at the top of Ursula's flat. The room was spick and span; there were new vases of eye-brights, marguerites and daisies all rescued from the mower at the Marzili Park – how lovely to enter such a welcome.

As the days unfold many people come to see us. We sit on the floor, surrounded by flowers, light two trays of candles before us, ignite some incense and sit together – wholly earthbound, universal. Sometimes talk is small and sometimes it is deep; somehow, though, one always feels the words are secondary and it is the 'being-ness' and openness which really matter. That feeling of Suchness as personal barricades break down and the world's colours merge into a shimmering silver. The edges blur and fade, body and background become one and the only objects which hold their form are people's eyes.

I hardly slept at all this night – the chimes of the Zytglogge informing me of the hours: one a.m., two a.m., three a.m., four – I dozed here and there and leaned against the wall but the mind was uninterested in sleep. Spring's surging passions sublimated and redeemed, transmuted and hooked into higher planes. "Away!! Away!" the heart cries out but it is gone, it is already gone; gone beyond, beyond the blue yonder. Yes!! What sweet intoxication!!

Travelling – trains and cars – meeting with good people. Broad mountains pass before us, glitter in bright morning sun, the shining lake, the troubled hearts – hovering in the vast and present. Switzerland – its neat and well-formed faces, its crags, its peaks and the awful loneliness of me and mine. How painful it is when we try to protect and possess the lovely just in order to be safe and to have time to play. The mountains sit so still and the fall-out from Chernobyl rains down. Patiently they sit, those oceanic heaving crags, and what do they care about the passions of the ants which crawl upon them? The poison rain falls down, permeating rich and poor, unwitting, unconcerned at our indignation. The silence of the shining mind, the unrelenting law of Truth, overlooks, upholds and is the fabric of our being. The life of the individual is so insignificant and small, but what joy that truly we are not that.

> The blossom falls
> The wind-surf crowded seas –
> Mont du Silence
> Why are you so empty?

★ ★ ★

At this time we were still in the process of organising a meeting with Joya, and it seemed unlikely that she would be able to get transport to Bern. She had moved, a few weeks before, into a community of disciples of the Mahavatar Babaji in a place called Schweibenalp, above Brienz. We made a few phone calls and decided that the best we could do would be to go there by train on the following day.

We swept down the valley to Thunersee and then headed on to Brienz, thundering through the blossom and the green. A man whom we met pointed the ashram out to us, high on the other shore beside a waterfall.

"That is our destination," he said, somewhat slightly glazed, leaning upon the window's edge, sweeping his arm outside and devotedly ringing a little bell.

Joya and her daughters met us at the station and we were driven up to the ashram by a man called John. At that time there was a weekend session being held, led by a famous mystic, Dina Rees. There must have been eighty or a hundred people there, crowds of children, clothes of colour and good feeling. It was not the kind of environment that Sister Cittapala had ever been in before, having lived as a middle-class Swiss housewife, but she loved it and Roberto and I felt quite at home, back with the love-tribe for an afternoon. Joya was very grateful we had come to see her and did all she could to help us feel at home. After some tea in the sun, listening to the chanting with Dina Rees, we went indoors into the main house where Joya stayed. Up on the very top floor we found the place where she lived with her two daughters, four cats and a tortoise. All up the stair-way haunting pictures of Babaji's eyes gaze out from skies, shadowy trees and concrete buildings hang there ringed in one iris.

Their practice is fundamentally that of devotion to the guru, to the manifestation of eternity within the time-bound. This kind of way appeals greatly to Joya's nature – she greets us with "*Om Namaha Shivaya*", their fundamental mantra, and already her room has several shrines in it. She gathered all her family and we began the *paritta* chanting, to bless their home and invite auspicious forces to aid their lives. Through the windows came the broad and gentle tones of Bach's "*Jesu Joy of Man's Desiring*" and, rather than try to shut it out, I thought that the mixture of the Asian and the European, the jumble of sound at once chaotic and fine, made a gesture which fitted perfectly their lives. Amidst an excess of good things all shaken up and mixed together, it is still possible to find peace and inner harmony. By the end of the chanting the music had finished and our voices on their own ended the scene. The tortoise had ceased its wanderings, the cats were still and a joyous calm hovered in the air.

It was getting late by now but was still bright and sunny so we went for a little walk around. As we emerged Sundar, the leader of the Ashram, bounded down from his house to come and greet us. Joya told us that he had a new-born baby and said to him that I would like to bless it. This was news to me but, being one who tends to go along with such things, I followed faithfully as Sundar invited me inside. It was full of people there so he asked his wife to come aside to a quiet room where we could see the child.

"*Om Namaha Shivaya*", she greeted us, with the softness and gentleness of total motherhood. Her voice was as quiet as were her eyes and she shone with the warmth of sincere devotion. New motherhood and bhakti yoga are quite a potent mixture and it made me feel a little like a rhinoceros in their midst.

"Would you like to hold the baby? I'm sure it is allowed," said Joya and next thing I knew there it was – this pink little thing, just three weeks into waking life, held up against the ochre of my robe.

"Smile sweetly and radiate *metta,*" I thought but, far from cooing and gurgling with delight at my all-abounding love, it immediately began to cry instead.

"Oh well," I thought, "chalk up another failure – so it goes, I suppose, ho-hum." I gave the baby back and we said goodbye, but the sense of ineptitude and failure stayed with me. The sense of insufficient love, of not being confirmed in that self-image was painful and seemed to loiter in the mind. On reflection, though, and sometime after leaving Schweibenalp, it all fell into a different perspective. The child's tears called out the sense of suffering in life, the truth of the pain of separation from the loved. In terms of the total love and devotion which is their community's ideal, suffering and conflict are resolved by being drowned in the radiance of the heart. But we are children and we can't always manage that – "Between the idea and the reality … falls the Shadow." In such a community, where life is moral but very loosely tructured, they must certainly have a generous share of ups and downs. To survive, one must abide in a pure acceptance of everything and not get entangled in the moods of those around you. A child cries: this is suffering, but to whom does it belong? If there is an owner, then birth and death begin right there. The Suchness of a child's tears, the Suchness of a smile, when there is no distinction both birth and death are stopped.

★ ★ ★

Our travels to Zürich and the East became almost a blur as the vernal spirits took charge of the world around us.

Quiet days in Meilen and Balgach – on this sunlit morning there is nothing in particular to do – the lake shines below, birds hop the roofs and apple blossom explodes quietly around us. Later this afternoon we will set off for Dicken and the week-end retreat which we will lead there – quiet times – spending a few days with long empty spaces, talking with our hosts and walking out in the burgeoning fecundity of spring. Warm, wet weather has brought the sprouting world out into an almost unnatural fertility and lushness. There have been steamy days of tropical heat, cascades of leaf and blossom. This is the land of the dandelion and the buttercup and, unlike the meadows of England which have mostly been fertilised into a sterile uniformity, the fields have a golden aura of richness which the bell-banged cows and bearded goats tug at with relish and contentment.

Meilen is a village-like suburb of Zürich and as we walked around people greeted us with a gentle "Grüzi". There is a homely atmosphere and a softness of manner here absent in the roaring city streets. However, one little boy we encountered expressed *his* views very frankly: (Roberto's translation)

"Why haven't you got any hair!?"

"Why don't you wear proper clothes?!?"

"I **don't** like you!!."

Some Swiss are very conservative, even at five years old.

The retreat flew by in a fingersnap and, for the last time, the three of us were on our way to Bern.

A crowded, sleepy train-ride took us through more bursting green, in the fields and woody lowlands by the railway. Green upon green, green upon green, well-kept factories pass by and misty rivers. Ursula was waiting for us in the underground concourse of the railway station in Bern. The hooting and hollering drunken remains of the afternoon's football crowds were strung through the arcades, echoing round us in the halls.

"E'wasch gurus!" gaped one amazed and half-delighted reveller.

"Incredible," I thought, "what a scene."

When we got back, Ursula confessed she had a surprise for us.

"It's to do with nuts," she said and went off to arrange things,

"Curiouser and curiouser," I thought.

Eventually she took us down through the flat and up to her room on the other side. There, spot-lit in the little dormer space, was a smiling Buddha-rupa, four feet tall. I recognised it as the one Urs had pointed out to us in an antique shop the other day. It was a Burmese standing Buddha made of gilded wood. She had emptied her bank-account to buy it.

"It was crazy, I know, completely nuts, but I couldn't resist. The idea hit me last weekend when I was in Germany at a conference with the Dalai Lama. I just woke up in the morning and knew, 'That's what I'm going to do,' so I went to the shop as soon as possible. When they told me the price I wasn't sure I had enough, but we contacted the bank and what I had there was right to within a few francs."

"Well," I thought, "Why not? If we want to start a monastery in Switzerland, what better way to begin than with a Buddha?"

We were all stunned as we sat beneath this figure, talking on and on late into the night. It was getting close to two a.m. when I finally went to sleep, swollen with a warm contented glow. Acts of faith like that have a way of touching people. To trust in the heart and be so gloriously insecure: to give away all your money for the sake of others. How heart-warming and fine – and what an honour it is to be involved in this ripening of the virtues of the Buddha.

★ ★ ★

The last days and hours in Ursula's flat sizzled with ardour and benevolence. A flood of people came to say goodbye and to sit up late into the last remaining nights with us. Eventually, however, we had to go....

Ochre tourists in summer clothes choke the paths and halls at Gatwick, incongruous we three mendicants in winding sheets – one white, one brown, one gold – slowly pacing through the throngs – patience – trying to keep cool and steady, unflustered by the surging forms around us – mendicant life amongst the lotus-eaters; I wonder what our appearance says to them?

"Weird, very weird."

"What do they think they look like?"

"I wonder what they are into?"

"I wonder, do they know something I don't?"

We return, gift-laden, from the Land of Milk and Honey, and melt back into the sea of the familiar.

Meaning in Myth

A public Sunday afternoon talk given at Amaravati, September 1993

THE TITLE FOR THIS TALK is 'Meaning in Myth' – because of the work of people like Freud, James Joyce and Joseph Campbell, this is quite a popular subject in current times. This century there has been a whole re-emergence of the understanding of myth and what its usefulness is, what its place is in our culture and in our way of thinking.

Oftentimes within our ordinary patterns of speech, we take the word 'myth' to mean something which is false or untrue, or a fabulous lie; it is quite common to say, "Oh, that is a myth!" or in books such as 'The Myth of Mental Illness' or 'The Myth of Freedom', these are using the word to indicate that this is not real or this idea of freedom or mental illness is not the truth. If we look more deeply at what we mean by myth, we can see that in its original purpose it is not just pointing towards something which is fanciful or untrue, but it is more a pattern which is symbolic, evocative of a greater reality. A mythical tale is not necessarily aiming to be factual or historical, it is simply an archetype which is portraying some common experience of humanity, some common experience of our mind. In that way it is not intended or necessary for it to be historically accurate in order for it to be something which is useful, meaningful and helpful to us.

In any religious scripture or in looking at legends and mythical tales, we can see that there are basically three different strands involved: firstly, there is the aspect of archetype, there is an image which is being portrayed of a common human experience; secondly, there is the historical aspect, i.e. events that actually happened, if a person like Ulysses really lived, or what events really occurred in the life of Jesus Christ or the Buddha; thirdly, there is the psychological aspect, how that same pattern is represented in our minds – how the events of the life of the Buddha or of a particular story match our own experience, what does it say about our own psyche. Through any kind of tale, any kind of religious scripture or suchlike form, there are these three different strands involved.

187

In modern times, with the arising of analytical study by historians, theologians, archeologists, anthropologists etc., searching for what is true in terms of what can be historically and scientifically verified, it has been assumed that if you can not pin an event down to a definite date and certain historically corroborated characters, then it is not true or it is to be discarded.

From my own limited perspective I think that this is taking things too literally, because even if one can prove that it was impossible that the Buddha was enlightened at that particular spot or that Jesus was definitely not born on the 25th of December or that Jesus never existed at all, still there can be some usefulness to the story. This is because it can match experiences common to all human beings. Stories such as these are carried through time, we remember them because they have meaning for us in that they are symbolic of aspects of our own nature. The reason why we remember myths then is that they give us an inroad, an access point into our heart. They are pointing to general experiences of life and, by making them conscious in graphically portraying those events, those triumphs and crises, the comedies and tragedies of heroes and villains in history, we can see the events of our own mind occurring. It is by making things conscious, by bringing them into our minds, that we can begin to objectify them, understand them and learn to harmonise with them.

I found out a while ago that in ancient Greece the theatres, which had strong religious connotations, and the hospitals were always built close to each other. Spiritual and physical health were both very closely related to the use of theatre; it was not just entertainment, but rather the comedies and tragedies that were portrayed in Greek drama were there as a type of psychiatric treatment, as a way of helping to understand and balance out our mental life. This is very much how one should understand the use of myth and legendary tales: they can be employed as a way of understanding our own life in a direct and complete way.

★ ★ ★

Since we live in a very multi-cultural society, we are in contact with a great variety of influences; we are surrounded by different stories and we have access to ones that not only come from our own European or Asian backgrounds but we live in the middle of a whole confluence of different cultural patterns. One can see that there are fundamental human questions, problems or qualities that appear all over the world. Different traditions, different groups have evolved stories and ideas to help symbolise these and to effectively bring them into consciousness.

Wherever humanity has appeared, one of the questions that has arisen is, "How did we get here? How did humanity appear? What made the cosmos happen?" Everywhere in the world, each culture has its own creation myths of how the universe came into being. Then, even if we have some sort of idea of how and why we got here, the next question is, "What am I supposed to do now? What happens next? What should I do with my life?"

In the Judaeo-Christian tradition there is the creation story of Genesis, the story of God creating the world (somebody sent me a postcard a couple of days ago from Israel saying, "Five thousand seven hundred and sixty-two years ago God said, 'Let there be light.' Happy new year!" I thought that was a very sweet way to put it!)

Scientists and historians can say, "This is absolutely ridiculous; there is no way that the universe could have been created five thousand seven hundred and sixty-two years ago, we can easily prove that was not how it was!" and one can discard such a story as being absurd just as one can any other aspect of scripture. We can dissect it, take it apart, say that it has all been cobbled together from a variety of sources and that it is therefore invalid or unimportant. Rather than looking in that way, however, the whole usefulness of a myth is to apply it reflectively so that it works on an intuitive level.

If we compare this story with the Buddhist tradition we find that the Buddha avoided such proclamations, he did not make that kind of story prominent. He is one of the few religious teachers that did not make very much of a creation myth. In fact, he made a point of saying that the ultimate beginning of things is fundamentally inconceivable, it is one of the imponderable things. Which does not mean to say that he did not know the Truth but rather that this is something that can not be put into thought or word; the thinking mind can not conceive the reality of the situation.

The way that we see the universe in terms of human-centred perceptions of time and space is restricting to the quality of true vision, so the Buddha said to not bother trying to figure out how it all began. He actually said that if we try to, we will either go crazy or our head will explode into seven pieces. He avoided talking about the ultimate beginning of things, but then he also said, "If you want to know how a universe comes into being at the start of an aeon, how a universe arises, it's like this...," and he describes how first of all different beings arise in the high heavenly realms and then as time goes by they appear in lower and lower realms, then the physical world comes into being and eventually reaches a point of degeneration as the universe expands to its fullest extent. It then starts to collapse again – this is called a period of universal expansion and contraction – and such cycles have occurred innumerable times. Interestingly enough, this pattern matches quite well the scientific model of a Big Bang and then a Big Crunch. I find it quite marvellous, however, that the Buddha described this but indicated that this is just the way a universe happens and that this kind of knowledge is not really important.

What the Buddha was trying to point to was that it is not a matter of how it all began in the first place, or how we can develop a universal picture of it, but to recognise how our experience of the world arises; this approach brings it more inside. In the Buddhist approach he talks about the genesis of problems, how our experience of separateness and our difficulties in life arise. So, rather than having an average creation myth, the Buddha taught what is called Dependent Origination, which describes how it comes to be that we experience dissatisfaction or unhappiness in the moment. How do our sense of alienation and our problems arise? And how do our problems cease? That is the significant thing, isn't it? It's not a question of "How does a tree do its thing?

How does a star be what it is? Why are electrons the way they are?" Nobody knows basically!

★ ★ ★

It is interesting that we can look at the biblical myth of the creation of the world in seven days and at Dependent Origination and find many correspondencies. The Buddha describes how ignorance, not understanding the truth of things, is the cause of alienation and dissatisfaction. From ignorance comes the apparent separation of mind and body, and of self and other. Attachment to the senses becomes solidified, which leads to deepening of sense contact, and the concomitant feelings of pleasure and pain become something that we absorb into and attach to, so that we run away from pain or we chase after pleasure. The mind thus becomes caught up with self-based desire of one sort or another; attaching to that desire then causes us to invest further in trying to possess the beautiful and escape the painful. When the beautiful slips through our fingers or the painful catches up with us, then that is what we call dissatisfaction or *dukkha*.

It struck me a number of years ago how accurately this model matches the story in the first three chapters of Genesis: from the Buddhist point of view, ignorance and desire are portrayed as the cause of suffering and alienation, and in the Judaic myth it is pretty much the same.

It has always seemed to me to be a disastrous mistake to think that Genesis is referring to historical events rather than being a meaningful myth to symbolise some deep truths about us. Rather than looking to it to describe the origins of the human race, the Jewish people and so forth, the first three chapters of Genesis seem to be talking about this same process of Dependent Origination: whereby out of God, out of Ultimate Reality, not only the human race arises, with all the creatures, plants and animals of the world, but also so do alienation, suffering, misery and pain.

It is true that the familiar expressions of Dependent Origination all begin with *avijja*, ignorance; however, as the Ven. Ajahn Mun pointed out – "Ignorance has to have a mother and father just as we do, and we learn from the scriptures that *thitibhutaṁ* is its mother and father. *Thitibhutaṁ* refers to the primal – Original Mind."

At the source, all there is is God – Ultimate Reality. Then "In the beginning God created the heaven and the earth," I understand that in the Hebrew version of Genesis, rather than "God created" – as a being that acts on a volition – its meaning is more like "Out of God, heaven and earth arose,"which equates more with the kind of pattern that I have been describing. Heaven and earth, here and there, represents the basic division and separateness of 'sankhara', heaven and earth are set apart from each other. The spirit of God moving on the waters is like arising of consciousness in that world. The land is then separated from the sea and all the creatures are brought forth into the world. Here again is the same sort of branching, complexifying elaboration of the pattern, to the point where there are creatures and Adam and Eve living in the Garden.

This takes us through the levels from *viññana*, *namarupa*, *salayatana*, *phassa* and *vedana* – the mind and body, the six senses, sense contact, to the level of feeling. So that, symbolically, living in the Garden of Eden is like living at the level of pure feeling, being responsive to the world in a state of innocence and invulnerable pleasantness where we are not being driven by desire or fear but just being responsive to life.

If the mind is really sharp and aware, we can actually live at that level of pure sensitivity where we are not driven by desire, fear or aggression. Ajahn Buddhadasa would regularly encourage this – to try and cut the cycle between feeling and desire, before feeling turns into desire. If we can just live at the level of feeling, where we are mindfully responding to pleasure and pain, attraction and aversion, not acting on desire, then we are in Eden before the Fall – we are able to live in a contented, blissful, naked and harmonious way.

Then the serpent arrives on the scene … the fruit of the tree of knowledge is 'advertised' and Eve is persuaded; this is the arising of desire. Following that desire, the attachment to it leads to the choice to eat the fruit, *upadana* or grasping. The actual eating of it is *bhava*, the moment of knowledge arriving – the impact of getting what you are after. Then *bhava* leading to birth is when we hear the voice of the Old Man,

"Adam, where are you?"

"Oh God!"

The point of no turning back has been passed, they have emerged into raw knowledge; which then leads to the two of them being driven from the Garden. Alienation, separateness, "All the days of your life you will toil with sweat and bring forth children in pain…," etc., etc.

So one sees the same pattern being portrayed in this mythological form. For all of its faults, it must be a primary myth that exists in our society because of its ability to identify that same pattern. It is a tying together of the relationship between absolute transcendent Truth, selfish desire and alienation, suffering.

You might think that all of this is complete nonsense; however, one can also see that these are simply different ways that we can use to describe and understand the arising of suffering.

The other of the two questions – "Where do we go from here?" or "What do we do now?" – is dealt with in the central myth of Christianity in the crucifixion and the resurrection. That is the crucial point of the life of Christ and the main symbol of the religion, the cross is always used in Christianity as the central image. The scientists, theologians and historians all have a great time taking apart the crucifixion and resurrection story. It may be completely unprovable factually but it is much more significant if we think of it in terms of what it might be symbolising and embodying. This event is the parallel of the Buddha's enlightenment, the experience under the Bodhi tree; both are about the conquest of death. The crucifixion and the resurrection of Jesus shows how, through the experience of suffering, persecution and humiliation, the sense of self is transfixed, pinned down and has to be completely transcended for the resurrection, for salvation to occur. The self or the ego had to die completely for the deathless Christ-nature to be realised.

In the Buddhist scriptures and commentaries, the accounts of the enlightenment under the Bodhi tree depict the assault by the hordes of Mara: his name means 'Death' and he is also the Lord of Illusion. The Buddha-to-be is attacked by the forces of fear, the forces of desire and then the forces of duty. First an army of demons comes at him, then the daughters of Mara, trying to seduce him, and finally the visions of his family – his old father trying to call him back to Kapilavastu to take over the throne. Just as the crucifixion and resurrection are, these are pointing to experiences within our everyday life: the Buddha symbolises the mind in all of us which is awake, which is pure and aware; that mind is constantly impinged on, assaulted by the hordes of Mara in perhaps more subtle and not so graphic ways but certainly we are assailed by feelings of fear, feelings of desire and feelings of responsibility. Just like the Buddha, the only way we can skilfully respond to that is to sit unmoving under the Bodhi tree of awareness and say, "I know you Mara!" What causes Mara to be unable to harm the Buddha is simply that sense of recognition and awareness; death is powerless against it. Similarly with Jesus on the cross, when he completely surrenders, he lifts up his head and says, "It is finished." Evaṁ – his work has been fulfilled and the illusion of death destroyed.

★ ★ ★

One can take a myth, a story, in many different ways and it is always up to each individual to see how these different images affect us. In a way, however, because these are talking about deep and complex aspects of our own being, the patterns can help and guide us even if conceptually we cannot follow it or put it all together. Stories point directions for us and tell us what to expect in many different ways.

Another of the most famous and powerful myths in our time is the story of the journey home of Ulysses from the Trojan wars. This story and its archetypal value is something that James Joyce picked up on in his great novel. He portrayed it as a journey through a wild night in Dublin in 1904 but, in the same way, he was trying to take what is a universal symbol and put it into a context of ordinary everyday life to make our life more understandable. This kind of representation is talking about you and me and the events of our own world, our own minds. Similarly in George Bernard Shaw's play 'Pygmalion', originally a Greek myth about a sculptor who falls in love with a form he has carved and whom Aphrodite eventually brings to life as Galataea; Professor Higgins falls in love with his creation, a cockney girl who, for a bet, he trains to behave and speak like a duchess.

The story of Ulysses contains powerful religious symbolism: in many ways our spiritual life is built around the sense of longing for home – we feel a bit like Adam and Eve outside the Garden, we have been chucked out, we feel separated from other people and uncertain of ourselves, we feel insecure and have a sense of longing. We long for security and comfort, we long for that feeling of "Ahh … we're HOME" – like returning after a long journey or just that feeling of getting back to our home after work. It is that same heartfelt quality that is expressed in this story – "Ahh … safe, we're home at last, this is **good**." This is a religious symbol in that a spiritual homecoming is a realisation of the true nature of what we are. The experience of being pulled constantly homeward, that quality of longing for home, is in a way the spiritual longing that we have for Reality, for completeness, for fulfilment.

It is interesting that in the story of Ulysses it takes him ten years to make what is, if you look at it on a map, a journey that should have taken him just a few weeks. But he is drawn in by all kinds of events both painful, beautiful and disastrous – being attacked and imprisoned or being distracted, seduced, being shipwrecked and so forth. When looking at the trials of his journey and comparing that with our own spiritual life one can say, "Yes! That is what it is like"; sometimes we are beaten up by some angry god, shipwrecked and set loose to float in the ocean. It is also interesting, however, that Ulysses had Athene the Goddess of Wisdom as his protector, his mentor, she was always there looking out for him and making sure that, even if everything else fell apart, he would somehow manage to survive.

In looking at the different events of his journey, even though it took about ten years, seven years of that were spent in the company of an island of nymphs. Calypso fell madly in love with Ulysses and he lived with her and her companions for seven years. It was a blissful existence: a lovely Mediterranean island, surrounded by beautiful people, an idyllic, dream-like existence, but after seven years of this he feels in his heart, "I want to go home. This is all very lovely but this is not home, I want to go **home** – I have to return to Ithaca."

I won't go into all the other aspects of this story, but such things as being trapped by Polyphemus the Cyclops, and being caught between Scylla and Charybdis, the sea monster and the great whirlpool, these all represent the trials and difficulties of our spiritual development, when everything goes wrong and we feel attacked and oppressed. Ajahn Sucitto once compared meditation to the journey of Ulysses and his sailors past the Sirens. The Sirens represent the desire mind. Ulysses knew that the only way that he and his crew could defeat and get past the Sirens was if one of them could hear the Sirens' song and not be entranced by them. Passing sailors would hear the Sirens singing their beautiful intoxicating songs, promising bliss and knowledge and then would land on the shore of their island. These beautiful sea-nymphs would then turn into terrifying monsters and summarily devour the sailors.

Ajahn Sucitto was commenting one day how the spiritual powers and faculties are very much like Ulysses' crew – they filled their ears with wax so they could not hear the song and then they tied him firmly to the mast. They then rowed past the island and of course the Sirens start calling to them, singing their bewitching song. Ulysses is straining at his ropes trying to break free but the crew just rows on. He is desperately yelling at his crew, saying "Come on, it's all right lads! Change of plan, I'm sure this is going to be all right. Untie me!" But the crew just hauls away. The ropes are the Five Precepts and the crew are the Five *indriya*: faith, energy, mindfulness, concentration and wisdom – these are our spiritual powers, they are the things that power us through even though the desire might be overwhelming. The fickle mind is tied to the mast and screaming – this is what it feels like being on a meditation retreat sometimes, strapped to the mast and screaming to be let out, but it is only by being patient and letting the spiritual powers carry us through that we actually get past the Sirens. This represents how we have the ability, if we have good friends, a moral commitment and the right spiritual powers at our disposal, we can get through the most intoxicating, bedazzling, entrancing pulls upon our hearts.

It is also an interesting aspect of the story of Ulysses that, when he finally arrives back at Ithaca, he is fast asleep – that he is carried there by some friendly, nearby islanders. He has become totally exhausted by this time and, as the story goes, they sail the last stretch then pick him up and carry him onto the beaches of Ithaca. When he awakens there Athene puts a haze over his eyes so that he cannot recognise where he is. Even though all the way through the story he is referred to as 'noble, long-suffering and resourceful', she realises that if he wakes up on the beach and realises he is home at last he is going to lose control, he will be so happy he will get careless and is therefore likely to get killed. He has been away by now for twenty years and things have changed on the island. She thus puts a haze over his eyes so that he discovers slowly where he is and that the island has been taken over in his absence. A whole gang of suitors have been trying to win the hand of his Queen Penelope.

He eventually meets up with his son, Telemachus and a few other friends: first of all he is recognised by his dog, who has waited and stayed alive until Ulysses came home and at last, overjoyed when he sees him, finally lays down and dies. His old nurse also recognises him, from a scar on his leg, but many of his old servants and friends have turned against him and are now helping the suitors and trying to get the most out of the land that they can.

Some others, however, like Eumaeus his swineherd, are still faithful – after all this time he is still looking after the pigs. In his disguise as an old man, Ulysses goes and stays with Eumaeus; they sit and talk through the evening, but what really impresses him is that, even though it is late at night and it's dark and cold, Eumaeus says, "I have to go out and look after the pigs. I should not just stay in here chatting." Symbolically what all this means is that it is only those qualities of being faithful, humble and simple that enable the recognition of Ulysses, the King, to take place.

I will not go into the details but, eventually, all the suitors get killed in a gory finale and Ulysses finally resumes his throne. Thinking about this some years ago, when I happened to be reading the Odyssey, it struck me that it was very like the stages of enlightenment: Ulysses leaving Troy and heading for home indicates the entry onto the spiritual path and from there the whole story unfolds as a spiritual analogy. When he arrives on Ithaca, he is home but there is still danger, he still has not completed the task. This is rather like the third level of enlightenment, what is called *anagami*, non-returner – he is home but there is still work to be done. The main opponent, the main obstacle to regaining the throne is what is called *asmimana* or 'the conceit of identity'. This is the final battle: even if we have developed enormous virtue, clarity of mind and purity of heart and we are home, back in Ithaca, if we do not deal with the sense of self, with the conceit of identity in a very intelligent way and we are incautious, then we are going to end up getting skewered by the sense of 'I' and we are never going to make it back to the throne. Perfection here is symbolised as the rightful king back on the throne of his kingdom with the country at peace and in harmony.

It struck me that this was very much the final battle of spiritual life. The last three of what are called 'the ten fetters', *asmimana*, *avijja* (ignorance) and restlessness, these are the final tasks that are laid out before someone on the spiritual path; of these, the sense of 'I', the sense of identity, is perhaps the main protagonist that one faces. Confronting it can be a gory business, but with wisdom, symbolised by Athene, on one's side, with humility, simplicity and faith, the hero of the saga must win out.

(You can probably tell I have a fondness for mythology. Actually it was the only kind of thing I read as a child – I never read the usual adventure stories or normal things that boys like – I was buried in fairy tales and myths from the age of about four onwards, so this has always been a main reference point for me in my life. These stories work on an intuitive level; they are there, they are absorbed and they give us models to work with.)

★ ★ ★

It is also interesting to see how myths arise within our own life in unexpected ways and present themselves to give us direction. I remember some years ago Ajahn Kittisaro talking to me about an unusual experience that he had had. He was taken by a friend of his, who is an artist, to visit an exhibition of sculpture in London. This man had said, "There is an incredible sculpture there, you have got to go and see it!" It was Jacob Epstein's 'Jacob Wrestling the Angel' that he was referring to, and it was on exhibition in London for a while.

He said, "You're joking! We are down here in Devon. We can't drive all the way up to London to look at a piece of sculpture, that's ridiculous," but his friend replied, "You've **got** to see it, it is incredible, amazing," so, eventually he agreed to go. Now this particular monk used to be a wrestler himself, and when he saw the sculpture, he was stunned. He later described to me the effect it had had on him, and there had obviously been a very strong spiritual message there for him. The two figures, which are physically identical to each other except that one has got wings, are locked together in a hold. He was able to see that Jacob had obviously been trying to go for a certain hold on the Angel. In this manoeuvre you get your arms under the armpits of the other person and then you flip them over – if you can do it, it is very dramatic and you completely defeat the opponent in one glorious slam. But you have to get your balance just right – if you don't, then you put your own position greatly at risk.

In this statue Jacob has obviously been going for this hold, trying to flip the Angel over, and he has lost it. Jacob's hands are thus underneath the Angel's arms. The hold has just been broken and his hands have flopped down, he has lost the advantage. Meanwhile, the Angel has got him in a bear-hug. Now in a bear-hug you have to have your hands locked together to crush the chest of the other person, but he noticed that the Angel, having just broken Jacob's hold, rather than the hands being locked together, they were fingertip to fingertip. He realised that the Angel was not crushing him – it was an embrace – and the Angel is looking right towards Jacob with a piercing gaze. Jacob meanwhile is looking up to heaven, so the moment of defeat has actually turned into a moment of embrace and exultation – Jacob thought he had lost, but it wasn't the contest he thought it was!

As he was telling me this story I remembered a dream that I had a little while before. For years I had had a recurring dream, a nightmare of sorts, where I would be in conflict with some people or some other person. I would always be bashing away at them, or trying to knife them or shoot them, chuck rocks at them or something! And the other person would always be just standing or sitting there completely unbothered by what I was doing, just smiling benignly or with a look of, "When is he going to stop this silliness?" There would always be a sense of anxiety, fear in me that I had got to keep this opponent off, "My life is in danger, I have got to keep them away from me!"

The language of myth is the same as the language of dream, and I could see that these dreams were indicating something to me, but at the time I could not figure it out – "What is all this violence? What is going on here? I am not a violent person … am I???" This dream, however, would come back over and over again; every few weeks it would return in one form or another, which was quite disturbing. I could not figure out what it was about. I would think, "Who is this opponent? Who are these people I keep thumping away at, and why are they never the slightest bit bothered by what I am doing to them?" They would never retaliate in these dreams; I would never get hit or hurt by them in any way but I always seemed to think that they were a terrible danger to me.

Then one night the dream came again, but it was in colour and very, very vivid. I was wrestling and was locked together with some other person; and then I thought "It's that dream again!" It was so clear, I woke up inside the dream and asked myself, "Who is this that I am wrestling against anyway?" Then the other person raised their head, looked me right in the eye and smiled, and guess who it was … it was me. Oh ho! "Well if that is me **there**, then who is this **here**???" Very interesting.…

About a year after that I had another dream wherein I found myself in the opposite position. I won't go into all the details of it but I was instead the one that was being ineffectively attacked by an enraged figure. It was someone well known to me who was an incredibly arrogant, conceited person. He had very good qualities in other ways but he possessed a monumental ego. He was in a state of rage and started to attack me; I let him bash away for a while, but it was not really having any effect at all, even though he was thrashing furiously away trying to hurt me. I thought, "This is a bit pointless, I might as well leave." I just walked peacefully away and left the situation unharmed, not feeling any fear or negativity to him at all.

So, when Ajahn Kittisaro talked to me about the statue of Jacob wrestling the Angel, I went and looked up the story in the Bible. It was quite remarkable that I had had this dream without ever having seen the statue or thinking consciously about this story. What it seemed to be symbolising was the ego wrestling against the true nature of things, or the sense of self wrestling against the Dhamma. No wonder that no matter how much the ego was bashing away trying to protect itself, the Dhamma, that which is true and real, the natural order of things, was neither being aggressive towards the ego, nor was it needing to retreat; it was utterly un-bothered by what the ego was doing, just mildly and affectionately amused. Witnessing that in the dream then enabled me to contemplate it and question, "Which is the real me?"

The face that I had seen in the wrestling dream had been utterly peaceful, happy and contented, and very different from the agonised, anxious, frantic state that I felt my 'self' to be in. One could see that this was talking about the interplay between identifying with the egoic mind and identifying with the Dhamma or Buddha mind – the mind which is completely attuned to Nature, the transcendent knowing mind. This all seemed to show that sometimes these stories are in the air, in our blood, in our race memories; they just arise in this way and play themselves out in the world around us when we need them.

★ ★ ★

As a culture, we can make good use of this process – it is not to be underestimated how much bringing our attention to these different stories can guide our lives in a very helpful way. I was very impressed recently on reading an account of the Royal Shakespeare Company performing the works, often the tragedies, of Shakespeare in psychiatric institutions. There was an account of them performing 'King Lear' in Broadmoor, a hospital for the criminally insane, which one would think would be a very dangerous thing to do. However, just as Greek theatre was very much tied up with mental health, what they were doing was portraying the very things that these people had done, the very things that their minds were filled with, in front of their eyes, and in that portrayal a healing occurs. Apparently the players felt a rapport with the audience, a commitment to the depth of their acting and an understanding of the material far greater than they had ever experienced before in any kind of major theatre production. The audience understood what the horror and the tragedy were about because they had been there. After the play they would have discussion groups, workshops wherein the players, the inmates and the staff would all talk with each other. One of them said that three different people, all of whom had killed their parents, came up to them separately after the play and said how much they wished, like Cordelia who makes good with her father King Lear at the end, that they could go to their parents and make good with them in the same kind of way. Simply by witnessing the whole situation they were better enabled to understand their own lives.

It was said that one or two could not cope and just took themselves off and cried, but even that, just being able to let the tears out in the sense of regret, allowing it all to surface, is a tremendously powerful aspect of spiritual training. In Buddhist practice, on the internal level, this very much relates to what is called 'wise reflection' ('*yoniso manasikara*' is the Pali term), whereby we bring consciously into the mind the things of our life which are important or difficult for us – things which are hard for us to understand, or which are painful, things which are powerful in our minds. We use our reflective abilities to look at that, to raise some image up and get to know the feeling of it, to witness and acknowledge it, because the very act of attention, knowing, is itself the healing agent.

If we are very upset about something or very angry or depressed or we are very excited, just to be able to raise into the mind the recognition: "Here is excitement. This is what excitement feels like," or "This is a tragedy; everything has gone wrong. This is a total failure, a disaster" – to raise that up into the mind and then to simply recognise that "This is what disaster feels like – it is like this." We are not pretending that it does not matter, but by making it conscious and bringing it up into the mind in that very clear and distinct way, we are able to free the mind of it. It becomes an object; it goes from being 'what I am' to being part of Nature.

Just like the people in Broadmoor, or in listening to different myths and legends, or reading religious scriptures and other tales, having these inner forces portrayed in an archetypal way and brought up into consciousness so graphically, it enables us to digest it, it enables us to say, "This is part of Nature" – "I have done something terribly wrong with my life, I have made a terrible mistake," or "I am a great success; this is absolutely glorious, my life isfantastic"– by having it portrayed in front of us we can see, for example, "Here is someone else who has had a fantastic victory, but look at what happened to her!"

So we can objectify the events of our life and understand them as a more comprehensive picture, rather than being swirled around as if we were in a whirlpool, being carried around by the successes and failures, the pleasures and pains of what we experience – we are not a victim of life, we are able to see it in a more clear and objective way and thus not suffer over it.

This is an aspect of Buddhist meditation that is often neglected, but it is something that Ajahn Sumedho often teaches about; personally I have derived an enormous amount from developing this approach. It makes such a difference to look upon our life in this reflective way, to bring it all into consciousness. The rôle of this kind of portrayal in stories, myths, dreams, poems, etc. is a very powerful medium for us. It may seem of secondary importance, but if we do not bring these same things to light, what we find is that we are very ill-equipped to deal with life. If we have not done that somehow then, when we meet with tragedy it is **my** tragedy, it is not just Nature; if we meet with success then it is **my** success, it is **my** glory, and we get carried away by it.

There was a very interesting study done once by a psychiatrist called Bruno Bettelheim who did a lot of work with autistic children. This was in the 1960s and, at that time, people were very concerned to have everything politically correct and modernised, civilised and egalitarian. So they started to straighten out the fairy-tales that they were telling the children in the hospital unit where they were working. They re-wrote all the fairy stories – they took out all the violent ogres and witches that ate children's heads, together with all the ghastly, unfair, cruel and shocking elements. They dressed them up and made them a little more nice and polite.

They ran this programme for quite a number of years, but there were other centres that they were looking after where they did not use this approach. About twenty years later they made a psychological profile of these different groups of children and they found that the ones that had had the sanitised fairy-tales were much more helpless in terms of real life, they were much less able to cope. The ones who had had a full dose of evil dragons, gore and rough justice knew, when the boss came at them in a rage, "Do not panic. Reach for the magic feather! There is a way out of this." This struck me as being a very good way of understanding the process.

★ ★ ★

The situation that we have in the West nowadays is that we are losing our myths, and the ones that we have do not really apply so well. Because of this we find ourselves adrift as a society, we find ourselves very much at a loss as to how to steer ourselves. There are whole areas of our life where we simply do not know what to do.

In Asia many of the ancient myths are kept very much alive through dance, classical music and theatre. Just yesterday I was at an event in Leicester at a Hindu temple; it was part of a conference on religious faiths and the environment. They did a puppet show of the Ramayana and the woman who was narrating was a very gifted storyteller. She got to the place in the story where Rama and Sita and one of his brothers are living in the forest together. The evil demons were coming to try and trick them and carry Sita away. One of them appears as a beautiful golden deer in the forest, Sita sees the golden deer and says, "Ooohh! How beau-ooo-tiful, oh! I must have it...," and the story-teller modulated her voice into the unmistakable sound of an Indian woman walking past a jeweller's shop, pointing out a golden necklace to her husband: "Ooohh! I must have it!" All the women started chuckling and so did the men – it was all so familiar! One could see very easily how something in the tale was portraying a very everyday occurrence for them – and the dangerous results of deliberately following desire!

I find it a shame that our culture has lost a lot of its old myths even though, as I was describing, we do still produce them, our minds still naturally formulate them. In the media sometimes stories that capture the imagination are portraying where we are at as human beings and as a culture. Occasionally these can have a great effect in helping to heal or steer the society; for example, Arthur Miller's play 'Death of a Salesman' in the 1950s put a completely different light on the American Dream. I was also quite struck last year how people became obsessed with the film 'The Silence of the Lambs' – everyone was talking about it. When I read about what the plot of the film was and saw the kind of fascination, obsession or horror that people had with the film, what arose in my mind was that this is actually a very clear and graphic portrayal of Western life today. Western civilisation is embodied as the eloquent, polished doctor, one who understands the body and the mind and yet is completely mad, and devours the very thing which it is his duty and his occupation to cherish and protect. Isn't this a portrayal of where Western civilisation is at? We are like a brilliant, deranged being that is coolly devouring and despoiling the very life it is our duty to protect.

I do not know how one can go about creating helpful new myths, but it struck me that one thing we are particularly lacking in the West, and what we do not have a mythology for is spiritual heroes. Our heroes seem to be people like Arnold Schwartzenegger, Madonna, Clint Eastwood and Kurt Cobain – these are our society's public heroes. Mahatma Gandhi, Mother Teresa, Martin Luther King and perhaps the Dalai Lama are given some prominence, but we lack much in the way of spiritual heroes for the manyfolk.

We also lack any mythology for death now. Death is looked upon as a life having failed. A society that rejects death has no way of understanding and accommodating the fact of it.

The other great area of lack that sprang to mind is that we look upon elderly people with disdain, they are seen as young people who have failed – if we are old, we are a failed young person. We are looked upon as a spare part in society. We have lost our mythology of the old as being worthy and wise; we have lost our sense of the older generation being our sources of wisdom. I was talking yesterday with a representative for the Sikh community at the conference I mentioned, he was saying how he likes to hang around with the old people, the old members of the Sikh community just because he soaks up so much goodness and wisdom from them. I thought, "How rare!" One just does not find that in Western culture very much; even elderly people themselves are so indoctrinated with this attitude that they too think, "I don't want to be a bother, please put me in a home, your life is more important than mine." One understands the practicalities of it, but it is a shame that we do not look upon our elders as our guides and our sources of wisdom.

Yesterday I saw an advert for a Building Society in which there was a white-haired man in a leather jacket standing next to a very fancy Harley-Davidson motorbike. The headline was "Grow old disgracefully." This seemed to say it all – do not let yourself grow old, fight it, "rage, rage against the dying of the light"; fight against old age rather than see that oldness and the kind of wisdom and sagacity that come from having lived for many years is a beautiful and worthy treasure. To look upon old age as a time when you can and should carry on playing at childhood is a great shame. I do not know how one can turn things around, but I see that until we do develop ways of generating respect and value in these areas, our society is going to continue to drift, degenerate and wander off course. So I leave these thoughts for you to consider for this afternoon.

Beata Beatrix and
the Proud Professor

(On a dream sequence and an Epstein)

Whose side are you on
of the flower and the stone,
or is some other angle yet unseen?

Jacob wrestles with his Angel:
   rock-carver battling
   raw crystal, white –
   pounding it with bolster
   soothing it with sand.

Rough chunks fly of Word made matter
   hewing raw matter
   shaping Mother stone.
A man coaxes meaning from the fabric of the earth,
releasing sense and sinew from syllables of stone.

Twin forms humanoid – winged/unwinged –
   locked onto each other
   at the moment of release.
No spine cracking in an icy hawser hold
but a softening embrace and the moment of relief.

   – Surrender –

"Let me go for day breaketh"
   the eyes roll heavenward,
   the thrashing battle over:
   the moment of release
from pounding, kniving,
heaving against Nature,
   who now, as always, answers
   with silence and a smile.

– Release –

hands drop, the gasp of revelation
face to face
line for line
grip for grip

"Here am I
battling against Truth –
indomitable, pure
inviolable, whole –

but who is there to fight
and what is there to fear?"

– Transformation –

Now the Beast –
audacious, arrogant
engorged, enraged
and purple with affronted pride
beats upon **me** painlessly
and so away I slide…

For certain this one knows not why
contention does not make us free
but, how humbling, there go I
but for this shift in loyalty.

Those who lingered met disaster –
the Beast has swallowed every bone,
the house is void, the Beast is master –
Wisdom says: Leave well alone.

Leaving:
not through lovelessness,
the looking-glass has been traversed,
allegiances have simply switched
and isolation's bubble burst;

thus alone into the world I go

– Unchained –

unburdened save by Beatrice –
fragile blossom of the rock
like the wild orchid, shy
with loving, lovely blessedness;

like the golden-headed Spring
leaning from her upper window
showering her blessings down –

blameless beauty
endless love

all is lost
  without
    your smiling
      light

★

Amaravati, Spring 1991

The Contemplative Heart

From a talk given on the Easter retreat, Amaravati, 1992

SOMETHING THAT COMES UP very frequently around the subject of formal practice is the idea of 'good' meditation and 'bad' meditation. There are some bright or concentrated qualities that we appreciate and that get praised, and we call this 'good' meditation, and then the other – a mind which is busy, confused or over-active – that we tend to call a 'bad' meditation. It's a good idea, however, to look at how we use those terms and why we are making those judgements. Are they really worthwhile? Things can be very deceptive. Even though one recognises that to have a bright, clear mind which is wise, compassionate and selfless and so forth is a worthy thing, and to have a mind which is filled with selfishness, greed, confusion, agitation, doubt, insincerity, one can reckon well, yes this is probably not such a good thing – but we can often get deluded by the appearances of things and make very superficial judgements.

It is possible to develop a concentrated mind just by applying will-power. By being disciplined and practising meditation with diligence and energy the mind can become quite a still, clear space. But what one can also find is that, even though the mind is quite alert and no thoughts are being allowed in, what we've actually got is a police state. We're unconsciously running an autocracy where any kind of intruder is immediately annihilated; it is a sort of spiritual fascism. The result is a very nice, clean, well-ordered country – everything is as it should be – unfortunately, there are a lot of corpses needing to be whisked away and a lot of heavy karma being created. But we've got our clear space, and that's what makes it all worthwhile!

When we investigate we realise that this is a state of suffering – there's perfect control, but no joy. So one has to guard against that, or at least notice the sterilising, numbing effect of all of the annihilation and suppression that we're doing in order to create that particular mental state.

Another frequently discussed subject is that of having some sort of good experience during meditation, where the mind becomes very pure and blissful.

This may not have been induced through suppression or suchlike but is instead a direct experience of the mind in a pure, bright, natural, peaceful state. This of course is extremely delicious and wonderful – very pleasant – but we're not quite sure why exactly this state has arisen. Maybe for a whole retreat we might have managed to drop into this mode – from day three we cruise there for the rest of the retreat. And so we think, "Oh, this meditation business is really good, I like this. I'm going to come back for more." And then of course what happens, even if it has only been for the period of one sitting, is that we're tormented for the next ten years, doing everything we can trying to replicate that wonderful state.

I don't know if this is a true story, but I was told that Leo Tolstoy, who was a Russian nobleman, used to like to work in the fields with his farmworkers. One day while he was scything corn with them, he dropped into a state of absorption, he became completely absorbed in the scything. He worked all day long without a break – just his body moving smoothly and scything the corn. It was completely effortless, he cut masses of corn and all the time his mind was in a blissful, one-pointed state. So, of course, at the end of the day he thought, "Wow," or whatever that is in Russian. Anyway, after that, I'm told he spent many, many years cutting acres and acres of corn desperately trying to get back to that same experience, but he never actually managed it.

Whether it's true or not, it's a good illustration of the hunger to reclaim the wonderful experience. We think, "Well just a minute now: it was a morning sitting so maybe that's why the afternoons don't work so well. Maybe it's the morning sunlight that's got something to do with it," or, "It was in the autumn, maybe the season's got something to do with it," or, "It was a monk teaching last time, now we've got this nun, maybe the feminine energies do something to interrupt," or, "Well, I had a stool then and now I've only got this cushion and maybe if my back was just a little bit…" – endless manoeuvrings and adjustments, trying to figure it out!

We can go into agonies trying to replicate those same precise conditions where we experienced the wonderful feeling. So what was originally a very pure and fine, wholesome experience becomes a cause for incredible misery – tantalising us with a sense of longing.

We can still make a problem out of it even if we do find ourself in that kind of calmness and brightness. Someone I was talking with today was saying how he had never experienced any kind of blissful or calm mental states before and then, for the first time, on this retreat, suddenly there it was – but then he thought, "Oh dear, what do I do now?"

For so many years we've had to wrestle with thoughts and feelings, agitation and restlessness, so that's what we've come to know meditation to be. And then suddenly, "boop" – nothing to wrestle with – and we feel, "Oh dear." The restless feeling is still there: the feeling of, "I should be doing something, I should be working with something here," and so we end up being at a loss with how to handle it. Even though there is a bright mental state there can be a ground-swell of disquiet, uncertainty and disorientation. So even though the mind is concentrated and clear we find ourselves unable to really be with it. We feel that we have to fiddle with it or put something in to it or protect it from leaving.

So, what all of this goes to show is that what we think of as a 'good' meditation can easily be not so good at all.

The same is true of what we think of as a bad meditation. Often we have got a whole lot of mental stuff – repressed emotions and feelings from the past, memories, experiences, anxieties about ourselves or about other people, about the future, and a lot of unacknowledged, unnoticed conditioning and attachments that are there. Meditation is a very good way of freeing all that up.

It's rather like scrubbing a cooking pot. It's only after a lot of scrubbing that you get to the black, baked-on stuff down at the bottom and it only starts to get loosened after some time. Meditation is rather like pot cleaning; we're getting down to the serious grime, the stuff that's been there for years. So, to be sitting for a period of meditation and just be experiencing a whole maelstrom of feelings and thoughts can actually be the result of good work that's being done. This is the muck that's coming off the bottom, it is part of the cleansing process, the deconditioning, liberating process.

So if we think, "Oh dear, it's all going wrong. My meditation is useless," we're perhaps judging the experience in the wrong way; it can easily be a very good thing. Perhaps we're finally releasing our grip on all this stuff and allowing it to be made conscious. We need to open the mind and allow whatever is there to surface, so then we can acknowledge it, understand it and let go of it.

This is such an important aspect of meditation that it's actually a very helpful thing to do deliberately. There are many different ways of cultivating this, but one of the most accessible is to use deliberate thought to make ourselves conscious of desires, fears, doubts and the attitudes of mind that we have. To make those conscious we bring them into the forefront of the mind and think out all the worst possibilities, all the things that we most dread. Or to think through the most painful memories or the strongest attachments that we have – just to make them clear.

One first needs to establish a basis of tranquillity in the mind; then one simply drops in a particular thought or idea. Often one focuses on areas of emotional strain or struggle, because it's usually in the emotional world where we experience most of our suffering. As a society and as a culture we tend to be quite unconscious of our emotional world, or at least at a loss with how to handle it. So one can just introduce a thought or an idea; or bring up the face of a particular person – our father or mother, our husband or wife, our child or our lover; or we can bring up a particular doubt to voice to ourselves – whatever is the thing that most strongly affects us. Then, as we bring that idea to mind, one brings the attention down to the area of the heart.

The heart is the centre of our feelings, but in this practice we're not trying to analyse them. If you think the thought, "Did my mother really love me?" – that's a good one, nice and easy. "Does my husband really love me?" or "Do I really love my husband?" Whatever is your favourite flavour: "Should I be a

Buddhist nun?" "Should I disrobe?" Whatever we use, we're not trying to analyse or even to figure out the question conceptually. We just raise the question and then bring the attention down to where we feel the emotional response to it. Then we're able to witness the flow of emotion that occurs around those questions, around those areas of our life that we can't see clearly when we are actively involved, e.g. if we are around a particular person where there is a strained relationship, or where there is some heavy memory.

When we're in a meditation sitting we're in a benign situation, we're not faced with that particular person, we're not having to perform in response to them – instead we can just witness the habitual reactions that are there. If you remember a scene of violence in your childhood, or you remember someone who has hurt you badly, or you think of someone that you're passionately in love with – you can watch the play of those emotions as they occur within your heart so that you can get used to them. We can get to know them in a safe environment, they're not having to be acted upon. That way we can understand them, get to know them better.

So, for example, we might have a lot of regret about the past; the mind dwells upon how things might have been…. "If only I hadn't done **that**, then everything would have been all right." One can just raise that thought: "If only I hadn't married xxxxxx; if only I **had** married xxxxxx, then how different it would have been…." Then notice the feeling that is there – what comes with that? So we're not trying to justify it or judge it or criticise it or make anything of it but are just getting acquainted with the power that that has in our mind. And once we begin to know how it works, we are not so easily seduced by it. This process is something that I and the people in this monastic community are very much engaged in … a lot of our training is around using this kind of practice. But it's also something that is very basic to human nature – if we make things conscious, if we 'name' them, then somehow we have power over them and are able to live more harmoniously.

★ ★ ★

To equip ourselves in life for the things that we are going to face – all of the loves and hates, successes and failures – it's an important thing to make ourselves as fully conscious as possible. And to use thought to raise up, to look at and to inquire into all of these different areas of our life. We can also use thought to work with the feeling of selfhood. Not that we're trying to understand intellectually, "What I am," or what the self is, but simply using a thought or a question to illuminate the feeling of selfhood. One composes the mind and waits until it is quiet, calm and tranquil and then just drops into it a question like, "What am I?" or "What is a human being?" If there is a real quality of enquiry there, then we find that, for a moment, the habitual assumptions about what we are are interrupted. There's a moment of hesitation. The query opens the door to our intuition like a key. So when I say, "What is Amaro Bhikkhu?", before the intellect can come up with some very poor but relatively true answers, the very fact that we've raised the question touches our intuition of what we truly are – which is inexpressible, but it can be realised, it can be known.

We're using this form of enquiry to create a kind of gap, to open the door a crack so that at that moment we can break through our normal habitual ways of seeing what we are – as a personality, a woman or a man – and to awaken to that which is the transcendent aspect of reality.

One can use all different kinds of approach. We can use a question or we can just state what we usually think we are: "I am a man," "I am a human being." And even though we might think, "Of course I'm a human being. What else am I – a goat???", actually when we use that sort of statement reflectively, in a meditative space, then what is noticed is that the statement only refers to a little part of the picture; it's just one way of describing certain aspects of what is here but something in our hearts knows that the truth is much vaster. The statement cannot be the whole story.

Just to say our own name can have a most amazing effect. That which is the most familiar thing in the world to us suddenly starts to sound extremely weird. Because we've so associated the sound of our name with being what we are. "Of course that's who I am," and then we realise, "but it's only a label, isn't it?" It's just what we write down on our passport. But what actually is that label referring to…? At that moment the conceptual mind is interrupted, as if a door were swinging open, and then the light of what we really are is able to penetrate. At that moment of hesitation, the mind is in a state of openness. There is attention, non-grasping and non-discrimination. In the mind at that moment there is the sense of mystery, wonderment.

It's almost as if you're creating a doorway between the personal 'I' and the transcendent 'I', so you shift from being "I am Harry Jones of 22, Acacia Avenue" to "I am the Way and the Truth and the Life." That is the shift. (Maybe this way of speaking is a bit too dramatic…. Well, it is Easter and I'm a bit prone to melodrama – so never mind!)

But I stand by the principle – that's basically the reality of it. By questioning our assumptions about things on the immediate level we are then able to penetrate to the greater reality behind it. As, by making our doubts, fears and hopes conscious, we penetrate from the superficial idea of them to the direct awareness of them, so in the same way, we can use this process to illuminate the very quality of selfhood.

Now, emotions are a particularly tortuous area of life. They are generally complicated and it can be difficult to see what emotions are at play. This process of enquiry and making things conscious helps us to unravel the emotional world and its reactive cascades. Often what we think of as being a strong emotion in us is not the real problem. We can have an emotion and then a reaction to that emotion; for example, if we experience jealousy we can develop hatred for ourselves for feeling jealous. As jealousy arises we feel, "I shouldn't be jealous. This is terrible. I'm supposed to be a spiritual person and I just feel mean and selfish and jealous all the time."

So on top of what is a simple reaction we pile a reaction to the reaction. This can go on into reactions to reactions to reactions. I'm sure you're all familiar with the process: feeling anger, and then feeling guilty for being angry, and then feeling helpless because you feel guilty about your anger. The chain goes on. It's a helpful thing to bring attention to these chains of emotional re-action, because otherwise we never break free from the tangle.

Some years ago I found myself madly in love with somebody; this was rather inconvenient because I happened to be a monk at the time. Normal channels of dealing with the situation were not open, as it were! I found my-self completely, obsessively in love with this person, and she was around a lot of the time so it wasn't like I could just ignore it. I found it very difficult to work with – I tried everything I could do, everything in the book to try and deal with this in a good way, but it went on and on – for two years. It was a grim time, and quite agonising because I wanted to stay as a monk. My heart was in the monastic life but this passion was like having a rhinoceros in the shrine room with me; a presence that was always there, a pungent presence that one couldn't quite ignore and which demanded to be fed constantly. It was tricky.

During a retreat, whilst I was doing some cleaning, the woman I had this obsession with walked across the hallway where I was working. It was a re-treat time so my mind was quite alert to what was going on, and I noticed that on seeing her, before the feeling of desire there was the feeling of fear. I thought, "Oh, that's interesting." And then a little voice in me said, "NOTICE THIS." Now why should this be so significant…? This is interesting…. So I pondered it and realised that the problem was actually that of being afraid of sexual desire. "The natural attraction towards this other person is probably not that great, but it's being stoked up day after day with your being frightened of it being there, and not knowing what to do with it." And I knew – "YES! You've got it!"

It was quite ludicrous in some ways but something at last clicked, so in-stead of trying to deal with the feeling of desire and attraction towards the woman I started to notice and bring my attention to the feeling of fear of sex-ual desire, or the aversion to it or wanting to get rid of it. And in two weeks the infatuation was totally gone. It was incredible. If you put it in a movie, no-one would ever believe it. It was amazing – two years of solid anguish and then it was just, "Pop!" Gone. This was very impressive to me and it made me in-clined, from that time on, not to just keep an eye on the most prominent emo-tion or problem but to look at the reactions to that – how the mind is handling the situation.

★ ★ ★

We can look at the way we deal with physical pain in the same way. We can get so involved in dealing with pain itself that we are not really noticing our attitude towards it. We think, "I should be patient with it, I should be able to ac-cept and love this pain." O.K. But actually what we feel is, "I'll love you as long as you get out of here. I'll love you only if you'll leave me." And we start making deals with the pain, "I'll give you five minutes of affection and then **out**!" We ne-gotiate and struggle, and this just makes the whole thing a lot worse.

During the winter monastic retreats here, every so often we would have long sittings, for three or four hours in the afternoon. The rules of the four-hour sitting are that no-one is allowed to leave the room. It was, "You're in. One o'clock, click, doors shut, you're allowed to change your posture. You can even stand up if you need to, but no-one is allowed to leave the room." And the idea is that you stay with the sitting practice for that whole length of time. Now in the folly of my youth I decided, "Well, if these great spiritual warriors of our time, people like Ajahn Chah, can sit without moving all night long, I can at least sit for four hours without shifting." As soon as the thought was formed, my mind panicked. But I stuck to it and even arrived ten minutes early. Normally I can sit quite comfortably for an hour without moving, but on this occasion I was so anxious about the coming ordeal that after ten minutes I was aching and twitchy. Oh dear. My mind was racing and negotiating and desperately seeking some kind of escape – this went on for the first hour.

As we settled into the second hour my legs had formed themselves into a kaleidoscope of burning aches and my mood was less panicked but more like an internalised continuous whimper. At the end of the second hour I suddenly remembered where I was and opened my eyes for a while. It struck me that during the entire previous two hours I had not thought for one second about any of the other fifty people in the room. Was I the only one who was suffering? It struck me deeply how self-obsessed the mind had become in the face of anticipated pain and how it had neatly created a hell for itself. So … what to do?

I had begun to get pretty bored anyway with the endless "Poor me! O *me miserum*" monologue and so I decided that, if I had to spend the next two hours stuck in the same position, at least I could do something useful. So I began to practise *metta* for everyone else in the room – all the other monks and nuns, lay-people on the retreat.

After an hour of this my mood was considerably brighter and the pain in my legs was much reduced. Another three-quarters of an hour went by and I was flying – not literally – but I was having a great time. The pain in my legs had vanished and I was beaming *metta* out of every pore – I knew that I had better not lose my concentration for fear that the pains would return – but after a while I didn't even care if they came back: "Whatever happens, I am happy." By the time that the bell rang I was disappointed – "Oh dear, it's all over…."

It was a powerful lesson: it's only through whole-hearted, sincere acceptance that release is found, and the effect of putting attention onto our attitude rather than onto the big bother of the moment is the thing which eventually does the trick.

"Gold is where you find it"

(Written following a dream wherein a great and beautiful chestnut mare came and befriended me; at the time a voice said, "Her name is Udissa, Light.")

Always alone –
Udissa,
'Light' –
never with the heard.
But
what is that crystal song
an earthly sound of –
silence?
Or is it the first sound
to fall on the Awakened:
the air of gentle rustlings
of bodhi-leaves a-quiver
as, with somersaulting ease,
a breeze
stirs a morning cool in Magadha?
Dawn light
rosy horizon
blue moon
May morning.

Certainty, serenity,
stillness on the razor's edge,
lends an ear
lets fall a tear
for the faithful Earth –
hear.

Now
around these breathing branches,
filamentiferous interface
of earth and sky
where time meets timeless;
the infinite and bounded kiss
in spherical embrace.
At
this
zenith
of green and cold,
is fluttering the pulse and bud
of toiling, teeming,
restless, emergent, collapsing
fever
but

the silent light
illuminates unceasingly.

"Who is it?"
hovers in stillness,
the Wonderful,
and
thumb touches thumb
tip to tip

.

(*Amaravati, 1986*)

Suicide is not Painless

From a talk given in Diamond Heights, San Francisco, June 1993

Question: *I am curious to know – what is the attitude towards suicide in your Buddhist tradition?*

Answer: This is a question that is asked quite frequently. Every different religious system has its attitudes towards suicide, what it means and how it sits within our consciousness, because in every human society this occurs to a greater or lesser extent. From the Buddhist point of view that I am familiar with, in the Theravada world, the approach is quite pragmatic. There is not any kind of doctrinal line on the fate of someone who commits suicide – instead it looks at the mental state that causes a person to do that. We would not make a blanket statement about what would be the karmic result of committing suicide.

Obviously, if you are moved to take your own life, there has to be a degree of negativity, distress or destructiveness there. In Thailand, which is the country I am most familiar with, when someone takes their own life it is regarded as something tragic and painful. The person was likely to have been in a very confused, upset and negative state of mind, and the state of mind in which we die is seen as conditioning the next birth. If we go to sleep at night and we are in a bad mood, generally it is right there on the pillow next to us when we wake up; in the same way, the way that we die, and the state of mind that is there at the time, tends to affect what the mind is going to gravitate towards – at least that is the way it is spoken of.

When someone takes their own life there is not a critical judgement about them, there is no concept of it being a sin or a cause for damnation or anything like that in the Theravadan world. What one tries to do instead is to help that person understand that this has been a violent reaction that is necessarily going to have a painful result. It is recognised that rarely does taking our own life fundamentally solve anything and that, regardless of the causes for it, there is going to be some negative result.

For example, there was a woman who was close to our monastery in

Thailand who had terminal cancer. She was getting thinner and thinner, her body was wasting away and she was in incredible pain all the time. She had two small children and a husband who loved her very much, and she could see that it was very painful for them to see her wasting away in agony in front of them – she weighed about seventy pounds at the end. So she decided to take her life – she took her husband's pistol and she shot herself.

In Thailand what is always done for people who either kill themselves or die suddenly in any way, is that they do not cremate the body but they keep it intact for at least a year. The idea behind this is that, if someone has died violently or has taken their own life, then there is a period of time when their consciousness has the opportunity to get used to the fact of their death – the transition from the human state. Things have the chance to settle down; destroying the body immediately (apparently) throws the person into a greater state of confusion and disorientation, so they keep the body. The body of this woman was thus interred for a year, then after a year it was taken out of its coffin. In this particular case they kept her skeleton in the monastery because she had donated it to be a contemplation object but the rest of her was cremated in the usual ceremonial way.

In normal circumstances the person would just be cremated after a year; during the time immediately after the death, the family and friends would ask the nuns and monks to do a lot of chanting for the deceased person, more so than for an ordinary death. They would perform a lot of acts of kindness and generosity and dedicate whatever blessings came from that to the person who had died, because for a suicide they see that that person is more in need than an average person. There is no blame associated with the person who has killed themself but much more a sense of, "How can we help them?"

The understanding is that for a person who has died, and who is maybe stuck in some sort of confused realm of being, somehow they are benefitted by the loving attention of people that know them and whom they have left behind. Often in the monastery, people would bring a picture of the person who has died and put it on the shrine. Or in your own home you might make a little shrine with a photo and have candles and incense, flowers – to make a sacred space for them and to honour their memory. The family would ask for special funeral chanting to be done every night for a week, then they would bring offerings to the monastery a week after the death, then a hundred days after the death, and then on the anniversary of the death. In this way one is constantly bringing to mind the memory of the person who has died and associating that with things that are creating good karma in their name. Something which is painful and tragic is thus being associated with that which is joyful and restorative. This process not only, in whatever way, benefits the person who has died but it also helps those who remain behind – something which has been heartbreaking then becomes a cause for developing goodness in their own lives. It also becomes a cause to give oneself to the spiritual practice, coming to the monastery and spending time with wise and helpful people. This is the way it is handled in the Theravada tradition in Thailand.

In dealing with the feeling of loss or bereavement, particularly with suicides, there is always the question, "Why? What could I have done? How could I have helped?" Particularly for us in the West, we who are heavy-duty thinkers, there are always a million things that we are convinced we could have done. We get so caught up in, "How it could have been. How it should have been. What I might have done. Why does this happen? Why was this person driven to this? Why didn't I see it coming??" and so on and so forth. We become so involved in the sagas and the possibilities we are creating, that we miss the real grief itself. We fend off the grief by worrying, we fill our mind with thought so we do not actually allow ourselves to grieve and digest the experience.

Earlier this year the father of a very close friend of the monastery committed suicide. I knew him well because he and his family live very near to where my parents are in Kent, in South-east England; he often drives me from the monastery to visit them. His father had worked for over thirty years for a major industrial company as an engineer and middle-man between the manufacturers and the inventors, and it had been his ideas and projects which, for the last 10 or 15 years, had been the major money-spinners for this multinational corporation. At the age of sixty-three he was given three weeks' notice that his job was finishing and that he was going to be fired, and this was whilst he had been away on a tour of several different countries, including the USA, setting up the latest deal for a new project. When he got back, after working long hours and travelling thousands and thousands of miles, he was told, "You are going to be laid off in three weeks' time – thank you very much." He knew that he was approaching retirement age but this was an incredible shock – there was no explanation, no recognition of what he had done for the company. Naturally he was very upset by this.

He struggled through December and January trying to find things to do. He was involved with a local music-therapy group, but his sense of worthlessness and betrayal and depression just got darker and darker. The day that he finished a particular music project, his wife went out to work in the local school, where she had been teaching for years, and when she came back at lunchtime he was hanging in the hallway – a terrifying expression on his face and no note, nothing left behind.

This happened during our winter retreat. I got a call from this friend saying that his father had committed suicide that morning. I talked with him for a long time and then went to the funeral a few days later. It was very moving to see how the family had handled it: this friend, who had been meditating for many years and was very close to his father, said that it was such a shock that he went totally physically numb. He sat in the spot in the hallway where his father had killed himself, his body became ice cold and he could not move. He just sat in that spot for three hours without moving. They made a shrine in that place in the house; they had candles burning, he and his brother and his mother kept a vigil around the clock. When they brought the father's body back, they kept the coffin in the house with the lid open. They surrounded it with flowers, brought all his favourite things into the room and they kept a vigil by the coffin for the whole week. They asked us to do lots of chanting at the monastery, even though this man was not a Buddhist.

Theirs had been a most loving marriage and loving family – it was amazing to see how, in the midst of something so extraordinarily painful, that they just kept returning to the feeling of grief and allowed themselves to digest it fully. It was also compounded by the fact that, not only did the company that he worked for not even send a representative to the funeral, they did not send flowers or even a note – nothing – so there was plenty of opportunity for rage. But they just stayed with the whole thing and digested the painfulness of it. It was remarkable to see how they did not dwell upon the whys and wherefores and what they could have done, but they kept returning themselves to the reality of: this has happened, this is the pain of life, this is tragedy. It was very sad and painful to be there, but it was also wonderful to see how human beings can be with a situation like that and can fully embrace it.

These are the kind of reflections I would bring to mind around suicide. Everyone has to work with their own intuition, every situation is slightly different, but basically it is more important to open our heart to that very feeling of the painfulness of it, than to try and justify it or explain it or to do anything with it. Just to feel that quality of loss and to realise that one of the karmic results of loving someone is the painfulness of losing them, especially in such a tragic circumstance. Then, in response to that, to dedicate your acts of kindness and goodness to that person.

The younger son of the family I have been talking about, late one night shortly after his father's death, felt he had to express what he was feeling. He sat down in front of a typewriter and wrote this piece: talking about his father and the events that had occurred. It is a most clear and beautiful expression of the painfulness and yet, strangely, the rightness of what had happened, and the refusal to blame. Through it all, determined to honour the father's decision, regardless of how painful it was for all of them – that is what he chose to do and we are not going to wallow in our own sense of loss or criticism or worry, we accept that this is how it is, this is what we have got and now we go on from here.

Let us, who have respected Don's judgement so much throughout his life, respect it now and let him go with our blessing. Let us be grateful to him for what he has given us and not sorry for what we may feel he has taken away.

With the gentle, kind and non-judgemental spirit of my father, the family forgive all of those who may feel any guilt or sense any failure for not having saved him from his despair, as we forgive ourselves. We would like this spirit to find its home within you and help to guide and strengthen you as it has us. Let this and not the self-recrimination that so tortured my father be his offering to us at this time. He withheld the depths of his suffering from us with love. Now let us in his memory have the same compassion for ourselves.

Let us be sad but not too sad.

Andy Price

Dark Mother Dharma

(*A sestina on Prajñaparamita and Mother Kali*)

Pure water, clear as empty space
flowing slenderly in fingers through our mother;
from the timeless field springs living earth,
the deepest humus, beginningless and black,
from these lips comes both the kiss of death
and the sweet liquor of every spirit's song.

Over my head the air is filled with song,
holy vastness, star-drenched edgeless space –
for the hesitant and wolf-suspicious, death –
infinite sky, the cavern of Dark Mother.
With half a smile she parts her robe and into black
black, through singing space I tumble far from earth;

somersaulting, is it I or spinning earth
that folds the envelope of void ? The song
dissolves and merges with electric black
whorls of matter, dark mysterious space
inside and out, there is only Mother
Nature, the curling currents of her hair – no death

deceives for she is the Source – she stamps a clashing anklet. Death
and birth are but the flashes of her eyes; blue earth,
the peacock iris gate through which every mother,
father, daughter, son and war become her song.
Every child of Nature is but a chord in space:
every mountain, murderer and starlit black

and swelling sea is gathered into that maw so black
the promise of it only could be death –
instead, beyond her scarlet lips is vibrant space
thrice measureless, and there is only She. The earth
cries and sleeps and sings its holy song –
YES – knower, knowing, known are sacred Mother.

A tumbling massacre, the hair of swirling Mother;
I drown in fragrant waves of inky black,
dissolve into the source of every song –
all here conceived as 'I' is only She, and death,
that darkest word of all the tongues of earth,
is but a turquoise crackle in the combing out of space.

Mother essence dark, no hiding place for death –
Black One your beauty shines – a thousand-coloured earth-
song, ringing in a vast and listening space.

Amaravati, April 1994

Emerald Buddhas

This is an account of a teaching tour made in Northern Ireland in the spring of 1988, shortly after a terrorist attack on a Catholic funeral in Belfast. Anagarika Jakob and I spent much of the first week in the company of Paddy and Linda Boyle and their four daughters.

THINGS SEEM QUIET in the city. After the uproar of the killings last week there was apprehension about our visit, but once here we have found life carrying on regardless. There is tension and suspicion as ever. Nervous glances at the airport – eyes darting into the car as we drive past – everyone is watching everyone, but in a situation of danger this is only natural. People learn to live with the stress, or survival would be impossible. Paddy mentioned yesterday that Tommy, a member of the Buddhist group, and his family had been right by one of the grenades which went off in the graveyard. I asked him –

"How are they coping with all that?"

"I think they've forgotten it already. You just get hardened to it, you have to."

The Buddhist group's little centre, The Asanga Institute, is a good symbol for the situation here: inside a tall ragged house on the Antrim Road – the ground floor windows barricaded with sheet metal – the door armoured as well – up the battered stairway, in a small room at the top, is a clean bright peaceful place to shelter. A symbol of the heart, it is a place of warmth and brightness amidst the forbidding ice-walls of suspicion and fear. It is a place to go and remember the possibility of quiet and illumination, where the powers of goodness can be recalled and cultivated. The symbol of The Refuges is very vivid here.

★ ★ ★

Paddy played videos of the two incidents which had ignited Belfast over the last week or so. These were very disturbing and it was good to have Tony (who had been at the first funeral) right there to talk it over with. It had been pretty hard to cope and he and Tommy had both been quite caught up with it all –

"We know all these guys, we were at school with them, how can you not be involved? If you live there, to a greater or lesser extent you are in it; these are the people you share your lives with, they are your folk, y'know."

It is so easy to forget how much it is the tribal and protective instincts which keep driving this monster of destruction. A few days later I talked to Tommy about all this: he said the Falls Road area had exploded with rage that night – hooded men hijacking cars, throwing petrol bombs off motorway bridges onto the traffic below. He had ridden off to the mountains on his bicycle, hoping to burn off what energy and emotion he could. In trying to come to terms with it – and then the murder of the two soldiers – he said he kept thinking of Enniskillen, where an IRA bomb had killed eleven innocent people and injured many more on Remembrance Day last year. He had never really accepted that his people had perpetrated that outrage – but he realised now that the people in that town felt just as he and his did in the Falls after the graveyard killings. When he mentioned this to others, most were sobered by the thought, realising that the situation was identical.

A day or two later we went to Enniskillen to give a public talk. Once we arrived in town and met up with Bob Kelly, we were whisked off to his family's lovely house, perched on a steep hillock above the church of this village, Ballinamallard. He and his wife welcomed us with great respect and cordiality. Their daughters were very shy at first but after we had eaten, as I was talking with Bob over a cup of tea, I noticed a small furry creature edging across towards me. Silently it inched closer and I recognised it eventually as a skunk. It tilted its little nose up and cocked its head in greeting – doing the job for the little girl whose hand was animating it. I greeted it and asked its name –

"Flower," came the whispery reply. Soon my conversation with the skunk proved unnecessary as the two girls became brave enough to talk to us direct.

This town has had a shadow on its name since the bombing here last year but, far from being shot at – as some in England had predicted – the talk at the public library was a pleasant and calm event. About thirty people turned out, a massive number apparently, and the talk and questions seemed well received by all. These things are always a bit frosty at the start, but if you keep pouring it out eventually things begin to melt. By the second hour I felt like I was with my oldest friends, which on reflection I guess I was – the presence of Truth, the great friend, how good to see you again.

★ ★ ★

The morning after the public talk Bob drove us to a large forest on the southern shore of Lough Erne. We followed a narrow lane through several miles of pines to a cliff edge high above the water. Below us was spread the great stretch of blue with large islets scattered here and there. We wove our way back to Ballinamallard through the long rolling roads, rapt in conversation on Buddhist life.

After packing up and farewells, we took the long road back to Belfast, passing through Armagh and Newry down by the border with the South. Traversing this country there is the constant feeling of being in two parallel worlds: the land of perfect little hills and pocket-sized farms, ancient hedges, empty roads and crystal air; a land of unhurried and gentle folk, strong in heart and spirit. On the other hand, it is a place of rain and black helicopters, police checks, barbed wire and bullet-proofing. We passed the church hall in Enniskillen where the bomb had exploded; like a headless corpse the whole of the roof and upper walls were as if they had been sliced off, the gaping innards of the place opened to the sky.

★ ★ ★

The next couple of days were spent in and around Belfast, spending time with people from the Buddhist group. The presence of the Troubles and divisions in the society made a continuous impact on the mind.

During the afternoon we walked up to MacArt's Fort, on top of Cave Hill, which overlooks the whole of Belfast. It was a shining day of vivid blue skies, arcing over all the land and sea below us. The city seemed so innocent from that height. The slate roofs of the Ardoyne, combed like a well-ploughed field, the gentle blue haze settling in still air, the thrum of engines from the motorway – who would have thought that the human mind could have turned such a haven into a horror story. From above there was no sign of anything but charming busy-ness; drivers and pedestrians, workers and children, as blameless and empty as wooden dolls. This distance epitomised the principle of detachment – with aloofness you could see all the drives and strains, compelling strictures and values of the system, were nothing but human creations. But it also echoed the insensitivity of selfishness – a person distanced from the feelings at the heart of the city.

North from Belfast the towns are more often decked with loyalist Union Jacks, red white and blue kerbs, well-tended murals of William of Orange, "1690" and "No Popery Here!" It is hard to believe how strongly we need to defend our identity against the foe; fear, suspicion, mistrust, centuries of aggression and catalogues of misdeeds all mingle to form the position-taking of today. Rays of hope get extinguished as fast as they are kindled; however, it is for sure that peace is possible – in the wake of all battles eventually flowers return.

★ ★ ★

A day travelling around the countryside of the North softened the jarring images which had dominated the trip so far. This led us gently into the atmosphere of the retreat which was to be held in a woodsman's cottage, beside a large forest, at the southern end of Strangford Lough.

This house could not be much more perfect: a lot of work is required to keep the wood fires in, there is no electricity and only gas-light downstairs – this lends itself to the rousing of mindfulness in getting around in the dark, conserving batteries and developing general care and sensitivity for the physical supports.

Running up to the retreat there was often the feeling – "These people are depending on *me,* it's their first long retreat and *I* have got to produce the goods to help them. What if I fail? – If they all get fed up and leave? If it just becomes a crushing endurance test? Oh dear … and it's all up to *me!*" the proliferating mind burbling on. The sound of 'I am', 'me' and 'mine', a resounding foghorn of wrong understanding.

Listening to this kind of mental creation, there comes a natural response of letting the self-centred elements dissolve. Why turn an idea about the future into a personal problem? I began to reflect: "I am not going to Ireland to zap these people with ethereal vibrations and entrancing Dhamma talks, nor to rescue a nation from the grip of savagery. I am not even going to try to teach anybody anything." I made the intention clear to just go and spend a week in the woods with some friends; the time would pass, efforts would be made to cultivate the good and whatever came out of it I would endeavour to learn from. As the retreat began I said all this to the retreatants and encouraged them to regard the forthcoming time in the same way – simply to be there and make efforts to learn from life, however it happened to be. It makes such a difference when life is viewed in terms of universal nature rather than self.

★ ★ ★

Clumps of celandine and saxifrage border the well-beaten tracks of this forest and, from the bramble-buried mass of an ancient log, a colony of wood anemones peaks out. The air is dense and still, full of the growing light of an April evening as spring roars into its full spate. In this land of spirited and powerful people, the imagination soars to convey the wonderful balances, formless, vivid patterns that spin out of each moment as it comes. So simple yet so mysterious, awesome, testing, frightening, beautiful and terrible – familiar and safe, the oldest friend, yet a yawning, hungry chasm of possibilities. When you can't go forward and you can't go back and you can't stand still, what do you do?

Vanish – the Truth supports itself.

I tried to guide the retreat so that there was not a 'super-concentrate and get high' environment, but rather that of focusing the mind to see what is habitually done at the interface between the mind and the world. It seemed a crime to be on the edge of this lovely wood and not to take the chance to meditate amongst the trees; so, once people were well settled in, we spent most afternoons there. With the mind open – feeling the moment with the whole being – all positive and negative aspects would naturally fall into alignment. You would find yourself at the centre of some vast arboreal mandala – a spread of projection, perceptions, proliferations, all strung together in a web of intricate harmony. Leaves glittering in unison as a billow of wind would stir the forest. Love and hate, anxiety and hope all shimmering in their individual perfection.

★ ★ ★

It is evening now on Dundrum Bay. I write this leaning on some dry seaweed perched on the edge of a sand-dune. A few feet in front of me a small river runs its last race before merging with Father Sea. The tide rushes in to meet it, now well astir and surging in the stiffening breeze, quick and vibrant in counterpoint to the dark Mournes rising from the horizon to our south.

After the retreat Jakob, Nick Scott and I headed off for a few days' walk, along the coast and up over the Mountains of Mourne. The retreat had been good, but I am sure it was hard work for everyone – as a first retreat, though, that hardly came as a surprise. To wish it otherwise would have been a frustration – what a relief that we do not take unremitting success and happiness as our refuge. Perhaps we set too much store by the examinations which we create

with our thoughts and then feel we have to bluff our way through with hypocrisy and deceit – maybe they do not mean so much after all. Does this cliff, this sea, these lichens, this seal who watches us at breakfast, do they really know or care about all the attainments and problems conjured into being by the mind?

Next morning the sky came clear and blue, the day warming to Mediterranean heat. The boots Paddy had lent me fitted well enough, but large blisters had appeared which I had swathed in padding for protection – all to no avail – each step was painful. We turned off the main road, and joined an abandoned railway line which took us all the way to Dundrum town. Even though this was leafy and thick with the delights of new spring growth, I was quite blind to the bursting greens around me. I noticed my thoughts were becoming childlike and frustrated – a regression to simple self-hood followed pain, whining and complaining like a spoilt five-year-old.

"My feet HURT. I want to stop. It's not FAIR!!"

We reached Dundrum and, with a change into my sandals, the world took on a different face. The sands of Murlough Bay were completely empty. During the walk along the beach, amidst the vast open sunlit space, with the cloud-capped Mournes before us, all the negativity of the morning slowly played itself out. One step after another, the mind's additions to the moment became quite clear.

Avril, who had been on the retreat, had invited us to stop by her parents' house in Newcastle. We spent a while with her mother who chatted with us with great interest. Avril was utterly delighted that we had come, it turned out that it was her birthday, and she glowed with gladness at this brief visit. As Nick pointed out, for many people interested in Buddhist life, to introduce their families to what is so significant to them is very important.

★ ★ ★

Newcastle sits at the very foot of the Mournes so, after leaving Avril and family, we climbed solidly until we reached the tree line below Slieve Donard, the highest peak.

Next morning we aimed to break camp quite early and climb to the top. By then the cloud had dropped to swirl around us but we could see a peachy glow beneath, showing the lowlands to be sunny and clear. Through the cloud we reached the pass below Donard and, although it was in the direction opposite to the one we wanted to take, we decided to climb it anyway. Now and again a break would appear and a sudden flash of the valley and mountain-sides would strike us.

"Eet is like a mirakle", said Jakob in his gentle Slavic accent. "Now you see it – now you don't!"

We left our packs at the base, ascended through the thick white whisps and soon found ourselves at the summit. We sat at the foot of the cairn we had seen from so many miles away and could only make out a fifty-foot circle around us. This bore a striking resemblance to how it often is in the religious life: all the work can be done, but until the natural conditions come into line and support it, there need be no vision to bear witness to the Truth.

It was curious how all through the day – and to be truthful through the whole journey to these mountains – a song about the Mournes that I knew from years before, rang through the mind more than the feel of the mountains themselves. When we get used to thinking about life all the time, all we notice is our thoughts, not life itself. This also appears as a perpetual search to know – "Where are we?", "What time is it?", "What is this thing called?" – seeking for names and knowledge to capture the hidden spirit and fix, in this uncertain mysterious world, some vestige of permanence and solidity. It is more inviting to drift into some sentimental idea about the hills, than to absorb the rocks and heather, the mighty crags, the whispers of grass bending to the wind. It is strange how the mind goes: we are more ready to worship our images of the Buddha than to realise Buddhahood itself.

> Don't you go followin' them fashions now Mary McRee,
> In the place where the dark Mourne sweeps down to the sea.

★ ★ ★

Our journey ended safely with a long drive back to Belfast, a good bath and a softer bed for the night. The next day our flight to England was due so we bowed out, taking many fond feelings with us.

Here, at the germinal stages of things, is the promise of great goodness. I feel honoured in helping to set the seed and to cultivate the ground. As I leaned on the Mourne Wall up at Hare's Gap, I felt my heart melting deep into this land – pouring in through the treasured jewel of these mountains, pouring through to permeate the nation. Ireland's good spirits have done us proud, this whole adventure has been a charmed and blessèd event. In this land the spiritual life has long been valued and now this branch of the Sangha, having sprung from the forests of Thailand, has endeavoured to practise the Buddha's Way and offer it to the people here. This most precious of treasures now comes into Ireland, a fitting shrine for an offering from the land of the Emerald Buddha.

Life Without Sila is Like A Car Without Brakes

A talk given in Diamond Heights, San Francisco, Summer 1992

HE SUBJECT OF *SILA*, or virtuous, beautiful conduct, is a very tricky area which people often misunderstand. It is therefore an area where we can benefit from some guidance and instruction – some understanding about how to best conduct ourselves in the manner in which we relate, both to our own life and to other people.

Often, we are attracted to the Buddha's teaching because it cuts right to the very heart of our experience. I was certainly drawn by the ultimate and incisive nature of it – in particular, the teachings on emptiness. This seemed to be one of the most important aspects of the teachings – i.e. that which pertains to transcendent, ultimate reality.

In Western culture, we tend to not want to settle for second best. We want to aim for the top and we can tend towards the same kind of attitude in our approach to religious life. Why bother with the provisional teachings, the kindergarten stuff, when we can go for enlightenment just by the use of these powerful insights into selflessness and emptiness, or into the essential Buddha nature of all beings? You come across this in different Buddhist traditions, particularly Zen Buddhism and Tibetan Buddhism. This aspect of the teaching, that all beings are Buddhas and everything is perfect just as it is, was stressed in Buddhism's early years in the West. "We just have to awaken to the perfection that comprises everything around us. And once we have that realisation we can act in whatever way pleases us. If we are all Buddhas, then we act as Buddhas and everything that a Buddha says and does is perfect." So, the teaching was often interpreted in a way to justify any kind of activity. With the back-up of Ultimate Truth, everything is perfect. So, no matter what I do or how it looks to you, or to the police, it's all perfect.

On an ultimate level this is true. But this truth is something which has caused a great deal of confusion in the Buddhist world. Even though it's a very attractive, powerful, and liberating aspect of the Buddha's teaching, it can be badly misunderstood. I remember years ago being given a book called 'I Am That' by Nisargadatta Maharaj. Reading this book is like listening to God speaking – mighty stuff. In one passage somebody asked Nisargadatta about his own spiritual training. He very rarely referred to any kind of training at all but just to the act of being awake. He said that if you just wake up to the reality of what you **are**, then everything is fine. The questioner persisted and eventually he said: "The teacher told me, 'You are the Ultimate Reality – do not doubt my words.'" Nisargadatta's comment then is something like: "So, I just acted accordingly." End of subject! I remember thinking, "That's it!? That's all there is to it? Maybe **he**, as some special kind of person, was the Ultimate Reality, but what about all the rest of us?" It was so raw and direct, but, eventually, something in my heart said, "Yes, it's true – for everyone. That's all there is to it."

But then we tend to find that what may have been a valid insight, after a while, just becomes a memory of some thing that we believe we have accomplished. We take it as some kind of credit card that we can keep spending on and never pay the bill – because there's no-one there to send it to. It is just as if you received your account from Visa and returned it to them saying, "There is no-one here. No-one actually owns this card. Therefore here is your bill returned." If you did this you'd soon receive a visit from someone in a uniform!

This interpretation has been a common occurrence in the West, causing a lot of distress: people have taken some big mystical experience, or ratification by a spiritual authority (such as being named a Dharma Heir) or some approval by a teacher of great reputation, as an indication of their enlightenment. I've heard of people saying, "You don't understand what I do because I'm enlightened and you are not. Therefore, you can't understand the motives of my actions. You should not question what I do." **Anything** can be justified by this outlet.

In Christian history something very similar to this was known as the 'Antinomian Heresy' (literally it means 'exempt from the law'). There was a group of early Christians who believed that anything done in the name of Christ was a pure act. They caused a lot of trouble and were eventually squashed by the church. I find it interesting to see that the same dynamic occurred so long ago (and has done a few times since then in the Christian world). Individuals thinking that, if they have some kind of credential or authority behind them, like Jesus or a great Guru or Roshi, who says, "Okay, you've got it. Well done, I'm right behind you. You are the owner of the lineage. It's not you acting, it's just the Buddha nature within you" – taking that for granted, we don't necessarily recognise our own, ego-motivated actions, desires, opinions and views. Or we justify them as being 'Sleeping Buddha' or 'Angry Buddha' or 'Lustful Buddha' and drift further and further off the path. And usually we find that we've taken a number of people with us.

I'm sure many of you are aware of the distress caused in Buddhist circles over recent years around this point and this misunderstanding. As I have said, this ultimate viewpoint is valid. It has its own verity – that qualities of good and evil are only relative truths. Somewhere in Shakespeare's 'Hamlet' it says, "There is nothing either good or bad, but thinking makes it so." That is certainly true from the ultimate point of view, but from the relative perspective there is definitely good and there is bad, right and wrong. There is beautiful conduct and that which is ugly. So we must not only take things from the ultimate perspective, but use a bit of common sense as well; not just operate from idealism but look at life in terms of realism and practicality too.

It is stressed over and over again in classical Buddhist teachings that a deep insight does not negate the need to behave respectfully and carefully towards other people, to the things of the earth and towards social conventions. One of the disciples of a Master of Ch'an meditation was telling me that, even though his teacher is spiritually very highly accomplished, he very rarely gives talks on emptiness. This despite the fact that he is eminently capable of doing so. In most of his Dharma talks he teaches about doing good and keeping the Precepts. Regardless of his audience he tends to stress the need for a profound sense of moral integrity.

This monk also told me an interesting story about their early days, in the Sixties, when their monastery was situated in an old mattress factory down in the Mission District of San Francisco. In those days, amongst all the other luminaries of San Francisco, there was a character called Sufi Sam. He was one of the psychedelic gurus of the time. Sufi Sam was quite a wealthy man who kept open house and provided free psychedelics and booze for anyone who wanted to come and join the party, that is, be part of his group and/or join in the general spiritual free-for-all. He pulled in quite a few people and actually helped a good number of them. He was very much a do-whatever-you-want-to-do, be-whatever-you-want-to-be kind of teacher, as far as I understand. And he taught that we are all God/Buddha/The Great Whatever-it-is – however you want to name it.

As the story goes, one day Sufi Sam fell down the stairs and died. The following day about 20 of his disciples – slightly starry-eyed, long-haired colourful characters – showed up at this very strict Chinese meditation monastery. They explained that on the previous night, following the death of Sufi Sam, eight of them had all dreamed the same dream. In their dreams, Sufi Sam appeared saying, "You should go to see Master Hua and you should take refuge with him. Don't carry on the way I've been teaching you. Go with him and tidy up your act." It was interesting that, coming from a very liberal and open-ended approach, Sufi Sam should say (albeit under slightly exotic circumstances – from the other side) that what his disciples should do is learn how to contain and restrain themselves and guide their lives in a more wholesome way.

When Ajahn Chah came to the West he noticed that many people asked questions about selflessness, emptiness, and Ultimate Reality. Yet he could see how people were, how they operated, and he started to stress the keeping of Precepts – he tried to bring people down to earth. He saw that what we did **not** need was more of a passport to ignore the practical realities of human living by spacing out into some pseudo-transcendental realm, making that our aim whilst neglecting the world of relative truth.

The reason why the Buddha put a lot of emphasis on the Precepts, and also why the more orthodox Buddhist teachers stress them in other groups in the West, is precisely because of the pain and difficulty caused when we don't abide by some kind of guidance system. You can liken not adhering to a moral discipline to driving a car without brakes. (This is a very apt symbol for San Francisco – you've got some pretty impressive hills here!) If you imagine what driving a car without brakes here would be like, it doesn't take much to recognise that you could really pile up seriously.

So, that's what the aspects of self-control and self-discipline are about within the Buddhist training – just making sure that the brakes on your car work. Having a car that can accelerate and go places fast is fine, but if you don't have brakes, when the road bends you will be in trouble. When we reach a stop sign or a crossroads we need to be able to stop. Life is not all empty roads and green lights; other traffic, red lights and so on abound.

What you find in the Buddha's approach towards *sila,* or virtue, is that it is not an imposition upon life – as if he were thinking, "All religions are about telling people that they can't have fun, so I suppose mine will have to be that way too." His approach was neither an effort to put the dampers on everything people find enjoyable, nor was it a gratuitous imposition of rules upon people. But my experience of it (and what initially attracted me to the Teaching) was that it was a simple effort to pinpoint the areas of life where we get ourselves into trouble most easily, where life is most karmically loaded; so it's more like pointing out the danger spots and encouraging us to be careful. The Buddha wasn't saying that something is inherently bad or wrong, but that if we don't develop some kind of sensitivity to these difficult areas of our lives, if we don't look out for trouble spots and problems, it's like driving with your eyes closed, or like driving without brakes. "You're going to be fine for a while, friend, but don't expect me to be around to pick up the pieces when you collide with something."

Looking at the Five Precepts for the Buddhist laity, they are very much presented in this spirit. They are there as guidelines to help us, not as the voice of the Lord dumped upon us. So, often people are concerned about what sort of standard to follow, how strictly to apply the Precepts. This is, of course, up to each individual. The Buddha presented them in quite a formalised way so that there is a clear standard, but we can apply them in differing strengths. In different cultures, what is considered right and wrong varies somewhat.

The first precept is not to take the life of any living creature. This comes from a basic respectfulness of life and is about controlling aggression. If it is taken very scrupulously, then we avoid all unnecessary taking of life – even the tiniest insects, mosquitoes or the greenflies who are doing terrible things to our roses. The precept is there to make us think about what is most important to us. "Are my roses more important, or is the life of this creature?"

I once had a potted plant, a chrysanthemum. At first it looked vital and healthy with lots of flowers, I suspect because it had been jammed full of chemicals in the flower shop. Then, of course, it got a bit exhausted. As you might know, when a flower gets weak the greenflies sniff it out from across the garden. After a while this poor plant was covered in greenfly. I wondered what to do about it. First of all I picked the greenflies off with a feather and took them outside. This was quite laborious because they multiply at an alarming rate. Eventually, I looked at my plant and said, "I am not going to keep a plant anymore. I'll look at it as a greenfly farm. I'll just keep pet greenflies instead!" (Did any of you ever read e e cummings' poem about his uncle Sol's worm farm?)

I am not necessarily suggesting that this is the approach one has to take. But, certainly, we can terminate a lot of suffering by changing our attitude to what we expect or want out of life.

Last weekend we were down at the Ojai Foundation having a meditation day, but we were not allowed to use any of their buildings. It seemed that they'd had some problems with the planning authorities so we had to have all of our sittings outside. In that area of the State, there is a very potent biting fly. We could feel these little flies landing on us as we tried to meditate. It was very good for concentration as we felt these little critters land and sink their jaws in. Quite naturally, the first reaction is, "These flies are obstructing my meditation practice, they shouldn't be here." But then I realised that I was just getting annoyed with them for biting me. From their perspective, **we** came and sat on **their** hillside, a five-star food source, radiating heat and all sorts of interesting smells. So they think, "Well, whoopee. Drive-in, free burgers." If we just change it around and consider instead – "I'm not here to meditate, I've just come to feed a few flies. I'm having a fly-feeding day. Of course, if I am going to feed such flies, it is going to hurt a little bit. That's just part of the deal." By changing our mind around we can relate to the whole world in a very different way.

I've just used these examples so we can see how to work with the precepts and use them to help us live in a much more unselfish way. But the precepts don't only relate to external things, they also relate to the inner world. We try to refrain from killing off anything in the mind, like wanting to kill our selfishness, anger or jealousy. Rather we try to develop a mind which is able to work with, accommodate and deal with things in a non-competitive, non-confrontational way. We learn to work with the differing aspects of the mind rather than attacking and aggressing against them.

The second precept is about acquisition or greed, the desire for owning things. The text of the precept is: "I undertake to refrain from taking that which is not given." Which means that we need to learn to live just by what comes to us, to live without taking more than we need from life. So it not only means refraining from stealing possessions or money or defrauding people, but also developing a sense of contentment with what we've got, learning not to chase things just for the sake of acquisition. In this culture, this is a highly rebellious principle: most of us here this evening are not hell-bent on becoming millionaires by the end of the year, but still, the whole ethic of 'more is better' easily creeps into us. Even if we're way above wanting fancy cars or loadsamoney, we can still want loads of spiritual acquisitions – sublime states of mind, beautiful Buddha images, or wonderful spiritual books. Often there is greed for significant experiences; these we can end up using solely to gain a reputation for having great wisdom, or to inflate our egos or to impress our friends. So the second precept is helping us to guard against greed of all kinds, and accumulation for its own sake.

The third precept is probably the most tricky one. I have heard tell how, when Ajahn Chah came to the United States in 1979, he was teaching at IMS and giving a talk about the precepts to an audience of around 100 people who were on retreat at the time. When he got onto the third precept, which is about sexuality and the proper use of sexual behaviour, he went on for about twenty minutes without giving the translator a chance to get a word in. He really got into his stride! It was quite a task to convey it all in English, but one could see that this was obviously something that needed to be explained in detail. It's an area which is very personal to people and it is difficult to have an objective standard for it – particularly in today's society where many of the traditional boundaries have shifted radically.

I've contemplated this question a lot because people have asked about it so many times over the years. To use a classical standard – e.g. to say that people should not have sex before marriage – is so completely out of tune with the way life is in the Western world these days that if I promoted such a standard there would probably, and rapidly, be a much smaller group of people who gave any credence to the things that I said! Even just the idea that a relationship should be between one man and one woman is a great presumption nowadays. Because to be in a partnership of a man with another man or a woman with another woman is pretty common – particularly in this town! So one needs to have some sort of objective standard, whereby sexuality is not just being used as a distraction, for some selfish end, or simply to maximise pleasure for oneself, but much more with a quality of responsibility and commitment. A standard that I might suggest (and this is just for everyone to consider...) is to refrain from engaging in sexual intercourse with anyone you wouldn't be prepared to spend the rest of your life with. Not **intending** to, just *prepared* to. This is only a suggestion – I don't want to give anyone heart failure.

Now it might seem to be a bit of a cheek for someone who has been celibate for the last fifteen years to put such a thing to you. However, even though I was quite libertine in my ways, this is actually the standard that I used to live by before I was a monk; and this was before I was even a Buddhist. I did slip occasionally(!), particularly if I was blind drunk, but I must say that I found it a really helpful standard to consider: "Well, would I be prepared to spend the rest of my life with this person?" If the answer was "No," I found it much better to relate on the basis of friendship and to avoid going into the area of sexual engagement.

This is just a standard for you to contemplate; it might seem somewhat extreme but it does carry the use of sexual energy, and the sexual nature of our bodies, with a due sense of responsibility. So that sex is not just used for pleasure-seeking and so forth, but is a way of bonding ourselves to another person in a way that is wholesome, supportive and beneficial to both sides.

The internal aspect of this standard is that we're not just trying to maximise the pleasure principle generally; instead we're inclining more towards a sense of responsibility, of caring for all things mental and physical rather than just using different kinds of pleasure to distract ourselves from boredom or for taking our mind off more painful things.

The fourth precept is on 'right speech'. In some of the Buddha's descriptions of the Five Precepts, he spent more time on this precept than he did on the other four precepts put together. This was quite striking to me when I first came across it, because what it said to me was that speech is our primary area of contact with other people, it is how we relate with others most immediately, most directly and most repeatedly; it is also the most loaded area of activity. Who we think we are and how we present ourselves to others is largely represented by what and how we speak. So the Buddha encouraged a great deal of care and sensitivity in our use of it.

The precept of 'right speech' is not just a matter of not lying, it's also to do with not gossiping, not back-biting, not talking about people behind their backs, and not using abusive or vulgar speech. In this way we're being careful and not letting those tendencies of the mind spill out into a more karmically loaded situation. We're not bringing those things into being carelessly. By applying sensitivity in the way we relate to other people, we're guarding those unwholesome tendencies of mind and restraining ourselves from just dumping them onto other people. We're not relating to others in a dishonest way, or in a selfish, spiteful, aggressive, or abusive way. Those tendencies of mind are checked at the mind door and not spread out into the world.

The last precept is to refrain from intoxication. To refrain from drink and drugs which cause the mind to become heedless. The popular interpretation of this is that it only means to not get drunk. But the wording of it is pretty clear: it means that one should avoid altogether that which causes us to be heedless. Again, I should reiterate that these sort of standards are not absolute; however, this **is** the pattern laid out by the Buddha, and he did so for a reason. The usual way of thinking is, "Well ... the occasional glass of wine over dinner ... it is uncivilised to say 'no'. People take you out and want to give you a pleasant evening and then you go and upset them by refusing their offer of a glass of Chablis." We can feel that it's quite unreasonable to refuse alcohol, or to not 'allow' ourselves a drop now and then ... or a few mushrooms....

But this is a standard that we're creating for ourselves because we see that, if we are heedless and careless with life, then we inevitably cause problems for ourselves and for other people. If we're more mindful, then we're much less likely to cause the same kind of problems. It's a simple equation – when we're mindful, we don't suffer. There might be pain or difficulty, but there's no anguish. The more heedless and careless we are, the more anguish and difficulty we generate. It is a very direct relationship. If we are deliberately clouding the mind and causing our natural qualities of restraint to be squashed, we might feel great at the time, but I am sure everyone is well-acquainted with what it feels like later on when we realise how we spoke, the things we did and the things that we brought into the world in those less guarded states.

Again, I don't want to present this as a moralistic put-down, I simply bring attention to this so that we can notice what we do when the mind is distracted, confused or is modified in that kind of way.

In the formal ceremony of taking the Refuges and Precepts there is a little chant that the person who is giving the precepts recites. It says, "*Sila* is the vehicle for happiness; *sila* is the vehicle for good fortune; *sila* is the vehicle for liberation – therefore let *sila* be purified."

According to the Buddha's teaching, the whole process of liberation necessarily begins with moral restraint – a respect for the way that we act, speak and relate with each other. We might feel that to follow our feelings, fears and desires – to act in a free and uninhibited way – is Right Action in the sense that we are 'honouring' those feelings. However, that restraint and inhibition can be a very wise sense of right and wrong, and is what the Buddha called *hiriottappa*; he described it as 'The guarding and protecting principle of the world' – *lokapala*. It is that simple feeling of 'This is the right thing to do, this is good, this is noble,' or 'This is wrong, this is ignoble.' To act in a restrained and careful way, keeping the precepts, isn't something which is inherently good – there is no such thing. But what it does is to free the mind from having to remember and live through the reverberations of unwholesome karmic action. If we're unkind and cruel and selfish then we have to remember that. So it's not that 'goodness' is something absolute; more accurately, it is that if we behave in a good and wholesome way, it leaves the mind clearer and more peaceful than if we behave in a selfish, greedy or cruel way, which leaves the mind in a turbulent state. It's a very straightforward relationship.

So we can see that, just by keeping the *sila*, observing the precepts, the mind is naturally freed from remorse. There's nothing horrible that we have done that we have to justify or remember. When the mind is free from remorse then we feel a natural contentment, a sense of gladness that alleviates self-criticism and depression. (This is perhaps a revolutionary approach to the psychotherapeutic treatment of a negative self-image.) In the same vein, along with that quality of happiness, the body and mind become relaxed and at ease with life. We're not caused to be tense and agitated. When there is that kind of physical and mental ease, then we really begin to enjoy the way we are and the way life is. The mind is open and much more bright.

If the mind is content and joyful with the here and now, then we find that it's much easier to develop meditation. If this 'place' is pleasant and comfortable we are not going to want to be off in the past or the future or somewhere else all the time. If San Francisco is a good town and you enjoy your life here, you don't feel like you have to move to Oregon or England, or to the South of France. This principle works in the same way with the mind.

This is why, if we ever want to develop concentration or good states of meditation, then we behave in a very restrained and careful way. On retreats we have a routine and strict discipline so we're not filling our minds with stuff which we have to remember, causing disturbance. The environment is carefully controlled so as not to create that kind of effect. In the same way, if our whole life is being guided by *sila*, then we're consistently providing a quality of joyfulness and contentment in the here and now.

With the development of *samadhi* – the more the mind is steady, stable and open to the here and now – the qualities of insight and understanding naturally arise. The more clearly we look at where we are and what's in front of us, then the more able we are to discern the patterns that are there – the way that life works and functions. And that quality of 'knowledge and vision of the way things are' then brings about a profound seeing into the true nature of reality. The tendency to reject or grasp hold of things is then weakened – as we see into the transient nature of things, we no longer try to possess the beautiful or run away from the painful – instead we experience it directly as a flow of different aspects of nature.

The more empty and serene the mind is in its attitude towards the comings and goings of the changes in the sensory world, the more the heart is at ease with life. There is a realisation of the innate, natural freedom of the mind – there are no obstructions to the natural peace and brightness of the mind. The mind's pure, original nature then becomes the abiding experience, and this is what we mean by 'enlightenment' or 'liberation'. No thing has been gained, it is merely the discovery of what was always there but had remained hidden.

These steps all occur as a process of evolution, one stage following naturally upon another. Just as we grow from babies into infants, into children, adolescents, then into adulthood and old age – so too, if we start with *sila,* then these other steps of the process will occur in time on their own. It is the basis, the *sine qua non* of the spiritual life – you can't get to be an adult without having been a child first. If there isn't that basis then, as far as I can see, we are seriously obstructing that whole process of evolution from occurring. We are disabling ourselves from fulfilling the wonderful potential that we have as human beings.

The Golden State

PART ONE – A FERTILE SEA

This is the first of two pieces which describe a visit made to the United States in the summer of 1990. This first part covers the broad spectrum of spiritual life which was encountered; the second part dwells more specifically on seclusion and monastic practice in the USA.

IT IS SAID that in the past – before the Europeans came – the San Francisco Bay area was so thick with life that the sky would be darkened by flocks of birds as they rose "with a sound like that of a hurricane". Streams were filled with silver salmon; the hills covered with forests of oak and berries, fields of flowers and bunch-grass; seals, grizzly bears, foxes, bobcats and coyotes abounded. It was "a land of inexpressible fertility".

In the last 150 years of 'civilisation' much has changed. But by some strange alchemy the fertility of the area persists: transmogrified from the rich life of local tribes and that of soil and beast, into the inner life, the hearts and minds of the people who now live there.

The USA, a land of opportunity, grew out of a revolution against European values. It was to be a country of freedom and equality. This ideal still pervades American society and probably nowhere more so than on the West Coast, where the majority of 'free spirits' have gravitated. Here especially is a place of freedom of expression, where dreams of all kinds are pursued.

In May of 1990, Venerable Ajahn Sumedho, Sister Sundara, Sister Jotaka and myself were invited to the USA to lead some retreats, participate in a conference on monasticism, and to give Dhamma talks to a number of groups on the West Coast. The invitation came from two groups: Insight Meditation West (IMW), founded to promote Vipassana meditation, mostly in the form of silent retreats and local 'sitting' groups; and Sanghapala, whose aim is to help establish a monastery in California under the guidance of Ajahn Sumedho. These two groups represent, to a large extent, the main sources of interest in our presence in the USA.

The two aspects of our life which they embody – serious meditation practice and traditional monastic form – are in fact closely linked, although the latter is less widely appreciated. It was to help people in the Bay Area have a fuller understanding of monastic practice, its methods and its results, that Jack Kornfield, the principal meditation teacher with IMW, convened the conference 'The Joys of Monastic Life' which we attended.

The practice which Ajahn Chah and Ajahn Sumedho have advocated involves taking Vinaya – the monastic code of discipline – as the basic lifestyle and, from that foundation, learning to appreciate whatever you are with. Putting this teaching into practice, we actually found ourselves able to feel at ease in a bewildering variety of environments: from the Esalen Institute to The City of Ten Thousand Buddhas; from the Zen Center AIDS hospice to a seminar with Huston Smith and a dozen academic philosophers; from a gathering in Chicago of all the Thai monks in the USA, to days of silence spent high in the hills of Northern California at the Bell Springs Hermitage.

The people we seemed to meet the most had been practising Vipassana meditation for a number of years – often through retreats at the Insight Meditation Society in Massachusetts or on the West Coast, with teachers such as Jack Kornfield, Joseph Goldstein, Sharon Salzberg, and Christopher Titmuss. In many of the West Coast urban areas – notably Santa Cruz, Palo Alto, Berkeley, Marin County, Portland, Seattle and Vancouver – fairly large groups of people meet regularly to meditate, listen to Dharma talks and discuss any problems in their spiritual life. These loosely-knit groups of people hold their focus around their teachers and meditation groups, and around Insight Meditation West. In addition to running retreats, IMW is in the process of establishing a sizeable meditation centre, Spirit Rock, in the countryside just north of San Francisco.

A prominent feature of this group's style of practice is the conscious movement away from traditionalist Theravada Buddhist forms. Spiritual practice is shaped around formal sitting and walking meditation, and blended with a Western psychological vernacular to describe the inner world being investigated. This has worked well – very many people have found inspiration and benefit from this approach – but it seems that for some we met, there are areas of spiritual practice left unaddressed … or, at least, some potential in their hearts which has not had the opportunity to flower.

One area where this difficulty appears is in the basic premiss which motivates the practice: i.e. what is assumed at the outset. By couching spiritual work in a psychological idiom – even though it is thereby more accessible – the practice can be construed in terms of 'me and my problems', which I have got to get rid of'. This is fair enough – 'me without problems' is much more attractive than 'me with problems'. However, the longer this premiss is followed blindly, the greater is the resulting anguish. According to conventional Buddhist understanding, the person doesn't **have** problems, the 'person' **is** the problem. It is because of conceiving everything in terms of 'me' and 'mine', in an absolute sense, that we continue to suffer and fret.

So, as Ajahn Sumedho pointed out over the weeks, we have to make a paradigm shift: from 'me and my problems', to 'the Buddha seeing the Dhamma'. Buddha-Wisdom is the ultimate subject – 'The One Who Knows'. And Dhamma – 'The Way Things Are', Nature – is the ultimate object, which can have no owner. As this shift is made, the heart is liberated. The world still is the way it is, but it's no longer a problem, and it's certainly not 'mine'.

A second area of hazy misunderstanding was devotional practice. As with all our retreats, at the ten days organised by IMW at Santa Rosa we had a period of chanting and bowing before the shrine at the start of each morning and evening meditation. We made it clear that joining in was not compulsory, and it took a good few days for many people to get a feel for the rôle of puja in relationship to meditation and self-knowledge. However, by the fourth or fifth day, we noticed more and more vigour coming into the pujas. Ritual and devotion can be a way of reasserting, on the emotional plane, the aspiration to enlightenment – a way of engaging the faculties of the heart, along with those of the head, in empowering the practice of the Path. Likewise, the Sangha embodies an archetypal principle, which can help unite one with the lineage of all who have ever practised as disciples of the Buddha.

The pujas were done in English, to lend a little more to their relevance, and they became a key-note in the practice for many people. They made such an impact, in fact, that by the end of the retreat some of the sceptics professed themselves to have been thoroughly 'sold'. Several Buddhist groups that we subsequently visited particularly requested that we do some chanting, or that I speak on the subject. There is a natural need in us to honour that which is good, higher, more noble, and it seems that people realised that making appropriate gestures of respect on the material level can be something beautiful. In our hearts we are bowing to wisdom, truth and virtue, to purity, radiance and peacefulness, not to a golden idol.

Balancing the intellectual and emotional elements in harmonious measure is also developed outside the shrine room through the work of serving others. In the Bay Area, service was found particularly in the area of hospice care. The growth of Buddhist involvement in care for the dying has been seeded from the long-standing efforts of such people as Steven Levine and Ram Dass. In the last few years, however, it has taken shape as a full-blown hospice programme in three locations under the auspices of the San Francisco Zen Center. The two doctors looking after the hospice ward in a local hospital are Zen Center students and much of the daily care and counselling, assistance to the nurses, etc. is given by a team of some forty volunteers, most of whom are with the Zen Center or IMW.

The joint involvement of Zen and Vipassana students is something that has actively been encouraged by the groups. Not only is the burden of work shared, but meditators are also able to engage their talents in helpful service. Formal meditation and silent retreats can lend a somewhat introverted tone to spiritual life. Generosity and service impel our attention outwards and, to our surprise, we often find that simply by not thinking about ourselves so much many of our mental terrors vanish. Not only do others gain but we do also – the wondrous arising of the 'win/win' situation.

★ ★ ★

The last week that Ajahn Sumedho and the nuns were in the USA was spent visiting Seattle. It is quite a cosmopolitan city and very reminiscent of San Francisco. Liberal and environmentally conscious in atmosphere, it too was a place to which people interested in Buddhist meditation had gravitated. The public talk which had been arranged attracted quite a large number, about half of whom had come down from Vancouver for the occasion.

Our hosts, aware of our full schedule in San Francisco, were keen not to exhaust us with too many events. Thus, most of the days were spent quietly, talking informally with the local Buddhists or travelling around the area.

When not obscured by cloud, Mt. Ranier is a vast volcanic snowy bulk which dominates the city. On the day we went to visit it, the dense cover broke just long enough for us to glimpse the peak. All around, and across thousands of acres of Washington countryside, evergreens carpet the land. In sharp contrast to California, the 'Golden State' (don't say 'brown' when looking at its meadows in the dry season!), Seattle is aptly named 'The Emerald City'. Bearing the brunt of a huge rainfall off the northern Pacific Ocean, it is thus blessed with a dripping lushness all the year round.

The others bade farewell and took off for England. After a brief but very fine visit to Portland, I returned to San Francisco.

★ ★ ★

The people we visited in the Pacific North-west, as well as those we met around the San Francisco Bay, live far from the 'shop-til-ya-drop' mentality of materialistic America. And, even though nowadays a lot of self-based and materialistic thinking has transposed itself into the psychological realm, it is clear that for many, simply making a meal out of neurotic hang-ups in an attempt to solve them is no solution either. Being "a brilliant wounded fragment" may provide some temporary purchase for the need to claw onto life, but bring peace it does not. Early on in our visit – leaning on a balustrade overlooking the Bay from a Tiburon headland, watching a few pleasure-boats scoot about on the water – a broad mustachioed man who had been in Berkeley since the Sixties said to me, "Y'know, America is like a slightly drunk teenager behind the wheel of a BIG car – ya kinda hope they will slow up, wise up or sober up, or at least run out of gas before they crash and burn." If America does have any spiritual hope, one feels it will be through the likes of these people. America is a young country, and just as youth can be obsessed with intense sensuality and materialism, it can also have an intense spirituality, openness of mind, eagerness to learn and readiness to change.

This maturing of values resonated through all the established groups we visited, and also amongst those who came along to the regular talks and retreats that I was invited to give around the Bay Area in July: twice-weekly evening talks, and three evenly-spaced week-end retreats. During this time I was based in San Francisco, in a small apartment just around the corner from 10 Arbor Street where the meetings were held. The aim was to have something of a temporary monastery, where those who were interested could come and talk with the monk, meditate, or just step out of the momentum-driven world for a spell. Being in residence, I was also able to receive people who wished to offer alms, accept invitations to eat at people's houses and conduct blessing ceremonies for babies, houses and the newly-opened Bell Springs Hermitage.

A small amount of publicity had quietly filtered through local Theravada Buddhist circles. At first the numbers of folk coming were low, but it was encouraging to see how, in just a short span of time, the level of interest expanded quite markedly: for a while my list of engagements reached 3 or 4 a day and, by the time I left for England in early August, the shrine room at Arbor Street was getting to be too small to contain everyone.

★ ★ ★

The Bay Area is truly a hot-house for spiritual seekers, yet the people we met did not seem to be those searching for the quick, hassle-free solution to all life's problems ("Free credit – pay nothing 'til April!"). Many had been steeped in one kind of spiritual medium or another – from psychedelia to therapy and meditation – since the late Sixties. These approaches had all promised freedom; many had helped but not quite succeeded in bringing the carefree fulfilment longed for.

While it is true that people will always come and check out a new product on the market, the interest directed towards us seemed to be more than just skin-deep. Buddha-Dhamma is not a cosmetic teaching. It was apparent that the example of the renunciant life, the surrender that comes from participation in a traditional form and the power and directness of the teachings, provided people with something that made a difference.

In this respect, the time I spent at the Esalen Institute is of interest. I was invited to spend a few days there, about 150 miles south of San Francisco on the Big Sur coast – one of the most beautiful spots on earth – miles and miles of rocky bluffs sweeping down to the ocean. Esalen has been the birthplace of much Californian spirituality – in particular, most of the novel approaches to psychotherapy were hatched there.

The spiritual and terrestrial influences mingle at the institute very much like their statue of the Buddha, almost hidden amidst a swarm of flowers, sitting serenely at the heart of the garden. Quite by chance, my visit coincided with a concerted move by the staff to establish more of a daily meditation practice for themselves. They were keen to invite monks and other meditation teachers to come and give them more consistent guidance. Like so many other spiritual communities, they had been through struggles and conflicts, and now felt the need to establish more clarity and cohesion. The Director and other staff expressed their hope to me that, should a monastery be established in the area, we would come and teach there periodically. Therapy is not enough any more!

American culture, for the most part, tries to dispense with the old, and to renew/reform/progress. This theme carries on as strong as ever, but it is significant that the current problems of ill-health, pollution and waste-disposal are reaching impossible proportions and people are waking up to the need to readjust their values. The adjustments have an American flavour, of course, which was evident in the large billboard advertising a **bio-degradable** throw-away camera, or the poster for a new low-fat yoghurt-based ice-cream substitute proudly promising "All of the pleasure, none of the guilt".

The few weeks we spent in the USA brought home the realisation that the rising sensitivity to nature, and respect for the origin, substance and fate of the things we use, was reflected in a true change of attitude in the American Buddhist world. For, rather than just trashing the traditional ways of doing things – leaving classical monasticism and devotional practices entirely behind for the sake of a new, rational and hierarchy-free Buddhism – some people are finding it worthwhile to recycle the old. After all, like other things we try and dump, the old doesn't just go away – it has an annoying habit of hanging around for a long time before it decomposes. What if it turns out that there is a lot there that's still of use? It would be such a waste just to sling it out.

People seem to be looking at traditional monastic practice with a fresh eye; its relegation as a culturally antiquated, worn-out form is being revised. Certainly, some aspects of Buddhist custom *are* redundant and inapplicable to Western society. But, as our experience in Europe has shown, these elements are not related intrinsically to the Dhamma-Vinaya as described by the Buddha. And, as many eminent teachers in Asia point out, it might be good if such aspects of Buddhist custom were discarded in Asia as well.

This visit to the West Coast was arranged in order to provide access to the Sangha and to see if the traditional unit of monastery and lay-supporters had a useful place in American society. The impression that has lingered is not one of friction with people, or of materialistic and violent horrors – even though these perceptions were plentiful enough. These impressions fade, and what fills the heart is a quiet delight, echoing with endless highways of space and light, thick with oleanders ... or islands rising in the early morning out of miles of opal fog.

This is a rich land and there is goodness here – goodness in the earth and in the hearts of the people – and it has been a joy to help the sincere find that which is truly Golden.

The Lesser, The Greater, The Diamond and The Way

A talk given on a retreat held at The City of 10,000 Buddhas, California, July 1991

HISTORICALLY THERE HAVE BEEN DIFFERENCES of opinion about the relative merits of Theravada and Mahayana Buddhism and, if you read much of the literature, they would seem to be quite divergent in their approaches toward Buddhist practice – yet there also seem to be some tremendous affinities.

When I arrived at the International Forest Monastery in Thailand, in 1978, I had never read any Buddhist books and I wasn't actually in search of becoming a Buddhist monk. I was a wanderer, a freelance spiritual seeker, and I just happened to turn up at this forest monastery that Ajahn Sumedho had established a couple of years before, basically as a place for a free meal and a roof over my head for a few nights. Little did I expect, some twelve or thirteen years later, that I would be doing what I am doing now. But when I went there and asked the monks about Buddhism, to explain things a little bit for me so that I could get a feel for what their life was about, the first thing one of them did was to give me a copy of a book of talks by a Zen Master, and he said, "Don't bother trying to read the Theravada literature; it's terribly boring, very dry. Read this, it is pretty much the same thing that we're doing, and it will give you a sense of what our practice is about." And I thought, "Well, obviously these guys are not too hung up on their tradition." The book was 'Zen Mind, Beginner's Mind.'

So, one could see right from the beginning that, even though there is a strength to the particular form within any Buddhist country, one is not necessarily constricted or limited by that. I was there for months before I even heard of 'Theravada' and 'Mahayana', let alone the differences of opinion between them. It seemed that when you actually lived the life, there really wasn't any great disparity, but if you thought about it a lot, and if you were the kind of person who wrote histories and books and had got into the political side of religious life, then that was where the divergences occurred.

I have heard Ajahn Sumedho recount a few times over the years that, for the first year of his monastic life, he had been practising using the instructions from a Ch'an meditation retreat given by the Ven. Master Hsü Yün, and that he had used the Dharma talks from that retreat given in China as his basic meditation instruction. When he went to Wat Pah Pong, Ajahn Chah asked him what kind of meditation he had been doing; at first he thought, "Oh no, he's going to get me to give this up and do **his** method." But, when Ajahn Sumedho described what he had been doing and mentioned that it had had excellent results, Ajahn Chah said, "Oh, very good, just carry on doing that."

So, one sees that there is a very strong unity of purpose; even though there might be historical differences between the two traditions, they are very much in accordance with each other. And one begins to see what the different Buddhist traditions are talking about. They get sectioned out into Hinayana or Mahayana or Vajrayana, as different types of Buddhist practice, but they are basically just different labels which are talking about attitudes of mind and, when the traditions are used wisely, then they will address all aspects of our mind, from the most selfish and mundane to the most exalted. They address all the different levels of our life, and it's only when they are not understood, when people take them as fixed positions, that there is any conflict amongst them.

Theravada Buddhism, for instance, is often taken to represent the Hinayana position, the self-concern of "Quick let me out of here, I've had enough of this mess; I want this to be over as quickly as possible." One can see that that represents a very definite stage in one's own spiritual development. For example, we start out with just a worldly attitude; basically we're not interested in spiritual development at all. We just want happiness, however, and wherever we can find it. We have a worldly outlook and no real spiritual direction at all. So then our first kind of awakening to spiritual life is when we start to acknowledge suffering. We recognise the need to rescue ourselves, to help ourselves.

So, the Hinayana refers to this initial stepping onto the spiritual path and seeing that there's something that needs to be done to sort out our own life. It's a natural self-concern; you don't set about helping other people or being too concerned about the welfare of others if you yourself are drowning. You have to get yourself to some firm shore to begin with. But then basing your spiritual practice around self-concern, and just trying to make your own life peaceful and happy is obviously of limited worth. We can see that if we do get stuck at that level, there is a certain aridity and barrenness that will set in.

I had an interesting experience concerning this recently. Normally my personality is of a friendly, generous, outgoing type, and I've always had quite a fondness for the Mahayana Buddhist teachings. However, I found toward the end of last year that a certain nihilism was creeping in. The abiding tendency was one of "I've had enough of this; I want out." This was really quite unusual for me and it started to come on **very** strongly. The idea of living into old age and having to cope with human existence and the trivialities of life and the tedium of a boring monastic routine was NO FUN. It all started to look incredibly uninviting. It was like being stuck out in the middle of a salt flat with no horizon visible. It was a strong, grinding negativity. I didn't feel friendly toward anyone, I felt no inspiration toward monastic life. The whole thing was a tedious rigmarole.

Every two weeks we have a recitation of our monastic rules and it takes about 45 minutes to chant. This is the regular refreshment of the spirit of monastic community – renewing our aspiration and our dedication to our discipline and our lifestyle. And I'm sitting there reciting these rules and my mind is saying, "What a total farce, what a waste of time this is" – *and* trying to remember the words I'm supposed to be chanting at the same time. Also, this was at the beginning of the monastic winter retreat that I was supposed to be helping to teach; I thought, "This is **really** going to be difficult." I was supposed to be inspiring these young monks and nuns and my mind was going through this very negative state. I was watching this, but there seemed to be a lot of justification for thinking in this negative way. I thought, "Well, maybe I had it wrong all these years, maybe I was just being an empty-headed, overly optimistic fool and being a bored cynic was actually the right path all along."

Then one night I had a very vivid dream, in full colour. In this dream I ate my hands, finger by finger. I pulled off my thumb and then each finger and ate them. It was so vivid I could taste them and it was even a bland taste. I ate the whole of my left hand then started on my right hand, and I ate the first three fingers until there was only my index finger and thumb left. Then something in me said, "Wake up!" I woke up and there was a very, very clear memory of this dream. Instantly I realised what I had been doing. Out of heedlessness I had been destroying those very faculties that were my most helpful friends and assistants. The negative and self-destructive attitudes were covering up and burning away all of the good qualities. The spiritual qualities that were there were being destroyed. It was really a shock to the system, and I realised I had been taking the wrong track. Then something else happened spontaneously. I had not really been thinking about Mahayana Buddhism or the Bodhisattva ideal, but what happened was that I started to say to myself, "Well, I don't care whether I feel even one moment of happiness for myself in this life; I don't care if I have to be reborn ten thousand million times. If I can just do one kind act for one other being in a thousand million lifetimes, then all that time will not have been wasted." Thoughts like this began to come up spontaneously in my mind, and I suddenly felt an incredible joy and happiness, and a feeling of relief; which is strange if you think about it rationally: ten thousand million lifetimes of ineffective activity and complete pain and boredom. But the result was a vibrant joy and delight. It was the breaking out of the prison of self-concern.

When the mind goes into that kind of death-wish mentality, just waiting for it all to be over, then all you're concerned about is yourself. You become blind and immune to other people. Even if you don't want to be, you find that you're building all sorts of walls around yourself. And I could see that this was very much the cause of the spirit of the Mahayana tradition and teaching: to arouse that unselfishness, that readiness, even if it is a pointlessly vast task, to take it on anyway. It then releases the natural altruism and affinities we have for other beings. We recognise our interconnectedness with all other beings, all other lives, and out of respect for that, one feels a sense of joy in being able to give, to help and to serve.

It is interesting that, at about that same time, someone gave me a book which showed me that this principle was found not only in the Buddhist tradition. The author was talking about this principle and gave examples from both the Hindu and the Judaic traditions. He told the story of Sri Ramakrishna and how, before he and Swami Vivekananda were born, he had tracked down Vivekananda (who was his chief disciple) up in one of the high Brahma heavens – he was absorbed in meditation, utterly disinterested in the world, "Close to the mountain of the Absolute". What a great phrase! Anyway, Vivekananda was seated there, totally enraptured in bliss. Then Ramakrishna took on the form of a little child; he wove the body of a golden child out of the atmosphere of this high realm and he started to sing and play in front of this sage. Eventually, after some time, the sage's attention gets caught and he opens his eyes and sees this incredibly charming little child, playing and cavorting in front of him. And finally, with his eyes completely opened, he is looking at the child, and the child says to him, "I'm going down; you come with me." So, Vivekananda went down and joined him.

The other example was of a Rabbi named Rabbi Leib. He was telling some of his disciples, "Before this life I did not want to be born; I did not want to come here. This human world is so full of foolishness and crazy, idiotic people. I had had enough of the whole thing and just couldn't be bothered with it. And then one day this fellow comes along, he looked like a peasant, with a shovel over his shoulder, and he says to me, 'Haven't you got anything better to do than to lie around here all day just enjoying the bliss of eternity? I work non-stop just trying to bring a little happiness, a little more joy, into the lives of other people, and what are you doing? You're just hanging around!'" He said that he was so touched by this person that he agreed to go along. This fellow with the shovel was the Baal Shem Tov, one of the founders of the Hassidim. It is said that he roams around the upper realms of the cosmos looking for likely characters whom he can dispatch down to earth to take care of the likes of us. So, it is interesting to see that this same principle exists in human experience in different traditions.

★ ★ ★

Self-concern takes us into a desert experience – even when we notice that the more coarse defilements of mind have abated or have worn themselves out, when we're not possessed by too much anxiety or lust, greed, aversion, jealousy, or whatever, and the mind is quite peaceful. As you may be aware, now that you've been a week into the meditation retreat, you can be sitting there with your mind quite concentrated, quite still and, rather than feeling rapture or a sense of wholeness and totality, the feeling is one of, "So what? Is this really what the Buddha built his teaching around, this blank mental state, with nothing much happening?" With nothing much in the way of thoughts and feelings, no great passions to wrestle with, it's like being in some little grey room. It's not disturbing in any way, but it seems a pretty tame experience to build a world religion around.

You think, "This is a rip-off! I've been struggling away for five or six years with fear and lust and so on, and now I get to the free space – here we are out in the open – and it's a desert. This is **not** right!" But then, what you realise is that this is not what the Buddha was pointing to as the goal of the holy life, because even though one can't see any outstanding objects causing obstruction or defilement, what is there is **you**, or in this case, **me**. There is the sense of **I** – someone here experiencing – there's a person. This sense of identity, even though it is not outstanding, leaping out making itself vivid, is a constant presence. The ego is a psychological structure that is there like a wall around us, like a prison. And because we are so caught up with life in the prison, we don't notice that we are actually hemmed in. It is only when everything has cooled down and one has a chance to look around and take in the surroundings that one has a chance to feel the sense of limitation, barrenness; there's a boredom, it's just BLEAAGGHH!

Even in Mahayana Buddhism – which is outgoing, geared toward altruism, generosity, compassion, developing a spiritual life for the sake of all beings – if our practice stops at the state of 'Me giving my life to help all others', even if this is highly developed, at the end of it there's still ME and YOU – me who is helping all sentient beings. Even in that respect, even though there can be a lot of joy, you still find this barrier, a sense of isolation or meaninglessness. There's a separation there. So, it is important to use the meditation practice not just to absorb into altruistic thoughts and feelings because, if you notice, a lot of the Buddha's teachings revolve around selflessness, around emptiness, like the teachings on anatta. If there is no self, who is it who's going to be radiating kindness over the entire world? If there's no self, then who is sending metta and who is there to send it to?

One then sees that there is a level of understanding, of being, which is beyond that which is tied up with self and other. No matter how high, refined and pure our aspiration might be, unless we go beyond that sense of self-identity and division in that respect, then there will always be that feeling of incompleteness; the desert experience will creep in.

So, if we pass through that grand-hearted attitude of mind, then we realise that which pertains to the wisdom of ultimate understanding, of Ultimate Reality; that which is called the Vajra teachings. *Vajra* means diamond or thunderbolt, indestructible, supremely powerful, the adamantine Truth. This is the understanding of selflessness. When the attention is put onto the feeling of 'I', one uses the practice to illuminate the assumptions we make about our identity. We have to turn the mind around from external objects, to shine it back upon the assumptions that we make about the 'subject'. When the mind is calm and settled, it's very helpful to start inquiring, "Who is the person that is the centre of all of this?" "Who is it that is meditating?" "Who is it that's knowing this?" "Who is the one who knows?" "What knows thought and feeling?" It's when we look and challenge the assumptions about there being a discreet entity here, then suddenly the prison walls collapse.

I had an experience of this some six or seven years ago – when I first started using this kind of meditation on a long retreat, asking "Who am I?" or "What am I?" and using that to create a hesitation in the mind, to put the sense of self into perspective; it felt like stepping out of a grey prison cell into sunshine and a field of flowers. It was a tremendous feeling of refreshment and relief, like coming across an oasis in the desert.

The Buddha said that the greatest happiness of all is to be free from the sense of "I am". Now, this might seem to some people to be a bit farcical or pointless, because our 'self' seems to be the most real thing in the whole universe – "If anything is real, I am." But it's only because we have never really looked, or inquired into the feeling of **I**, of **me**, of **mine**. It's only because we have never really studied that and seen it clearly that that illusion is maintained. Once you look at it closely, then the illusion falls apart. You can't be taken in by that.

So, one uses enquiry to challenge the assumptions that we are making and the walls that we create within the mind. That challenging of those assumptions is what dissolves the illusion. The instinct of the ego, however, is to immediately start creating things which produce activity elsewhere so that our attention will be distracted, so that we will stop doing this. The ego is like any creature that is frightened of dying, and as soon as we start to challenge the supremacy and the centrality of it, then a panic reaction gets going. You will find that the mind can throw up all kinds of interesting and compelling thoughts to persuade you to engage in something else quickly. So, one requires a great deal of resolution just to say "**NO!**" and to bring the mind back to asking, "Who is this?" "What is knowing this panic?" "What is knowing this feeling?"

★ ★ ★

In the *Vajra Prajña Paramita Sutra* you find statements like "No mark of self, no mark of other, no mark of living beings, no mark of a life", or "All conditioned dharmas are dreams, illusions, bubbles, shadows, like dew drops and a lightning flash, contemplate them thus," or "Everything is made from mind alone." And in the Heart Sutra as well, which they recite here at the City of 10,000 Buddhas every day, there are sections of it which go, "There is no form, no feeling, no perception, no mental formations, no consciousness, no ignorance, no birth, no ageing, no death, no suffering, no attainment and no Way." What this is doing is stepping out of the whole conditioned realm, putting the whole conditioned realm into perspective – do not seek for liberation, for certainty, for security in that which is inherently insecure, inherently bound and tied up with time, self, birth and death. As long as we are seeking for happiness in the conditioned sensory world, then we are bound to be disappointed. We cannot possibly find it there. And things like birth, death, self, other, suffering – these are relative truths and ultimately there is no suffering, no-one is ever born, no-one ever dies. All there is is 'Suchness' or 'The Wonderful' or 'Universal Mind' or any one of a number of terms that are used.

The interesting thing is you don't find this just in the Mahayana or Vajra-yana texts. It is fully explained and spelled out by the Buddha also in the Thera-vadan scriptures, although it may not get emphasised enough. You even get teachers who say that anatta should not be taught, that it is a dangerous teaching. After a talk that Ajahn Sumedho gave once, a well-known Buddhist teacher who was there was incredibly upset and disturbed that Ajahn Sumedho was teaching anatta to lay-people. He thought this was most irresponsible (although he him-self was a lay person!). Also I've been told of an eminent monk in Thailand who feels the same way; he thinks that anatta is too potent a teaching to pass on to all of you people, but I don't think so (*laughter*). This is the supremely liberating teaching, and you find a lot within the Theravada that is glossed over, that does continually push the mind to this point of ultimate wisdom.

For example, there is an inquiry made to a monk called Anuradha where he's questioned by some Brahmin scholars on "What is the nature of an en-lightened being after death?" "What happens to a Tathagata, an enlightened one, after the death of the body?" "Do they exist?"

The monk replies, "This is not spoken of by the Enlightened One."

He is asked, "Well, do they **not** exist?"

"This is not spoken of by the Enlightened One."

"Well, do they **both** exist and **not** exist?"

"This is not spoken of by the Enlightened One either," he replies.

"Then, do they **neither** exist **nor** not exist?"

"This, too," he says, "is not spoken of by the Enlightened One."

So they say to him, "You must be a fool or one who is newly gone forth. You obviously do not understand the Buddha's teaching or you would be able to give us a decent answer."

Then he goes to the Buddha and tells the Buddha of the conversation he had with these people, and he asks, "Did I answer in the right way?" And the Buddha said, "Yes, Anuradha you answered well."

"Do you see the Tathagata as **being** the five *khandhas*?"

"No, Lord."

"Do you see the Tathagata, as **having** the five *khandhas*?"

And he says, "No, Lord."

"Do you see the Tathagata as **not** having the five *khandhas*?"

And he says, "No, that's not true either."

"Do you see the Tathagata as being **within** the five *khandhas*?"

"No, Lord."

"Do you then see the Tathagata as being **separated from**, outside of the five *khandhas*?"

He says, "No, not that either."

"Correct!" said the Buddha, "Just so – what I teach, both now and for-merly, is suffering and the end of suffering."

The Buddha advises us not to try to define the enlightened in concep-tual terms because any conceptual definition can only fall short, can only be relatively true. The Buddha made very clear in the Theravada teaching just as much as in the scriptures of the Northern school that the ultimate perspective on things is the perspective of no fixed position, of actual realisation of Truth, abiding in that position of Awareness, rather than taking any kind of conceptual or idealistic position. That is our Refuge. Taking Refuge with Buddha is being that Awareness. So that we see that everything to do with our body, our feelings, our personality, our age, our nationality, our problems, our talents, all of these are simply attributes of the conditioned world that arise and pass away and there is awareness of those. The whole point of the practice is to constantly abide in that quality of Awareness.

Life is going to be frustrating and painful if we are looking for certainty and definition in terms of being a person, being some place – a being in time. It's only when we let go of the sense of **I**, **me** and **mine**, of the sense of there being a person here who has anywhere to go to, or anywhere not to go to, that there is the clear abiding in Awareness.

The tendency of the mind is often to conceptualise that. You say, "OK, I'm just going to be aware," and you take that as an ideal and try to fill the mind with that thought. What will happen then is that the thought turns into an object, so rather than just resting in being the knowing, we try to see what it is that is knowing. As Ajahn Chah would sometimes say – you're riding a horse and looking for the horse. We wonder, "Who is it that knows the knower?" "Who is it that knows the thing that's knowing the knowing?"

One can get the impression that there's some sort of infinite regression happening here, and that it's like falling off a cliff backwards. But it's not – because what happens is that when we let go of our sense of identity, then there is just the clear knowing. The mind rests in the bright, selfless, knowing, timeless state. And then the idea arises, "Oh, there is knowing." So rather than just resting in that pure knowing, we attach to the thought that there is something that is knowing. We're just fixing on that thought and then stepping out into the conditioned world. As we attach to any thought we're stepping away from that sense of pure knowing. If there is just pure knowing, it's like being up against the back wall. As soon as we hold onto any thought we walk away from the wall. We're going out into experience, going out into attachment to some condition.

If we just allow the mind to relax and rest in that sense of knowing, in that purity of being, then there is liberation, there is freedom right at that point. At that point the mind is aware of the sense of unity, of Suchness, there is the unifying vision which in Christian terms they call beatitude. The beatific vision is the vision of totality, of wholeness, the disappearance of any separateness. In this realisation there is no self – it's not you being with Ultimate Truth – there's just **THIS**, the mind in its pure awakened state, Dhamma aware of its own nature.

★ ★ ★

With the early presence of Buddhism in America in the 1950s and early '60s, there was a tremendous amount of use of this kind of understanding; people were saying, "Everyone is a Buddha," "We're all Buddhas," "Everyone is perfect." And, instead of this giving rise to people having the conduct of Buddhas, which is modest, gentle, and restrained, what this was sometimes taken as was a justification of license. Whatever you do, it's perfect – sober is perfect, drunk is perfect, to do whatever you feel like doing, whatever you're inspired to do – it's all empty. It's all Suchness. For people who took that highest principle as a fixed position or identity to hold onto … you can see that just the idea of it was not enough, and it caused some of the brightest Buddhist lights of the Beat Generation to die as alcoholics. There was a great sense of freedom of spirit that was inspiring it, but the idea of us all being Buddhas and everything being perfect is not exactly the same as the direct realisation of that. When the mind truly rests with that realisation, then what flows forth from it is a purity of conduct, a purity of speech and action, a gentleness, a harmlessness and simplicity. The Buddha's response to his enlightenment, being totally free and beyond any suffering, was not to pursue physical pleasures or seek intoxication. His response was to live incredibly carefully and modestly, using the things of the earth with frugality. He could have conjured up anything he wanted, but he chose to live as a barefoot renunciant, a peaceful, harmless being.

One can see that some Buddhist traditions over the centuries have become caught up in this problem, whereby the principle is attached to and then taken as an identity – "I am a Mahayana Buddhist," or "I am a Theravadan Buddhist," or "I am a Vajrayana Buddhist." That's like wearing a badge that gives one a certain credential, rather than seeing that the terms referred to are attitudes of being. For instance in England, at the Buddhist Society Summer School every year, one group would go and have their evening meetings down at the pub, ostensibly because they "had got beyond form". So, they would have their evening Dharma discussions down at the pub, which is all right; they are free to do what they want. The Theravadans just sit around, chatter and drink tea. But you could see that the attitude was, "Well, we're of the Supreme Vehicle. We don't need to be bothered with the petty concerns of *sila*; we respect the ultimate Buddha nature of all beings." And one could see that a lot of their inspiration and noble energy was getting sidetracked into justifying the simple quality of preference: that they found it enjoyable to have a drink or two, fool around and have an unrestrained time. Again, they are free to do as they choose, but it's a sad mistake to label this as the practice of Buddha-Dharma.

The result of this – trying to realise emptiness within a free-wheeling life – means that we then have the challenge of realising the emptiness of the despair and depression that comes from following those desires. People are free to take on the challenge!!! But it's a related thing; we can't just absorb into pleasure without getting the other side of it as well. It's as if we're holding onto the wheel as it goes up the pleasure side, but we're still holding onto it as it goes down the other side. I'm not saying these things as a put-down but, having done this quite a bit myself, I realise that we just don't have the presence of mind to let go at the top! It's the way we'd like it to be, but it doesn't operate like that.

At the beginning of the retreat everyone took the Refuges and Precepts. This symbolic act is to refresh our aspiration toward being a Buddhist, toward being Buddha. It's not a ceremony that one goes through to become a Buddhist, like a baptism. It's much more that it's up to us to refresh our aspiration within ourselves. Externally, we can adhere to a form, to a tradition, to a pattern, but if we don't eventually internalise that, if we don't bring that within ourselves and make being Buddha – being The One Who Knows – the aim, then any amount of external dedication to a particular form or tradition will not avail us very much in the long run.

★ ★ ★

One final point that we tend to not understand is that – if there is no self, if one is aiming to come from this position of ultimate wisdom, then why do we bother with things like spreading metta? If there is nobody here and nobody there, then why go through all the trouble of sending metta across the universe? Or the sharing of merit: you know there's no-one **here** and there's no-one **there**, so what's the point? Wouldn't we be better off saving our energy and doing something else? This is important to understand – how the different levels of our life interplay with each other – because even though at some moment we might be seeing life from the level of pure wisdom, from that place of timeless-spaceless-selfless awareness, the rest of the world is not necessarily seeing things from that point of view. What you have within Buddhist practice is a way of tying together all the different levels of our being.

The Buddha used conventional forms, he used personal pronouns. When people asked him questions such as, "If there's no self, why do you refer to yourself as an individual? Why do you talk to other people, why do you name people?" And the Buddha said, "Even though fundamentally there is no self, I use common speech in order to communicate things to people on a level that they can understand." So, when we are thinking about things like spreading metta, creating good karma, sharing the blessings of our life, one puts forth the effort to do that. You put your heart into spreading loving-kindness. You **do** it.

We set up monasteries, we put effort into creating opportunities and environments for people to learn from. We teach, offer guidance and support and instruction. But, having brought those forms into existence, then one dissolves any attachment to them. We bring forth wholesome principles and energies into people's lives, but we do not give them a sense of ultimate substantiality. We see that they are merely shapes, forms, patterns of consciousness. The sounds that I say, these are ear-consciousness, sounds that you all are aware of. There is the expression that the Buddha was the supreme weaver of dreams in order to wake up the dreamers. His teachings, his words and actions, are a system of dreams. Dreamstuff. But the mastery of the Buddha was that he created dreams which enabled the dreamers to awaken; to lead us out of the dream world into real life, into the true world.

As an example, for many years I had no feeling at all for devotional practice. "Anatta, that's what it's all about!" Every morning and evening, as we did our traditional chanting I would go along with it, try to stay in tune and so on, but basically I felt it was all pointless. Then I began to realise that I was missing the spirit of the whole thing – if we have right understanding, then we can bring forth those energies into words, bring forth kindness and benevolence, bring forth things which are useful and helpful into the world – but then not to own them, to leave them as they are, that is the great art and it is also the greatest blessing. You can see why the Buddha taught in the way that he did. It wasn't for him. It was to provide things for those of us who would come after: forms, patterns, traditions, ways of living that help to spur us on; ways to encourage us, to inspire us to wake up, to break through the illusions that bind us so that all can experience the true joy of liberation.

The Golden State

PART TWO – A STILL LIFE

IT IS AN OFT-RECOGNISED FACT that, once a religion is established in a society, over the centuries its original values tend to be obscured. Cultural overlay, empty intellectualism, assumed importance and conceit all contribute to a process of corruption.

When a religion enters a new country, however, there is an opportunity for a reclarification of values – particularly if it has not arrived through missionary zeal but through the interest of the local population. Against the background of a new culture, whatever does not relate to the basic spiritual paradigm becomes illuminated – and can be questioned.

Most religious traditions employ similar 'tools' – self-discipline, kindness, devotion, contentment with little, contemplation, meditation – which historically have often been formalised into monastic institutions. As Buddhism enters Western (and particularly American) culture, however, these basic spiritual qualities are being cultivated via a variety of approaches. Some are conservative, traditional and origin-based; others are novel, unorthodox and based more in the effort to fit with present cultural values.

★ ★ ★

During our teaching tour on the West Coast of America, Ajahn Sumedho, Sister Sundara, Sister Jotaka and myself moved amongst groups of both sorts. On the 'traditionalist' side, we spent time at The Sagely City of Ten Thousand Buddhas, near Ukiah, Northern California, and at the Buddha-Dharma Meditation Center in Hinsdale, Chicago. We also visited the New Camaldoli Hermitage, a Catholic monastery on California's Big Sur coast, and Taung Pulu Kaba Aye, a forest meditation monastery in the hills south of San Francisco, established by a Burmese Buddhist master of the *dhutanga* or 'austere' tradition.

On the 'modernist' side – if that is the right word – we visited Spirit Rock, the centre being established by Insight Meditation West (IMW) and the Vipassana meditation students of the West Coast; Green Gulch Farm, a community associated with the San Francisco Zen Center; and Cloud Mountain Retreat Center in southern Washington State, used by both Zen and Vipassana students. We also conducted an inaugural blessing ceremony for the Bell Springs Hermitage, a retreat centre particularly for those with life-threatening illnesses.

Perhaps these two attitudes are extensions of the psychological tendencies of 'primacy' and 'recency': either trusting what was *first* experienced as most important, or trusting what has been experienced most recently. Both approaches are, naturally, blessed with benefits and problems.

Traditionalism (primacy) derives from a respect for one's origins. On the spiritual level, for Buddhists this manifests as respect for the fundamental, unconditioned Truth (*sacca-dhamma*) as the Source. On the conditioned plane, it means a respect for Gotama the Buddha, the whole dispensation which arose from his accomplishments, and the lineage of all who have lived according to the teachings over the centuries – keeping them alive and vibrant to the present day.

Such devotion to the roots of one's faith has a tremendous supportive quality: one is participating in a form which has existed for millennia, with the power to buoy one up and carry one along, like the flow of a great river. One has the right to enjoy the inheritance of one's ancestors, living in the way extolled by them.

Traditional monastic institutions automatically inherit the faith and devotion of the people of their country of origin, and can rely on a stable Sangha to back up any efforts in a new land – which often receive financial support from the laity. Adherence to the trusted standards of the 'old country' draws in those who already have confidence in that form.

The principal difficulty is that, inevitably, these well-established forms of Buddhism carry a cultural overlay. This can make their transplantation to another social milieu a very delicate operation. If those bringing it over have little conversancy with the new environment, the precious seeds of wisdom can remain trapped within a capsule of Asian custom and language. Or – like a rare and fragile orchid – it might take root as something exquisite and exotic but basically infertile, unable to withstand for long the rigours of its new location.

★ ★ ★

The City of Ten Thousand Buddhas is, as its name suggests, more than just a monastery. Alongside the facilities for the hundred or more resident monks, nuns and novices, there are also elementary and secondary schools, and the 'Dharma Realm Buddhist University'. It is the main centre for a group of orthodox monasteries spread along the West Coast of America and Canada. The spiritual guide and founder of these monasteries is the Venerable Tripitaka Master Hsüan Hua, a monk of Chinese origin who began teaching in San Francisco in the early Sixties.

The monasteries still have a strong Chinese flavour – all the religious objects, rituals, etc. retain the form developed in China over the centuries – but Master Hua has consistently pointed out the original forms established by the Buddha. Thus his monasteries adhere more closely to the Vinaya and observe a number of Sangha procedures more strictly than is done in present-day Taiwan, Hong Kong and mainland China. Along with translating all scriptures and rituals into English, this approach makes it possible for those attending retreats, ceremonies and Dharma talks to tie in the practice directly to the Buddha's own Way, rather than just to the obvious Chinese tradition.

Despite attempts to make the teaching more accessible, Sangha members commented that the average interested American still finds – perhaps standably – their form of practice somewhat impenetrable. However, things are constantly in a state of adaptation. In being faithful to a tradition, one starts out by sticking with the known and well-established – and makes changes later, to fit the time and place. It is a dodgy business to design ideal reforms from scratch; one does better to see what changes will be suitable first.

Americans, however, are used to the opposite approach: the ideal is laid out on paper and approved beforehand – rather like the U.S. Constitution. This may be fine in principle but, to be ruthlessly practical, one has to start from where one actually is. So getting back to the problem of importing a monastic form, although there might be all kinds of great adaptations that *could* be made, it is only by using what is there already that one finds out what *really* needs to be changed. In making changes in this usually painstaking manner, the trust and confidence of Buddhists in the country of origin is happily retained. Pioneer monasteries are much in the public eye back home, so if too much is altered too quickly, disaffection can set in on a dramatic scale. Once a community is well-established, however, important adaptations can often be made without such negative repercussions.

★ ★ ★

At the Buddha-Dharma Meditation Center on the outskirts of Chicago, the experience is similar. Established much more recently (1988) by Phra Ajahn Sunthorn Plamintr, the centre has aimed to be a resource as much for local Americans as for the immigrant Thai population. In June of 1990 I was invited there to attend the demarcation of an ordination precinct *(sima),* and the ordination of several men as novices and bhikkhus. Despite being quite a junior monk, I was accorded a place of honour amongst the many Maha-theras, and was asked to give one of the Dhamma-talks to the whole assembly.

The efforts and sincerity of the resident Sangha, and also the lay supporters, were immediately striking; so also was their concern to be more of use to English-speaking Americans. So much was this on their minds that, from the drive from the airport right up until my departure time, I was repeatedly asked for advice on this. The barriers of language and culture, I was told, meant that more than 99% of the people coming were Asians.

They had been trying very hard. On this week end, for example, they had ensured that most of the Dhamma-talks would be in English. They held regular meditation classes at the Center; they had formed links with other local Buddhist groups in the Mid-West Dharma Association and had invited well-known teachers of other Buddhist traditions to speak on their festival days. However, many felt that there was an inexorable inclination towards becoming little more than a Thai cultural centre, with all the trappings of a Thai 'city' monastery.

The future is, of course, uncertain, but my feeling was that this outcome is quite unlikely. These are the early days when, as mentioned above, one tends to stay close to the mould from which one has recently emerged. Gentle transmutations will come with time. Since the determination of the abbot and the closest lay supporters is to establish a monastery for all people, and a place where meditation is taught and practised, that priority will necessarily set the direction it will take.

★ ★ ★

Our contact with Brother David Steindl-Rast at the 'Joys of Monastic Life' conference led to a visit to the monastery at which he now stays. Although professed in a different order, he has been at the Hermitage of New Camaldoli for the past eight years. When the Camaldolese Order was set up in the 11th century by St. Romuald they were even then something of a reform movement. Eschewing leadership by abbots (who already had an aura of power and worldliness), they established a unique pattern in Christian monasticism. Their life is divided into three basic styles: that of the hermit; that of communal life in the monastery; and that of a house in the city. Each monastic spends varying periods of time in each situation according to their disposition.

It was this unique blend that moved Father Thomas Merton to urge the Camaldolese to establish a monastery in the USA. In his eyes, his own Trappist order was too isolationist and rigid to fully serve the American people as he felt a monastic community could. Unfortunately, by the time the New Camaldoli monastery was founded, he was too valuable to be allowed to leave his own community. Thus he never got the chance to live with them in the stunningly beautiful place they found, nestled on the hillsides overlooking the Pacific. However, that the monastery exists today and is one of great vitality and ecumenicism, would probably please Father Thomas more than his own getting to live there.

On their 800 acres they have a number of hermit monks living in the woods, and a main community of about 25 monks, novices and lay-people, most of whom are a lot younger than the average resident of today's Christian monasteries. They have a small house in Berkeley as well, where a couple of monks reside whilst engaging in studies at the University of California.

They still retain their traditional monastic habits and follow the Liturgy of the Hours, but they have also made a number of adaptive changes – particularly in providing ample facilities for men and women to come on solitary retreat, and in the ecumenicism of their services and literature. Their emphasis is strongly towards contemplative and mystical aspects of religion, and towards religious unification. The Prior, Father Robert, was instrumental in bringing about the recent meetings between the Pope and the Archbishop of Canterbury. And Tibetan Buddhist prayer-flags could be seen flying in the little garden behind his cell!

★ ★ ★

As contrasted with traditionalism, the modernist way takes its cue more from the current attitudes and understanding of those interested in the teachings than from the way the teaching has been presented and lived out in the past. The present environment is of primary importance. This derives from the

quality of ultimate Truth as "apparent here and now, timeless", just as traditionalism derives from its quality of being the source and foundation of all things.

At such centres one finds, in the main, middle-class raised, educated white
Americans. The teachings are presented in their own language, by teachers
from their own kind of background, and in a familiar cultural context. The
advantage of this way is that it is easily adopted and used by people who have
grown up in the West. It slips into their value system and is absorbed com-
paratively painlessly. It is naturally more understandable to many people,
being of Western appearance and less alien than forms with an Asian veneer
and decidedly conventional flavour. Also, the vocabulary used to describe the
world of the mind accords much more with contemporary psychological ideas
than classical Buddhist expressions do.

A big disadvantage is the disconnectedness from the historical Buddha that
naturally arises. Through claiming Buddha-nature as one's reference more
than Gotama Buddha and his whole dispensation, social links with the rest
of the Buddhist world are weakened. Moreover, skilful means, teachings and
traditions that the Buddha established – which serve the whole spectrum of
human life – tend not to get used to the full. On the practical level, the separation from Asian forms also means that devoted Asian people, who might be
delighted to support the efforts of others in their cultivation of the Path, often
do not recognise these groups as 'real Buddhists'. The spirit of generosity, so
much to the fore in Buddhist countries, is thus disabled from helping to
nourish these efforts.

Another, and perhaps the most important, disadvantage is that in adapting to
the surrounding culture, some moral aspects of the teaching which are crucial
to wholesomeness and liberation get passed over. Without the reflection of the
larger Buddhist community, and without the standards established by the
Buddha being given prominence, these groups are vulnerable to incidents
which can and have had grave consequences.

★　★　★

For a long time the Zen Center has been the most prominent Buddhist institution in the San Francisco Bay Area. Originally established by Shunryu
Suzuki Roshi – whose collection of transcribed talks in 'Zen Mind, Beginner's
Mind' graces many a Buddhist bookshelf – the centre was guided, after his
death in the early Seventies, by Richard Baker Roshi, his Dharma heir. The
centre went from strength to strength, establishing both Tassajara – a retreat
centre for more rigorous training – and Green Gulch Farm – a more informal
community of Zen students, based around a market garden as a means of
livelihood. In a Sixties-Seventies spiritual environment characterised by dis-
trust of most traditions in favour of a 'direct-experience spirituality', this Soto
Zen group had managed to strike a remarkable balance that allowed for tradi-
tion-based and disciplined practice to be integrated with the idealistic lifestyles
of the time. For many, it seemed the perfect blend, which gave birth to much
confidence in Buddhism as a spiritual path.

In 1984, however, the Zen community, and all Buddhists in the U.S., were stunned by the news that Baker Roshi had been relieved of his post as abbot, because of a number of serious transgressions against the community standards of proper behaviour.

When I visited Green Gulch, the main interest expressed to me was in Vinaya and community discipline. Zen's customary approach to the Precepts has been – in contrast to the rest of the Buddhist world – more as themes for contemplation, which you bear in mind whilst going about doing what you do, rather than clear guidelines to be followed wherever possible. This overly liberal approach was clearly one of the causes of Baker Roshi's downfall, and for the distress and confusion of their community resulting from it.

Norman Fischer, the head of practice at Green Gulch, spent as much time as he could with me, discussing the establishment of a more solid basis of moral conduct for this community. He pointed out that they now better appreciated that they were not monks at all, but should look upon themselves as lay-priests. It was quite a relief, he said, to recognise their proper rôle, and to establish their values accordingly as a lay community. It was his hope – even though some other leaders of the Zen Center group were at variance – that they would at least establish the Eight Precepts as the standard for practice at Tassajara. This came not from a disaffection with his own tradition but from the obvious need, within the spiritual life, for a basis of restraint and trustworthiness.

★   ★   ★

IMW and Spirit Rock have had no such catastrophic incidents. The plans for their Marin County site focus around a retreat centre, but also include a teaching area where people can come to learn meditation and to hear Dharma talks, and an area set aside to be a monastery or hermitage. This group's style is based around lay practice, and is guided by teachers such as Jack Kornfield, Sylvia Boorstein and James Baraz. It is a group that has served thousands of people, organising silent retreats and leading local Vipassana meditation groups on the West Coast. Because of its simple approach and absence of religious trappings, it has been an inroad into the training of the heart for many whose interest was, initially, in a more effective kind of therapy.

Its form of meditation practice is, however, akin to the methods of mind-training contained within classical Theravada monasticism. Because of this, and also Jack Kornfield's time spent as a bhikkhu with Venerable Ajahn Chah, it was no surprise that IMW should convene the Monastics' Conference, and that Jack was the Moderator of the event. His affinities with both approaches described here, together with the growing interest in morality and traditionalism aroused by the debacles of Baker Roshi and Ösel Tenzin (Chögyam Trungpa's successor, who recently died due to AIDS), made the conference both pertinent and timely. The event was not so much for monastics to meet and discuss with each other, but more for Bay Area students of Buddhism to have an opportunity to contemplate such questions as: What is monasticism for? How does it work? What are its results? Is it still a valid approach? What should be changed? – and to hear from the mouths of monks and nuns themselves the accounts of their vocation.

★ ★ ★

Those invited to speak and lead discussions were quite carefully chosen – not for their eloquence or attainment, but rather for their years of commitment to a communal, contemplative, orthodox monastic life. There were Buddhists and Christians; all of us were Westerners.

Approximately 150 people attended, most having had little if any contact with traditional monasticism. Although largely of Vipassana and Zen Center background, there were also a fair number of Christians. Of the main talks, even though all were fine expositions, probably those of Sister Sundara and Sister Columba, a Trappistine nun, were most memorable.

At the beginning of the second day, Jack Kornfield invited everyone to suggest issues that they would like to see covered. The list began: celibacy, equality for women in Theravada Buddhism, adaptability of rules, vegetarianism, differences between Buddhism and Christianity ... and on and on it went. It seemed that everyone had a pet issue. After about half an hour, Ajahn Sumedho and I looked at each other somewhat aghast – it would take months to deal with that lot!

Just then one of the audience announced that she had just had an insight. Silence fell and we waited.... "We want it all! We don't want to give up **anything**. This is real **American** Buddhism!" Everybody laughed and, for that moment, could see the tendency to search for a perfect Buddhism that matched one's own particular biases. Ajahn Sumedho turned towards her and applauded.

Nevertheless, the suggestions kept on coming and with the question of equality for women well to the fore. It was Sister Sundara's turn to speak next and Ajahn Sumedho leaned over to me with a concerned look: "I would not like to be in her position right now." After a short break, she gave her talk. She spoke movingly and magnificently. In many respects, she had taken the most tricky of issues and clearly pointed out the way to work with such things: there are no simple answers, only ways to practise wisely.

Sister Columba was deeply impressive, probably less for the wonderful words she spoke than for the purity and light that imbued all she did and said. She described her entry into her convent and the life that she and her sisters led. She fielded questions with directness, humour and honesty. Here was the result of a lifetime given up to pure conduct, simplicity and Truth – a being radiant, clear and sublimely happy. For many people at the conference this said more than all the words for, despite belonging to the most orthodox and austere of traditions, she had arrived at a state of being that freewheeling Californians have combed forests, hills, retreat centres and beaches endlessly to find.

★ ★ ★

At the close of the conference, Jack Kornfield asked the assembly how many would now consider entering a monastery, say, for at least a year. It was a testimony to the insight in convening such a conference, and to the capacity of the speakers to put their lives into words, that 70-80% of the people raised their hands.

A monastery's purpose is to provide opportunities for such interest to bear fruit. Even though, as some suggest, the future of Buddhism in the U.S. might lie with lay groups, the monastery remains a unique and invaluable environment for the development of the spiritual life – not only for those within the enclosure, as it were, but also for those for whom it is a reminding and encouraging presence in the world.

So how will things develop – who knows? What can be seen for certain, however, is that there is already a tremendous fellowship among Buddhist people in the West. During this visit I experienced only warmth, hospitality and respect from those whom I met. What we are experiencing here is a cooperative effort towards a common goal, rather than a contest to see who is right and best. Traditional forms and the spirit of the present can work together like an old, well-used tool in a skilful hand. The tool and the hand on their own cannot achieve very much, but in concord we can bring great beauty into the world.

Self-portrait

My father is a judge of dogs
My sister Katie dislikes frogs
My sister Jane is fond of horses
And mother dear, well she of course is
An angel who is past compare.
And then there's me... but do I dare
To claim that I am *that* or *this*
An 'I am' swimming in the '**IS**'?

The question is beyond the reach
Of petty mind for on the beach
Of senses beat the endless tides
Of births and deaths, the carpet rides
Of cherished thoughts and memories
Of wives and lives and families.

Waves washing in and washing back
Create a past and future, a sack
Back-burdening, a being blind
And gripping too intense to find
The architect of all their pain,
The singer of the sad refrain
Who builds these realms of birth and death –
Inhaling and exhaling breath,
Inhaling birth, exhaling death.

Confused, incomprehensibly bizarre,
Clutching waves we think we are;
So lost that we forget the eye
Of wisdom, which does not belie
The truth of waves and sand and seas
Yet is transcendent over these.

A song of Suchness clear and bright,
The boundless inner peace of light
Whose unremitting presence roars
Oceanic at its shores.

So what awesome space is this
Wherein the wheel revolves,
And who the ocean into which
This universe dissolves?

A subtle thief, the question "Who?",
It burgles with delight,
It pockets pain and happiness
Then slips into the night
Taking all identity
And leaving on the light.

Taking petty mind up to that watershed
Beyond which nothing can be said,
Where, if words were to apply,
They would create a 'you' and 'I',
A plotter and their plot;
Abiding at this spot,
Untouched by anything at all,
No dust, nowhere to fall.

(Devon, 1981)

The Real Me

From a talk given on the winter retreat at Chithurst, February 1991

THIS EVENING, on the verge of people entering into great conflict in the Middle East, I thought I would talk on the fundamental causes of war. Even though we are in retreat and somewhat secluded from the events of the outside world, still we keep our eyes and ears open and feel a sense of sympathy and compassion for all the beings caught up in this conflict. Our efforts in the spiritual life are not to evade such actualities in the world – just because these events happen outside the walls of this monastery doesn't mean to say that we feel exempt or not interested or not a part of it. How many times have we been in conflict ourselves, even in this life, caught up in contention between ourselves and others? Probably in hundreds of thousands of past lives we have taken up arms against others, shed blood and died ourselves in conflict.

In considering this, and looking at the workings of the mind, one sees that the fundamental problem arises from the ability that we have to discriminate and take sides. When the mind is clouded and caught up, then 'this' and 'that' seem to be completely different from each other, they seem to be inherently separated and apart. Black seems to be completely separate and different from white; 'you' separate from 'me'. The more caught up and clouded by ignorance the mind is, the more absolute that separation seems to be and the common ground that exists between us becomes invisible, we lose it. In a personal clash we forget that we are actually both human beings – both people who enjoy pleasure, who feel pain, who love life and fear death – and the particular point that we are squabbling about possesses our minds so much that it becomes the most important thing. Even if it was something absolutely minuscule, the mind can take hold of anything, make a cause out of it and become completely blind to the common ground, the common unifying bonds there are between us. This is how wars begin.

★ ★ ★

I remember, before I was a monk, I used to find that I lived in about five different worlds; there were five distinct circles of people that I moved around in and some of these were ideologically very opposed to each other. When I was a child I did a lot of horse riding; I grew up around horsey people and spent a lot of time going to horse shows, fox hunting and hanging out with horsey types, believe it or not! This is a group composed of very conservative country people who liked to ride and go hunting, out for a good day's sport. (This I might add is attended by such pagan rituals as 'getting blooded' – when you are in on your first kill you get your face wiped with the fox's blood – just one of the delightful aspects of polite country society!)

The other spheres that I moved in were: my family, my old school friends, my academic life at university and lastly there were the freaks and hippies – underground people in London living in squats and anti-establishment collectives. I often thought, when sitting slumped against a heap of cushions in some dive in Bayswater, "I wonder what they would say if anyone knew that three days ago I was having stirrup cup with the Master of Foxhounds at the local meet?" Or once, when I attended a press-conference at Whitehall for the Royal Tournament, still in an altered state of consciousness from an all-night party, "If only they knew.…"

It used to disturb me sometimes how easily I moved between these different realms. I noticed that each group seemed to be under the impression that it was the only thing in the world that existed – perhaps not completely but certainly to a great extent.

Within the sphere of the family I was the youngest child, the only son, so with the family that was my identity. They called me 'Jim' and there was the whole web of unique family relationships and family activities and events. When I was with my old school friends – who were heavy-drinking, materialistic, public school rowdies – I would become completely involved with that. When I was with the horsey people I would be fully involved with that; when I was with university people I would become a studious academic and attempt to be a scintillating intellectual; and, finally, when I was with the underground types, hippie radicals and so forth, I would become completely involved with that.

I used to think, "There must be a real me in here somewhere. Which one is the real one, and which ones are just a front?" I could see that there was a lot of contention and negativity between some different aspects of the worlds I moved amongst, but somehow I realised it was all quite all right. I wasn't being two-faced or hypocritical; there were very good aspects to all of these people and I really enjoyed being with them, the local hunting set, the academics, the pub-crawlers, all of them. What my mind homed in on was the good, appealing qualities, the friendly noble qualities that existed within all of these spheres of activity.

One could witness the judgements one group made about another. The conservative country people would make scathing remarks about hippies and condemn them, they would be critical because of superficial characteristics or through the emblems of that tribe being different from their own: beards, patchouli oil, hashish and 'The Politics of Ecstasy' rather than green Wellington boots, tweeds and 'Horse and Hound' (and gin and tonics, of course). One could easily see how people become divided and drawn into contention with each other simply through not seeing our common humanity, what actually lies at the heart of our life. Amongst every single one of those groups there were good people doing what they felt was right, living in a way that seemed a reasonable, wholesome and humane way to exist.

The causes of conflict arise from identification, blind adherence to a rôle, a position, to attributes of our personality or some aspects of life. There is an incredibly vast array of different things we can identify with. We can identify with our family and our name: "These are my parents, this is my relationship with them, I get on well with my father, trouble with my mother, bit of a dodgy relationship with my brother." The family bonding that goes on can seem very real, we can become deeply involved in the emotional pulls and struggles of family life. Reminiscences of family history can also be involved with sustaining who we think we are. I notice whenever I visit my family (I don't know if other people's families are the same) there is an enormous urge to fix everyone as a particular identity; stories about embarrassing things that we did when we were small get told repeatedly. Many times I have heard the tale of how my parents came back from a dinner party to find the baby-sitter watching television and myself on the kitchen table with the lid off the treacle tin, with me and everything covered in a black sticky mess. The tales are varied and numerous.

The family is a particular group of human beings and our relationships, our past, the events of our childhood, our upbringing and all those triumphs and disasters are the cement that helps us form together as a distinct group, so it can very easily become a strong identity.

The physical body is probably the most powerful source of identification we have: our physical frame, the appearance of being female or male, being young, being old, being attractive, being unattractive – these can make a tremendous difference to us. "I am young. I am old. How old are you?" We don't say, "My body is thirty-four years old." We say, "I am thirty-four." Our mind doesn't really have any age, only our body ages. The more concerned with appearance one is, the more the importance of the body inflates. When we're young, as teenagers particularly, there can be an absolutely earth-shattering terror of a spot appearing on our face, just when we have an important party coming up at the weekend. Some great blob tries to manifest around our chin, or in some unhideable place and we feel totally destroyed – God has betrayed us. The body becomes an enormously powerful influence on how we feel.

I have quite unusual physical features, so I grew up with an bewildering array of nicknames. I used to have long curly hair, which would turn blondish in the summer sun, a great crown of ringlets and a very muscular body, so one group of women friends used to call me Adonis – I quite liked that. Then there was another group of friends, some obnoxious males who, because of my long nose and prominent ears called me Dumbo – I didn't like that so much. (I think I must have been an elephant in a past life.)

Identification with the body is something that has a very powerful effect on us as we age, the feeling of seeing the wrinkles arriving, the flesh beginning to sag and the lustre disappearing from our skin, our health and vitality fading, our hair beginning to silver and disappear. Men will try to convince themselves that they have always had a high forehead rather than recognise the fact the hair is actually receding – "It's a sign of intelligence, a high forehead!"

We can also cause a tremendous amount of identification around health – fearing illness, fearing pain, wanting to be healthy and vigorous. A great deal of time and energy can be spent trying to become healthy, trying to overcome sickness, or in feeling hard-done-by if we have a sick body – feeling we have been cheated or that something terrible has been done by us or has happened to us because our body is so sick.

We identify with the personality: "This person is always such a nice person, so outgoing, so intelligent. I am such a clumsy, socially inept type." Or the reverse, "I'm so wonderful, I am brilliant. So and so over there is foolish and stupid, a hopeless case." One can judge oneself against other people very easily over personality characteristics. Are we quiet or talkative? Are we bright or are we dark? Are we moody or enthusiastic? It is very easy to judge, "This one is good, that one is bad. That one is right, this one is wrong. I like this one, I don't like that one." We can create endless judgements and comparisons. The materialistic society spends an incredible amount of time in judging people against each other in competitions, seeing who is the most athletic, talented, attractive, most appealing. We put billions into endless contests to spruce up, fire up our enthusiasm for making these kind of discriminations.

Another area is our achievements: the kind of things that we have done in our lives, our successes and failures. We catalogue our ambitions, what we hope will happen in the future and also all the terrible things we have done, the crimes we have committed. We can identify with and carry these things around with us perpetually. "I had an abortion when I was seventeen," "I am the head of the team" or "I was caught stealing comics from the local newsagents at the age of nine," a crushing moment, caught in the act. All the successes, failures, good and bad things in our lives one can home in on and make a big thing out of. We can see ourselves as a high person, a low person, a weak person or a strong person just because of the events that have occurred – whether we are a victim or whether we are a success, a winner or a failure. How well we do in the kind of profession that we have, our abilities in the social world – "I am a teacher," "I am unemployed," "I'm just a housewife," "I'm a Member of Parliament," "I'm a meditation teacher," "I'm a failed Buddhist" – all of these masks can be picked up and believed in endlessly.

There are also innumerable things in the social realm that we can tie our name onto and claim to be who and what we are: "I'm a conservative," "I'm a liberal," "I'm an anarchist," "I'm a royalist," "I'm for the war," "I'm against the war," "I think it's right," "I think it's wrong" – there are political opinions of an incredible variety of shades and strengths that we can identify with. Then there are things like football teams that we can tie ourselves to – "I'm an Everton supporter," or "the San Francisco '49ers are the best" – just to have a hero and to root for them.

There are any number of things that we can align ourself with on the social level and take that to be our group – "This is my team, this is important and real to me." So when the group wins, we are happy and we celebrate. Then when they lose we die, we feel sad and depressed; and in aligning with one group we are automatically in conflict against the others. If our mind absorbs into politics and we are into the Conservatives, then we inevitably feel pitted against the other political parties, and the more fully we adhere to that, the more full the contention is. Identification causes that absoluteness of division.

We can identify with our astrological make-up: "Well, of course, he's a Scorpio, I can't talk to him, you know what Scorpios are like – appalling!" We can get an enormous amount of mileage out of astrology, palmistry, psychoanalysis, the Enneagram and all the rest of the great variety of different ways of mapping our characteristics, giving them labels and categories and relationships. All of these have a certain validity, but the more we buy into it the more we can see this pattern of division occurring. Even if that to which one is adhering is wholesome and good and helps in some respects, still one sees, however, that the more we take it to be 'I' and 'me' and 'what I truly am' – "A Virgo with Sagittarius rising, the Moon conjunct with Uranus in Leo; Sun and Jupiter conjunct at the mid-heaven...." The more we take it that "This is what I am, this is the revelation of my true nature," the more we miss the point. It can never be the whole story, it can only be partial.

We could go through the entire list of things to identify with in our present situation and, as if that were not enough, we have got past lives to play with as well! "Well, of course, this life is pretty mediocre, I'm not really anybody special, but you should have seen me when I was Queen Nefertiti or Josephine, Empress of France, that was a real event – you should have seen me then!" We can make a big deal out of the idea of past lives; who we were can become much more significant than who we are. "Well, I was a priest at a temple in Lemuria, then I showed up in Egypt, got stoned to death for stealing a watermelon in Alexandria in about 2000 BC. Then of course I was a nun with the Cathars and got a bit of karma going with the Catholic Church when they walled me up...." We can really get some wonderful stuff going!

★ ★ ★

One can see that in the midst of it all there is the search for the real 'me'. Which one is the real me? It's like trying to figure out which one of the social groups that I was describing did I really belong to? Within all the different strata of our existence we can be hunting for the 'real me'; and the mind in its hunger for security and belonging will catch on to some aspect and claim it, own it, be it, saying, "This is what I am, this is my true self."

Anything that we identify with in this way, we find that it always leads us to a sense of separation, barrenness, loneliness, a sense of incompleteness and conflict, afraid of what others think, wanting to be whole, wanting approval, fear of attack and friction. As soon as I am isolated and separated from the rest, then there is suffering, dukkha comes into being, it's inevitable. So with the spiritual path, what we are aiming at is to penetrate the question of what we are. I came across a wonderful statement that was made by Sri Ramana

Maharshi – "Why are you so concerned about getting things and doing things when you don't know who it is that is going to get them? Why are you so concerned about knowing who you were in the past when you don't even know who you are now?" We can be so interested in doing and getting and becoming, so interested in who we were in the past that we forget – "Do I really know who I am? Do I **really** know? What is a human being? What is anyone? What is this?" The spiritual path is the path of enquiry into the very roots of our nature. "What are we…?"

In meditation one can develop this enquiry in a very distinct way, using the mind's reflective thinking abilities to look into 'who I am'. When the mind is reasonably calm and quiet, and we raise the question "Who am I?", we start to challenge all of those identities: the identification with the body, with our family, our gender, with our social group, our memories, our successes and failures, with our occupation and the whole array of different things. When we contemplate: "Who is it that knows masculinity? Who is it that remembers? Who is it that feels pain? Who is it that is sick?" – when we raise the question in that way, clearly and consciously bringing it into the mind, then there is a moment when the thinking mind stutters; just for a moment, there is a realisation, a recognition – there is that which is knowing and then there is that which is the feeling of pain or the idea or whatever. We bring our attention to home in more and more directly on that gap, that moment when the mind halts, because quickly afterwards it says, "Well, of course, I am Amaro Bhikkhu, I am 34 years old, I am a Buddhist monk, this is my father, this is my mother, I am living in Chithurst Monastery and today is Saturday. This is your reality, be satisfied with it!"

The thinking mind will rise up and fill the gap with all these conventionally true attributes, but there was a moment, there was a moment where there was a clear space and it was seen that the 'Knowing' was one thing and the 'known' another. And, most importantly, in our hearts we realise that the 'Knowing' is much, much more truly 'me', 'what I am', or what truly IS than any thoughts, any feelings, or any designation of young, old, happy, unhappy, depressed, elated. Those are seen more and more clearly as simply patterns of consciousness, patterns in the play of Nature that there is an awareness of. With the contemplative, reflective mind we can pursue this kind of enquiry, learn to keep challenging over and over again the assumptions that we make, and simply abide at the end of the question.

As the mind becomes more calm and we begin to use this practice in a systematic way, we discover a strange process occurring – we ask

"Who am I?"

After some time the word 'Who' starts to sound ridiculous

so then it changes to,

"**What** am I?"

Then the 'I' starts to sound very weird so you ask,

"What is **it**?"

which then changes to

"What **is**?"

which reduces to

"What?"

Then only

"?"

then just the

•

then the point vanishes,

and there is only pure Awareness –
we are left completely pointless....

This is a process that we can see distinctly when it is followed carefully and systematically; the mind is more and more firmly allowed to rest in the quality of pure 'pointlessness'. In some ways this is a good word, being pointless, because it means we are not making the mind have a point, an abiding place – we are allowing it to rest, simply aware of its own nature, aware of both its emptiness and its suchness, and the arising and passing of all things. We are not defining reality, giving it a limitation or a location.

★ ★ ★

Somebody asked Krishnamurti one time, "What would you say is the meaning of life?" He said **"MEANING!?!** – how do you think our puny little thoughts can cast the nature of life into some kind of words that can truly express what **IS**? Life **IS** – it doesn't **mean** anything! What does air or moonlight **mean**!?" This is very true; this is very, very true. To believe that we can express what life's meaning is is to assume that we can put into words, into some formula, the entire nature of the cosmos – the universe and the mind in all their infinite and inconceivable stratifications and their incredible complexity and interdependence – to try and put that into the expression of human mouth noises is just absurd.

When the mind is allowed to rest in that sense of complete clarity and choicelessness, we find that it is beyond dualism – no longer making preferences or being biased towards this over that. It is resting at the point of equipoise, where this and that and black and white and where you and I all meet; the space where all dualities arise from.

With the mind thus resting, all conflicts are healed. This is the way that war is ended; affliction and conflict are drawn to a close because the very root delusion of separateness has been dissolved. It would be like our left hand going to war against our right – it's not going to happen, even in the craziest of people, since the commonality is much more obvious than the differences.

The Flowering of
the Golden Secret

An afterthought on enquiry and healing – this followed on from the previous talk.

IF WE TAKE THE TROUBLE to enquire and challenge our assumptions, if we let the mind open up and don't just operate from a blind habitual level, then we have a chance to let life truly blossom. Some time ago I was contemplating these themes and also thinking a lot about Ajahn Chah, our teacher. For nearly ten years now he has been in great sickness, his brain damaged with a stroke, paralysed and speechless. I had been thinking a lot about his condition and how strange and tragic it was that this extraordinary, mighty being, this person so wise and so loving was in such a state of terrible ill-health, unable to speak, unable to move. He is still a very lovely radiant presence even though he is largely inert, completely incapable of any voluntary action.

My first spiritual teacher, Trevor Ravenscroft, was a man who trained for many years in the esoteric knowledge of the Rudolf Steiner tradition; he was also an expert on the legends of the Holy Grail. One of the books he wrote was a commentary on a famous Grail romance called 'Parsival'. In this legend one of the main characters is the Grail King, Anfortas. In some ways he was in the same condition as Ajahn Chah; even though he was a powerful and great king, guardian of the Grail, he was sick and laid out. He had been dreadfully wounded by a lance, jousting in mortal combat with another knight. He had won the battle but for years he had been in a state of ghastly sickness. The similarity between these two situations caught my attention. Also because I learned that the Buddha's alms-bowl was one of the origins of the symbol of the Holy Grail.

In Christian tradition it is the cup that Christ and the disciples drank from at the Last Supper, and was also used by Joseph of Arimathaea to contain the blood running from the wound made by the centurion's spear. So, in certain Christian traditions, the Grail was seen physically and metaphorically as the fountainhead of spiritual power. I went back to look at the story of Parsival again and was very struck by its relevance and profundity – particularly since I had just been to Thailand and seen Ajahn Chah in this physically devastated state.

The other main protagonist in the story is the Grail Knight Parsival, who is the classic ingenue, incredibly naïve; he is a great fighter but amazingly unworldly and innocent. He is also the archetypal seeker. 'Parsival' means something like, 'through the valley' or 'through the centre'. His coat of arms was a 'T' shape with a space down the middle like: ⫟, which also has resonances of

'One who keeps to the middle way'.

He sets out in search of the Holy Grail and after some trials and tribulations, he finds the castle of King Anfortas. He comes into the castle and there is a splendid, fantastic ritual going on in the grand banqueting hall. Lines of stately beautiful maidens carrying flaming torches, noble knights standing in formation, a solemn, holy array of gentle beings. In the middle of the banquet, laid out on his couch is the wan and frail form of the wounded king. Parsival, being a bit of a bumpkin, is more than somewhat overawed by the whole thing and fails to take in what is happening. He doesn't ask the one obvious and crucial question, but just makes polite conversation instead. Everyone is waiting for him to pose the question and break the spell but he doesn't realise what he is supposed to do. He spends the night there and, when he wakes up in the morning he is all alone, there is no-one else around, the castle is empty.

So he leaves the castle and finds himself in a wasteland. (This is the same wasteland that is the substance of T.S. Eliot's famous poem.) Eventually after wandering there for five years Parsival manages to find his way back to the Grail Castle, by now he has realised what he has to ask – then the healing of King Anfortas occurs. I have tried to gather all of this together into a poem about the healing power of enquiry; it is called

The Flowering of the Golden Secret

It has been so long –
the Master's body laid so low –
like the wounded Anfortas,
guardian of the Holy Grail,
neither quite alive
nor yet quite dead.

The wasted flesh shocks the eye,
the straightest mind is turned;
too awed and stunned by raw impact
to ask the question, "Why?" –
"What is it ails thee?"

Stopping at the senses' gate
the seeker gets repelled –
so, guileless and innocent,
is left to wander wasted lands:
brave, brave, brave
but slowly wise.

The one of steadfast mind
trends towards the bright,
circling the holy place –
the domain of the Lord of Light – but
"Who seeks it will not find it";
so near, yet always out of sight.

Five circles of the sun: despair
and hope pursue each other round –
a sorry pair.

Whomsoever seeks the Grail
must do so with a sword –
hating God, defying Truth
but determined to go on;
for there's no fixed law,
no formula of knowledge,
that ever could withstand
the power of revelation
of one faithful
to their own courageous truth.

Straight through the middle.
The test is to forget yourself,
and all your cherished goals,
to partake of the anguish
of another.

Straight through the middle
comes at last once more
to place himself
before the wounded one;
via painful passages,
far beyond the bounds
of space and time, causality,
to reach the realm of vision:
to reach the Master's hut,
the Grail Castle.

"*Oeheim, was wirret dier?*"
"Luang Por, what ails you?"

The question now illuminates
presumptions we have made…
"Do not weep for **ME**!
It's **you** who are in trouble.
You think this body's all there is
to 'Ajahn Chah'!"

The veil is pierced –

revelation
of the perfectly awake,
radiant reality
is here.

The wound is healed –
transfiguration, peace – no-one
whose beauty came from birth,
ever equalled Anfortas
emerging from his sickness
– *fleur* –
a golden lustre falls upon the scene.

No-one ever reached the Grail
not named for it in heaven;
the steadfast one
who holds the middle
now comes to the throne –
thus
here and there
and you and i
at last dissolve,
are
gone.

✿✿✿✿✿✿✿✿✿✿✿✿
✿✿✿✿✿✿✿✿✿✿✿✿✿✿✿

Amaravati, 1990 – with many thanks to
Wolfram von Eschenbach, Joseph Campbell and Trevor Ravenscroft.

In Search of Freedom

From a talk given on the winter retreat at Chithurst, February 1991

OUR LIBERATION depends upon restraint, commitment and upon renunciation.

It is a strange thing that freedom comes through restraint, but this is really what spiritual discipline is for – it's for freedom. It is for establishing a life which is clear, harmonious and full. A certain amount of self-concern and egotism, greed, hatred and delusion has to be barricaded against and illuminated if we want to be free. Unfortunately, our minds are often dominated by the hungry ghost of self-concern: the avoidance of pain, for ME; the gaining of pleasure, for ME; the accumulation of things which provide security, for ME.

These habitual drives dominate our minds very easily: "What I like, what I don't like. What I want, what I don't want. What I believe, what I don't believe. What I think about this person, what I think about that person. I want to be with this one, I don't want to be with that one." These attitudes exist like an autocrat in our minds; handing out *diktats* to try and control the world and to get what we want. On the social level most people regard a dictatorship as an inferior political system; one person calling all the shots and making everyone bend to their own ideas. Just on the level of politics and social life, this is something which is seen as a source of conflict and hassle for the society as a whole. It's going to be a cause for disharmony and resentment – and the more selfish and greedy the dictator is, the more trouble there will be within the society.

This is exactly the same as the way it works in our own minds. If there is a dictator in charge within us, the more greedy and selfish they are, the more pain and struggle we will experience in our hearts – it is just the same. So what we do is to organize a peaceful coup, we have a little revolution. We gather the forces of goodness and quietly surround the presidential palace. We indicate that the tanks are waiting at the gate and we invite the incumbent to go and live abroad somewhere. We find them a nice little place in a far-off country – a seaside bungalow or a little château some place – keep them carefully watched, well supplied with food and drink and things to amuse themselves with, and no visa back to their country of origin.

This is exactly what we have to do in our minds – to let our sense of self, the power of self-interest, live out its days and die peacefully, free from any control over our life and to let the forces of wisdom guide the government instead. Then we are at peace, at ease – we are guided by the pure and the good.

★ ★ ★

Our basic assumption in life is often that there are things around me that are stopping me from being free. Everybody wants freedom. All around the world, different countries want freedom. As individuals it is something that we all want too – and even expect.... Much of our life is tied up with the efforts that we make to be free, to live in an unobstructed way, but freedom is something that is very difficult to find and certainly very difficult to understand. How do we find it?? And what is freedom anyway?

During my last year at university I was living in London and becoming more and more enamoured of anarchy and anti-establishment thinking – and more and more critical of the social order as it was. I deeply longed for freedom and I was blaming the problems of humanity on (amongst other things) the fact that the whole world order was being run by a secret consortium of the CIA, the Mafia and the Catholic Church, the Rosicrucians, the Freemasons and Howard Hughes: the 'Illuminati' working together to undermine and profit from an unwitting humanity.

I was deeply enmeshed in all of this and feeling very negative towards the British government, despite the fact that I was actually living on a university grant. The food that I was eating and my whole education was being paid for by the same evil-minded, tyrannical government ... but I selected my perceptions, I neglected to notice that. I ignored all the other benefits and pleasant aspects of the social system and filled my mind with – "They shouldn't do this, they shouldn't do that. I want to get out of this place. This is a terrible country!"

A part of the reason why I left England and decided to engage wholeheartedly in the spiritual journey was because in my heart I realised that the logic behind the anarchistic feelings that I had – the rejection of the imposition of law by an external authority – was all very flawed. I was looking solely towards condemnation, a defiance of the establishment, as a way to be free.

In my heart, however, the more I looked at it, the more I realised that this wasn't going to work. There was always a sense of compromise: not only was I living on the university grant but I noticed that all the great leading lights of free-thinking anarchy in England were on the dole. It was quite remarkable to me that they quite publicly admitted the fact that they were living on social security, while simultaneously condemning the government. I felt more and more certain that just by condemning and defying the establishment all you ended up with was compromise and negativity. It didn't really set one free at all. That wasn't where I was going to find it.

So then I began to understand freedom more in terms of thinking or ideas. I began trying to live rightly by working on the internal world, being a free person within myself – not being limited by inhibitions and social conventions – to be a free spirit. But I found that I was still trying to be free simply by defying convention. This kind of attitude has had a very powerful effect in recent decades, pioneered in the Beat Generation by people like Jack Kerouac and Alan Ginsberg, and by the free-thinkers of the Sixties. "Throw all the rules out of the window. Just be a free person. You don't need structures, you don't need forms. Tune in, turn on, drop out. You don't need rules, just free your Heart and blow your mind!"

So I found myself attempting to do this – just coming and going in my own way and following whatever I thought was good and right in the moment – trying not to be limited by any kind of structure at all. But one finds oneself continually living with form, with limitation and structure. Sometimes it's just plain obvious that the way to harmony is to accord with the structure – even though ideologically it might seem like capitulation.

If we try to follow this line of thinking – that all conventions, rôles, forms or limitations are somehow wrong – then we end up with incredible confusion. Should we abdicate our right to total freedom when it comes to public toilets? If you've got a male body, convention says you go in the men's entrance. That's where you go. If we are driving a car on the road, we don't exercise our freedom by driving on the wrong side. Otherwise, we might not get arrested, but we will definitely crash into other people or cause all kinds of havoc and distress around us – this is common sense. We go along with the convention in order to get from A to B because it is more important to do that, and it causes less hassle along the way. So to try to be free solely by defying convention is obviously not it either: if we try and not be constricted by the limitation that a convention creates, that creates conflicts also.

★ ★ ★

Sometimes structures get taken away from us. Supports that we are used to get pulled away from underneath us. Forms that we like to have around, the things that we do find helpful, can fall through our fingers and disappear. So some limitation or form has been lost but, far from giving us a sense of freedom, we are left with a sense of hopelessness, insecurity and barrenness.

Around the time that I was at university, on a couple of occasions, I experienced a complete disappearance of the sense of self. In the Buddhist practice this is considered something really good – we put hard graft into our meditation practice for years to arrive at selflessness. But at that time the result was an incredibly deep insecurity and anxiety. My sense of being a person vanished completely. It was impossible to think of myself as a human being.

I remember staring into a mirror, looking at my face and trying to get this face to be 'me'. It was the most peculiar experience. I stared, "There is the face and, yes, it's got the nose, the mouth and the eyes, yes it's all there. It's not anybody else's face but, but, but what has it got to do with me? What has that got to do with anything real?" The convention of selfhood getting blown to pieces is the most terrifying, disorienting experience. It took me weeks and weeks to recover (maybe I never did…).

When the structure was lost the result was not bliss and liberation but terror and insecurity. There was a sickening feeling of meaninglessness: "But, if this isn't real, then what does anything matter? Everything is just an empty parade of dreams, smoke, dust; it doesn't mean anything."

This is a position that a lot of thinkers in this century have come to – seeing through the 'God idea' and materialistic values, seeing the limitation of conventions and structures and coming to the conclusion, therefore, that it's all meaningless. This is the conclusion that the Existentialist philosophers are regarded as having come to.

Heidegger said in 'Being and Time', "I am the null basis of a nullity"; Nietzsche announced that "God is dead"; Sartre wrote 'Nausea' and 'No Exit', descriptions of arid waste-land experiences. Samuel Beckett, I believe, said, "Despair is the only realistic response to the experience of living," and came out with a synopsis of human life as "giving birth astride of a grave". Whether they intended to be so depressing is another story – Sartre wrote a whole trilogy called 'Roads to Freedom' – however, the result of thinking in those ways, from my own experience, was an ocean of despair and pointlessness. So, even when there is the sense of no self, if there is not clear understanding, then what seems to be left is barren and meaningless. All life seems supremely insignificant.

★ ★ ★

Rather than seeing the convention as empty and meaningless, and assuming therefore that all there is is meaningless, the insight of the Buddha is that conventions are empty, but there is also that which is beyond conventions. There is the conventional reality, but there is the Ultimate Reality also. This liberating element is often left out by the other approaches.

It is like these twigs in the vase we have in front of the Buddha here. We bring in a twig off the tree, it's just a brown stick and seems like a dead, lifeless thing and of no importance to anybody. But when it's looked after in the right way then the potential that it has, the life that it has, can come forth. You put it in water, you give it some light and then for weeks you get these beautiful sprays of buds, leaves and lovely white flowers. We can look at the twig and think, "This is nothing; this is totally insignificant." But actually within that all the time there was life, there was beauty and fragrance locked up inside.

When right understanding is established in our lives we realise the quality of completeness that comes with seeing the relationship between convention and liberation, between the relative and the ultimate. It is a fullness of being – the potential that is there springs forth and then there is beauty. There is joy and life's 'meaning' is revealed.

★ ★ ★

One of the initial reasons why I was inspired by the Buddha's teaching was this very understanding of convention – of how such limitation is no real restriction but actually is the way in which we arrive at liberation. I had only been at the monastery in Thailand for a couple of days when the monks took me out on their alms-round into the village one morning. As we were walking back to the monastery Ajahn Jagaro explained the principle to me. "The monastic form is there in order to assist and support the insight into liberation –

that's its only purpose." When this was first explained to me I felt a strange and intuitive sense of recognition, "Well of course!" Actually I also felt like an idiot; it seemed so obvious, yet I hadn't seen it myself. I'd tried to understand this for years, it had been a burning issue in my life since I was about eleven. And then, in two minutes, this monk had solved the riddle for me: it's not forms, structures and social conventions that stop us from being free, it's our attitude towards them and how we use them that makes the difference.

As long as action is accompanied by right view, right understanding and non-attachment it can lead to harmony, it provides the conditions for clear seeing. So what we do makes a difference. Doing good, doing that which is kind, which is not producing pain, discord and confusion for yourself or others, that leaves the air clear enough so that one can see. We stop the mind rattling around and moving so much – like a camera in a shaky hand – and in so doing we are able to see more clearly. With that clear seeing, the mind has the chance to understand and to let go.

As long as our actions are accompanied by right understanding and non-attachment they will take us towards liberation. When we start to concentrate on our breath, notice how it easily it becomes 'ME breathing' – it becomes really clumsy and clunky. We can get so involved and caught up with holding onto the breath and concentrating on it, it seems such hard work, that we become quite amazed that we manage to do this all day long. Every breath seems such a concern.

As mindfulness improves and our attention becomes clear and refined, then the sense of self and its domination starts to disappear. Consequently, we're more and more just feeling the body breathing. The body breathes according to its own rhythm with no sense of self involved. There is mindfulness but no interference.

With that the body then adjusts: the breath becomes long, becomes short, deep or shallow, whatever the body requires. This is a principle that I feel is very significant, something that I have used and contemplated a lot in the past. We need to extend that same spirit throughout all our actions and speech so that we are speaking, acting and living as easefully as carefree breathing. In such 'living like breathing' there is volition and action, but it is empty. What is done and what is said derives totally from the conditions of the present; there is no prior planning, and no 'person' who is controlling.

Sensitivity to the conditions is then what brings forth the right words and actions into all our relationships and all our daily business. We can be fierce or we can be gentle, we can be loud, we can be quiet. We can use the qualities of our personality to act out, in a thousand different ways, what will bring the potential of this moment to fulfilment, what will accord with Dhamma.

When action accords with Dhamma, with Truth – when there is harmony in the conditioned realm – then we are capable of seeing clearly and being free. If there is no clear seeing, then time and self solidify and freedom is gone.

★ ★ ★

Another aspect of this process of learning to act without attachment is that we no longer take sides in the conventional world. As soon as we side with what is 'right', then we immediately create wrongness. We immediately create a separation – a false importance for one convention and an unimportance for others – "I am more real than you are."

What we see in the Buddha's teaching is a very clear refusal to take sides with one thing against another. There is a famous account in the scriptures where a quarrel had broken out in the monastic community at Kosambi, to the point where the monks were ready to cause a schism in the Sangha. They would not listen to the Buddha's advice and they carried on squabbling and fighting, arguing with each other. They were so absorbed in their wrangling about which faction was wrong and which faction was right that the Buddha left them and went off on his own.

Several months later he was living in a different monastery; the Kosambi monks had finally had the foolishness of what they were doing brought home to them by the lay-people refusing to offer them food. They were feeling chastened and regretful, so they went to the Buddha. When the other monks and lay-people at Savatthi heard that the Kosambi monks were coming, everyone was worried about what they were supposed to do. How were they supposed to treat them?

It's really striking how the Buddha chose to deal with the situation. It's also the principle that lies behind the reason why the Sangha takes no side with political parties, or with different factions of any sort – arguing couples who come to the monastery, trying to solve their problems – or people who ask, "Is this a socialist monastery? Is it a Green monastery? Is this a Conservative monastery?" Well, we don't take sides. What the Buddha pointed to was, "Support that which is in accord with Dhamma, that which is true, good and wholesome; and discourage, do not support that which is not in accordance with Dhamma." Very simple.

We are respecting the goodness that is there in the people who are on either side of the fight. Just like in this Gulf War – with the Americans and the British and the other Allied Forces fighting against the Iraqi people – rather than saying, "This side is right and that side is wrong," and rehearsing all the terrible things about Saddam Hussein, or all the terrible things about George Bush; what Buddha-Wisdom points to is that there are good qualities on both sides. Whatever good there is in the Iraqi people and in Saddam Hussein, we should encourage that and give life to it. Whatever bad qualities are there, whatever there is that is unwholesome, then that's to be criticised – and it's the same with the other side.

Remembering back to that time of my being very critical of the British government and the establishment: in my mind I was portraying those in government as evil-minded, greedy, corrupt people slavering with intense delight over the accumulation of wealth and power, and with absolutely no human, compassionate, gentle qualities. Then, when I actually met some such people, I realised that they were just ordinary folk who were trying to do the right thing. They had been involved in a particular lifestyle, had come from a particular background, and life had just steered them in this direction.

Almost always people are acting as honourably as they are able. I once met Air Chief Marshal Constantine – he was in Bomber Command in the Second World War and led or organised over 150 raids on Germany, including the one on Dresden. He approached me to have a chat when we met in an RAF hospital – he was a very fine man whom I felt honoured to meet.... There are a tremendous number of good qualities, wonderful, beautiful qualities within all people. We should not be fooled just by each other's actions – beauty can easily get hidden behind a wall of aggressive tendencies.

The Buddha points very clearly to the encouragement of the good, and not to condemn any person out of hand. When we hold the mind in this way we are able to understand convention correctly. We are not siding with this one against that one. We're not expecting a convention to be perfect in and of itself. We're not expecting a form to be what makes us happy, to always be right, or to be something which makes us free. We are no longer looking for a partner who is perfect, or a place, a political system or a teacher who is flawless and who will always make us happy.

I realise that this religious tradition, life in the Sangha, obeying these rules and practising these teachings is not what makes us happy. The liberating insight is that these things are empty in themselves. They have no life of their own, they are just conventions. When they are understood correctly they open the way for the mind to see that which is beyond convention, that which is not formed – the Uncreated or Unconditioned. To be able to know Nibbana becomes possible.

As long as we are searching for the perfect place, the perfect system in terms of some form, or are looking for freedom in terms of some action, some pattern of belief or political system, then we'll always meet with frustration. We'll always meet with disappointment – it's inevitable. This is not a put-down, this is just how life is – it is only through fully knowing the limited and not identifying with it that we experience the Unlimited. Then there is perfect freedom.

The Great Journey

Is there no journey
without a return?

A journey that leaves no remainder?

Everywhere we go
we seem to carry some trace
of the place whence originally we came.

Is there no place
where there lingers no shade of transition?

    – the islet we must leave
    to find food and shelter;
    the family that waits for us at home;
    the legal impositions of boundary and time;
    the travel plan;
    expectations;
    the reasonable....

Is there no journey
into the invisible, unnameable?
Where no-one **knows**;
where passports, money and minds don't apply;
where there is nothing to fall back on?

Telephones, embassies, roads all chain us
    to the known,
    to the secure,
    to **my** world.

    But the free fly,
    fly and don't look back –

they disappear into uncharted,
uncatalogued horizons.

Traceless they go into the endless tundra
to commune with the musk-ox and the wolf;
or over the last mountain range
mounted on a buffalo,
leaving scraps of wisdom
with a lone *douanier*.

Is there no such journey?

Does every single one have return,
limitation, compromise
embedded inextricably within it?

"If only I could go,
unbeknownst to anyone,
and wander the Mongolian wilderness:
swathed and nameless,
just a face across the camp-fire –
to disappear into the desert night...

    Or to the Andes
       or the New York underworld
          or some hidden corner of a Spanish forest..."

To get AWAY!

But the past haunts…

"Is there some place on this globe
where nobody will mark me?
Where I do not have to give my name and number!?"

"Perhaps it is a sign
of the nature of this world."

"Well what of death then,
is that not a pure and clean finality?
Beyond the last breath
there is no turning back."

"Maybe so, O nobly born,
but they also say
that whatsoever hope or fear
upon which the mind fixates itself
at the point of death
will bring forth a new birth –
a return…."

These little circulations,
across the world of birth and death,
always echo with frustration –
vortices trapped within a cage of time.

We're caught into their whirling
disabled from discerning
the power of the spirit
to journey into Knowledge –

the great journey –
and **here** there is true completion.

The Great Journey is itself 'return':
the rediscovery of Eden
with eyes grown wise –
a return to primordial simplicity.

The mind of the sage
is but the mind of the child
which truly understands its own nature;
innocent and wise,
beyond sorrow, it is free

and the free fly –

the infinite their home,
their food is faith
their guide is peace.

Behind – no tracks,
ahead – no road.

They have ceased to search for happiness
in the labyrinth of time
thus they wheel
and float the skies at ease.

– F r e e –

The Great Journey
is itself 'return',
not to the binding
but from bondage
into freedom.

Chithurst, winter 1991

Absolute Zero

From a talk given on the Easter retreat, Amaravati, 1992

MUCH OF OUR ATTENTION is normally taken up with the state of the world. In a retreat we become more concerned with our own inner lives, our own being, but outside a very specialised learning situation like this, our concern goes to the world around us. How to help? What to do? How to understand it? How to transform it? We see the struggle and confusion, the stress and difficulty inhabiting our own and other people's lives. So we try to do the right thing, we try to do what we can to help. This is the natural outcome of our meditation, and we use Buddhist teachings for exactly this purpose. So even though our work may be done in a fairly enclosed, specialised environment, the aim of it is to understand the world, internally and externally, and to be able to help transform it.

The process of understanding depends on mindfulness, on the act of attention, and it is described by the Buddha as being a gradation of qualities: first of all we need to simply apprehend what is going on, to have *sati* – mindfulness. As the mind apprehends, then that develops into comprehension, 'mindfulness and clear comprehension'. In Pali this is called *sati-sampajañña,* which means mindfulness not just of an object but of the context within which it appears, the comprehension, at least intellectually, of what is going on in the moment. This then leads to wisdom, or *pañña*. After comprehension, there is penetration, realisation – which means that having seen what the pattern of events is, then we look into its inner nature. This essentially means to realise the qualities of change, emptiness and selflessness therein, and also its Suchness – we see it as an aspect of Nature. Such illumination of experience with wisdom is what liberates the mind, and this is what we mean by enlightenment.

This process is thus describing the transition from a mind which simply cognises – which is a worldly quality, with nothing to do with anything virtuous or unvirtuous – into knowing with a sense of comprehension and meaning. Then, when we talk about being the 'One Who Knows', this means there is the quality of wisdom, true illumination and profound understanding there.

To feel things directly, to know directly, and in that direct knowing and understanding, the heart releases its hold and there is freedom.

There are many practical applications of this; one of the most helpful is when dealing with different emotional states: feelings of intense pleasure or pain, restlessness, grief, hope or regret, anger or jealousy; feelings of warmth and comfort, affirmations and delight – whatever the emotion might be, every emotion has a physical attribute to it. When we try to understand the emotions intellectually, or we try to unravel their causes analytically just using our brain, we are looking in the wrong place. For an Asian person, when you talk about the mind you point to your heart, not to your head. So we approach the understanding of emotional states not so much through the intellect as through the realm of feeling.

When we notice we are in a particular mood of anxiety or excitement, energy, laziness, restlessness – or nameless dukkha, our old friend, where we know we are suffering but can't quite figure out what it is we're suffering about … that feeling – rather than trying to analyse the emotion, we just bring it into our attention in the body. We use body-consciousness as a way of bringing mindfulness to that feeling. What does anger feel like? What does resentment feel like? Know it directly and feel it in the body. In many ways this bypasses the processes of entanglement that we create, because when we bring our attention into physical feelings, we can't buy into them in the same way. We feel the imbalance that attachment to the emotional state causes.

This is a tremendously useful way of training the mind to de-emphasise the intellectualising process, the attempt to solve our problems just by thinking about them. Often, even if we have solved the problem in our brain – if we were worried about something and with logic have removed the source of the worry – the body can still be filled with tension and anxiety. It is charged up to worry about something, so we just finish one worry, but since the body is all set to keep going, it causes the brain to cook up another one – it finds something else to worry about. Since the body is tense and agitated it can cause the merest thought to turn into a major problem.

If we bring attention to the body and contemplate, "What is worry like? Where does it sit in the body?", we can feel it like a knot of tension in the solar plexus, in our gut. Every time you find your mind worrying about something, bring your attention down to your stomach, your solar plexus, and notice how it feels; then just let it relax, take your attention off the thing you are worrying about, let your stomach soften and notice the effect it has upon the mind. It is a mysterious and magical thing, but suddenly it seems to be much less of a problem; the situation might still be there, but we are not so upset about it. We see it more clearly; this process opens us up to that spaciousness which is beyond the feeling.

★ ★ ★

This same process, of coming into a state of harmony by being fully conscious of things, is ultimately the purpose of all ritual, artistic form, music and poetry. These are forms that we create in order to help trigger a change of mood and attitude, and to take us beyond. Any true artform helps us to awaken to the fundamental nature of our own being. It leads us, draws us to that. It speaks to the sense of universal order within us, so that when we hear some music or see something which is beautiful, whatever form it may be, the mind is caused to pause, to stop at the moment of opening. It reminds us of that in us which is completely beautiful, completely wonderful – this is why we love art and music. It is not because we like the sounds themselves, we love music because of the place it takes us to. For many people music and art are the substance of, or substitute for, their spiritual life, because they take us to the same place that meditation does: "All is rhythm and centre, equilibrium and presence." There is beauty, order, rhythm, life, no sense of self. This is why it is so delicious: great art can have the same transforming, illuminating effect that meditation does. It is more dependent because we need to be seeing or hearing that thing, or feeling it; but we love it because it evokes that same quality in us. It takes us to that same place.

This is the same with many different aspects of our life: as someone once said, "The magicians and story-tellers open us up to wonder with their tricks. We are lured into the eternal reality through well-timed illusion." The mind's attention is caught by a good story, a beautiful form, an amusing tale. The illusions lead us to reality by tricking us into seeing beyond ourselves – often despite our efforts. Our defences are circumvented; for a moment we drop what we think we are, and we find ourselves open to something much greater. In the moment of that greatness we go beyond ourselves, we break through our limitations. Sometimes this is what we need – we need to be tricked into letting go because we are so sure of our opinions and what we think we know we want. We are so sure about what is going to make us happy that we ignore all the signals around us.

★ ★ ★

It is also important to consider – "What is it we are searching for?" "What is it that we want in life?" Well, we know that we want happiness, but the question is – "How do we find it?"

In a way, every search for happiness is a spiritual search, it just gets sublimated into different objects. We inadvertently take money or affirmation, prestige or being an effective helper as being the commodity that has meaning or value for us, but fundamentally our search is a spiritual one. We are all searching for happiness, for what is true, what is real, what is secure.

From a spiritual perspective, what we are searching for is Ultimate Truth: we are fundamentally searching for ourselves. Happiness comes from finding that; to search for it outside in external things is always going to be frustrating. We use the simile of the fish – the fish lives its whole life immersed in the sea, yet it goes around everywhere searching for this mysterious thing called 'The Sea' – it is very much the same condition that we find ourselves in. What we are searching for is ourselves, what we are searching for is the reality of our own being, the happiness, the joy of our own true nature. But we are so used to finding happiness in external things that we overlook what we are, we overlook what we are swimming in. We overlook the very fabric of our being and the medium of all experience.

So the Path is very much a matter of letting go of that pull – the habitual search for the gratification that we are used to getting from external things, or particular feelings in our own mind – to open the mind to the source of our own life, the source of our own heart. We often use the description of trying to find Truth as an external object as being like trying to see our own eyes. As in meditation, if we are trying to find the 'One Who Knows' – "If the thoughts and feelings are not me, then who is it that is watching it?" – any attempt to try and turn that Knowing, the 'One Who Knows', into an object, simply takes the mind out into the world of 'I', 'me' and 'mine'. Knowing is the fundamental ground; as soon as we try to objectify it, we step out into the world of things and relative truths. So our need is always to rest at that position of the Source. We can't see God but we can be God.

In any kind of mystical experience, the presence of Ultimate Truth as an object (as Nibbana, God the Father or Mother Kali or whatever) is the initial stage. At first there is you together with the Reality that is being witnessed by you. But the ultimate goal of spiritual life is where that duality dissolves: where there's not that Truth and the one who knows it – the mind dissolves in identification with the ground of its own being – there is no God, no Ultimate Truth, there is no you. There is just the awareness of the present; the duality has dissolved because, as Joseph Campbell puts it, "That to which the metaphorical image of your God refers is the ultimate mystery of your own being, which is the being of the world as well." This is the goal of spiritual life, this is what we call Nibbana, the ultimate happiness, the end of illusory separateness.

Now, to take the thought – "I am the Absolute Reality" or "I am God" and to identify that with our personality or our ego is to be crazy. As soon as we say, "I am Truth," or "I am God," or "I am the Messiah", then everyone automatically realises that we are nuts. So when we talk in this way, we don't mean "I, in my personality, am God, and you are not" – but all of us, in the very depths of our own being, beyond personality and ego, are THUS – this is our Nature, whether we like it or not. The source of our being is totally divine, transcendent. This is our home, our goal. All the efforts that we make in life towards happiness – the things that we choose to possess; the goals that we try to achieve; the homes that we try to create – these are all tokens of this fundamental home, the fundamental richness, security and meaning that is right here within our own hearts, behind our own eyes. So close to us that we miss it – closer to us than our own sense of self.

This is our true home, our abiding place. This is the only thing worth living for. If this is our goal, our aim, then happiness is what we will find. If our goal is to acquire things or experiences, or even to save the world, then happiness will elude us – it has to. There is no other way it can be.

When the urges to love and hate, formulate and opinionate are restrained, when there is no identification with existing things, the Heart rests simply aware of its own nature: clear light, absolute and zero, real and utterly free. To rest here is to realise Dhamma, The Ultimate Field, Ground Zero: this is home. And around this point all identities, entities, places and people revolve.

The spiritual life is to live realising and remembering this; and to trust that there is no thing, nothing that is worth holding onto. To develop this kind of forbearance allows a contentment with the way things are, for we are only ever HERE, the time is only ever NOW and there is no other place that we can be. Discontent has to lead to frustration, so we allow all identities and worlds – from the infinitely small to the infinitely large – we allow it all to dissolve into the centre, the sparkling heart of light.

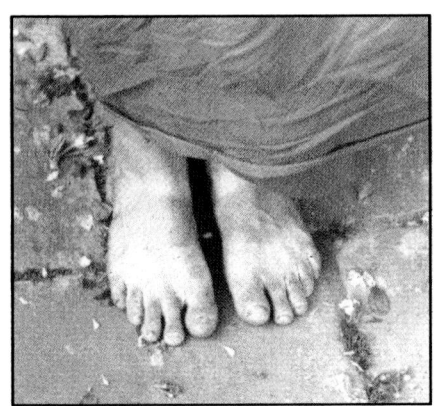